TEMPEST PILOT

SQUADRON LEADER C J SHEDDAN, DFC RNZAF
WITH
NORMAN FRANKS

GRUB STREET · LONDON

Published by
Grub Street, The Basement, 10 Chivalry Road, London SW11 1HT

First published in hardback by Grub Street in 1993
Paperback first published in 1997

Copyright this edition © 2003 Grub Street, London
Text copyright © CJ Sheddan and N Franks

British Library Cataloguing in Publication Data
Sheddan, C. J., 1918-
   Tempest pilot. – New ed.
   1. Sheddan, C. J., 1918- 2. New Zealand. Royal New Zealand Air Force.
   Squadron, 486 3. World War, 1939-1945 – Aerial operations, New Zealand
   4. World War, 1939-1945 – Personal narratives, New Zealand
   I. Title II. Franks, Norman L. R. (Norman Leslie Robert), 1940-
   940.5¢44¢993¢092

ISBN 1 904010 38 5

Cover design by Hugh Adams, AB3 Design

Typeset by Pearl Graphics, Hemel Hempstead

Printed and bound in Great Britain by
Biddles Ltd, Guildford and King's Lynn

ACKNOWLEDGEMENTS
When I was contacted by Norman Franks a few years ago, concerning a book he
was writing, in my reply I asked him if he would be interested in helping me with
my story. I had my memories but had no expertise in putting them together in
some readable form. Fortunately he agreed, so I must say a very big thank you to
Norman for all the work which has made this book possible. In thanking him
I must also thank his wife Heather, who in this instance, did all the typing.
   I should also like to thank my two old friends, Johnnie Johnson and Johnny
Iremonger, who independently both said nice things about me which Norman has
included as a Foreword and an Appreciation. Heady stuff for an old Kiwi.
Thanks too to Chris Thomas, who provided some extra photographs.
   Finally to my wife Joan for nursing me in 1944 and putting up with me ever
since.

                                                        Jim Sheddan, Auckland

CONTENTS

Foreword by AVM J E Johnson DSO DFC,
FIGHTER COMMAND'S TOP-SCORING PILOT IN WW2

AN APPRECIATION BY A POMMY CO.
G/CAPT J H IREMONGER DFC
Commanding Officer 486 (NZ) Squadron 1944

CHAPTER	PAGE
I FIRST FLIGHT	8
II ENGLAND	14
III FIGHTER PILOT	31
IV WITH 485 NZ SQUADRON	39
V DELIVERY PILOT	47
VI 486 NZ SQUADRON	58
VII ALL IN A DAY'S WORK	69
VIII DITCHED!	81
IX WOMEN AND OTHER TROUBLES	90
X THE TEMPEST V	102
XI DOODLEBUGS	111
XII OUR LAST WEEKS IN ENGLAND	121
XIII 2ND TACTICAL AIR FORCE	131
XIV SQUADRON COMMANDER	147
XV COPENHAGEN	156
XVI FINALE	177
APPENDICES	184
INDEX	193

FOREWORD

DURING my service career I came across several good men who were difficult to handle because initially they lacked discipline and refused to conform, and unless their latent qualities were recognised by their superiors, these 'prickly pears' failed to make the grade to their operational units: but if their squadron commanders knew how to handle them, they were usually worth their weight in gold because they were so bloody obstinate and pig-headed they were always to be found in the thick of the fighting when lesser men fled.

In fighter squadrons there was a great gulf between the veterans and the newcomers and, like Jimmy Sheddan, I was well aware of this unhappy situation when I joined my first squadron. However, in the late summer of 1940 the surge and press of war soon brought us together: two years later it was a different story and Jim was pleased to get away from 485 (New Zealand) Squadron for the more mundane task of ferrying fighters to the squadrons. He flew Typhoons, that ungainly fighter which, in 1942, was greatly troubled by engine and structural failures. Several test and squadron pilots had been killed when its tail broke away: the engine sometimes seized-up and caught fire; there was such a smell of carbon monoxide that pilots wore oxygen masks at all times, and the brute vibrated so much that it was said to cause sterility! Jim, however, responded to the Typhoon's challenge and volunteered to join an operational squadron. His CO, who realized the young pilot's potential, supported his application and in mid-1943, Jim, after a shaky start, was on his way.

When the war ended, I was commanding 125 Fighter Wing at Celle in Germany, and Harry Broadhurst, our AOC, told me that because the Russians were already in the Baltic, the Danes wanted an RAF fighter wing at Copenhagen. Since we had done pretty well he had selected 125 Wing for this delightful job: also the AOC added, a Tempest squadron, whose pilots had fought with distinction, would join the party.

Soon after, the Tempest squadron commander reported to me, and I was impressed with this well turned out young man who was very much on the ball and proud of his 486 (New Zealand) Squadron. He was Squadron Leader Jim Sheddan DFC, and here is his honest account of how this 'prickly pear' made the grade.

Air Vice Marshal J E 'Johnnie' Johnson CB, CBE, DSO & 2 bars, DFC & bar, DFC (US), AM (US), Legion of Merit (US), Order of Leopold (Belg), C de G (Belg)

AN APPRECIATION FROM A POMMY CO

I'VE known Jim Sheddan for sixty years, since we were at Tangmere when I took over 486 from Ian Waddy, and I'm happy to say that makes him and the rest of the Squadron my oldest friends. We've kept in touch all this time, though separated by 12,000 miles, when other friends closer at hand have somehow drifted away. I hope the family which is 486 will outlast our lifetime.

The tensions which built up during ops needed a release, and how each of us went about it was our own affair; that is, so long as others were not upset, or discipline and flying was not affected. Jim enjoyed off-duty life to the full, and had a great time encouraging others to enjoy it too. He has the gift of being able to get it all down on paper. How he's managed to do it I don't know, for I'm sure he never kept a diary, and his yarns have the freshness of good memory, savoured over the years.

I don't thing anyone need be offended by his tale of New Zealanders at war. They came half way round the world to our aid. They were entitled to reap the reward of all the fun which was to be had; and there was a lot of fun. Those who never returned missed their share of youth and zest, as they missed the trials and joys of the peacetime life which was denied them. That is a sadness for those of us who were the lucky ones and got home.

I write this on Remembrance Sunday, the day once a year when it is right to have such thoughts. It is my great privilege to have had, for a short time, the responsiblity of commanding such men—I dare not say of leading them, for they showed me the way. All I can say now is thank goodness Jim Sheddan never led me into trouble—reading his book, there was plenty about.

Johnny Iremonger DFC
Group Captain
OC 486 (New Zealand) Squadron 1944

CHAPTER I

FIRST FLIGHT

I was brought up on a farm by loving parents, one of six children, four boys and two girls, in a remote area of New Zealand. My education started well enough but due to changes in teachers, I did not progress as well as my folks had wished. Some of this affected me and I quickly developed a sort of protective screen to life in order to survive. All during my early teens, tales of World War One airmen had been avidly read by me which I suppose began my interest in flying. Man's ability to join the birds also began to intrigue me.

How a machine, which four strong men could not lift, could rise into the air and stay there as long as fuel remained, was a mystery to me. Thermal currents being unheard of, it was equally mystifying to watch sea birds hovering a few feet above a farm tractor while they waited for a tasty morsel to be turned up by the agricultural machine it was towing. Unbeknown to me the birds were using, in part, the uplift being generated by the warm air being created by the hot engine.

On one of my rare visits to Christchurch I decided to pay a call to the Canterbury Aero Club at Sockburn, (a field later re-named Wigram), and if possible try this new-fangled business of flying. There were many occasions, during my subsequent five years in the Royal New Zealand Air Force when my flying career was on the brink of being suddenly terminated but never more closely than on my first visit to Sockburn.

After calling on the one and only flying instructor, I made my way to the hangar only to be told that no aircraft were serviceable, but then, as if remembering a forgotten relic he added, 'The Old Hawk might be okay'. This was to be my first trip aloft and I did not fancy being taken up in some old aircraft which might or might not be serviceable.

The upshot of it all was that we made our way to an old aeroplane which had visibly seen better days and after much head shaking the pilot seemed to think that the old girl just might be capable of one more trip. I then found myself securely belted into the rear seat and the pilot installed in the front and after a few unsuccessful attempts he managed to persuade the motor to start. No sooner had this happened than the pilot decided that he must return to the hangar and I was left all alone, perched up there in what to me was almost a terrifying situation. The motor would let out a bang and the big propeller would do a full revolution—then a pause followed by another bang when the procedure would be repeated. All the while the airframe was shaking so much it was a mystery why the thing did not fall apart. It was only pride that kept me where I was and had I been able to have escaped from that monster without being seen, nobody would have ever persuaded me to go near another aeroplane.

Eventually the pilot returned and after a short run we were airborne. It was one of those perfect days when it was a joy to be aloft and so thrilled was I by the experience that I made up my mind that some day, somehow, I would learn to fly.

At that time the cost of learning to fly was well beyond what I could afford but fortunately for my dream the war arrived and I lost no time in making an application to join the air force as a pilot and after passing a medical examination I was accepted and then as a pre-entry chore had to do twenty-one assignments which were more or less a revision of our three years of secondary education. So far so good; it would seem that I had cleared the last hurdle and I eagerly awaited notice of when I was to report for training.

After several months I arrived at my father's home to find a notice instructing me to report to Timaru the following day to sit a pre-entry exam. In hindsight I could have found a valid excuse to have the exam postponed and thus have time to do some necessary revision but so keen was I to start flying that I took the risk and as was to be expected failed miserably. As a result I was down-graded to an air gunner. As could be imagined, the bottom seemed to have dropped out of my world and once again I was at a cross-roads, not knowing whether to chuck the idea of flying and transfer to the army or to play along in the hope of later becoming a pilot. Transfer to the army was always available so I decided to chance my luck and entered Levin to begin my basic training as an air gunner.

Luckily I have always found learning no problem but my tent mate and some of his friends were having their problems, so most nights I would hold a session and sort out any difficulties which they had experienced during the day. It is a recognised fact that the easiest way to learn is to teach, as before one can teach the subject must be understood and then reduced to its simplest form in order that the pupil can also understand it. The result of all this extra study was that of the fifteen two-hour exams, I did not drop lower than 90% on any of them and on quite a few I obtained the maximum which gave me an overall average of about ninety five. Out of one hundred and fifty pupils none had recorded more than sixty so, as can well be imagined —my results stuck out like the proverbial sore thumb. On the strength of this I was able to wangle a transfer to the pilot's lines. Another milestone passed on my way to becoming the 'man up front'.

Once confirmed as a possible future pilot the malady, which troubled most service pilots, started to take hold. Our first fear was that we would not solo in the old Tiger Moths we flew. This was a hurdle that a good many budding pilots failed to clear but once past this obstacle most seemed to sail along with few problems apart from the ever present ones such as sight and hearing which had a habit of appearing when least expected. The next major worry, well at least for the pilots selected for bombers, was converting to twin-engined aircraft. These aircraft were generally Oxfords which were flying from my old Sockburn airfield on the outskirts of Christchurch and which had now been renamed Wigram in remembrance of Lord Wigram.

It was at this station that my brother Alex, later to lose his life on his second operational trip in Bomber Command, was to come to grief. My brother, who had been nicknamed 'Altitude Alex', had no problems with the Tigers, being one of the first of his course to solo but for some reason he could not manage the task of putting an Oxford safely back on the 'deck'. In those early days, when sent off to do solo aerobatics, a pupil invariably tried to get as high as his Tiger would take him before commencing the exercise. In Alex's case his instructor, who was not a small man, took off in another Tiger to watch his pupil's performance but had to abort the mission as Alex and his aircraft were still climbing into the great beyond long after the second Tiger had refused to climb any higher.

Service training, which I did on Harvards, seemed reasonably free of minor problems as here night flying and close squadron formation were the most difficult to master and most accidents were usually fatal. I cannot recall a single occasion while at Service Training School when a pilot was grounded because he could not carry out the tasks allotted. The above also applied later to Operational Training where I was to fly Spitfires. The final hurdle was to be accepted by an operational squadron especially if it were one on rest and awaiting a posting back to a front-line billet. (I am, of course, referring now to fighter pilots).

The unhappiness was caused in my case by the arrival of any new pilot straight from OTU which was usually followed by the posting of a senior pilot to the Middle East where the squadrons seemed always to be clamouring for pilots. Strange as it may seem several pilots so posted were to sit around in Pilot Pools for anything up to eighteen months then return to England without ever having flown an aircraft!

The final calamity for some fighter pilots, as it would be for me, was to be taken off operations. Why this should be is possibly hard for the layman to understand, as such a posting meant that they could plan a future which could stretch ahead for years. On a front-line squadron each sunrise was possibly going to be your last. But for so many of us to be in action was the ultimate.

Amongst the aircrew training to be navigators were a number of ex-trainee pilots who only a few short weeks before had left Levin for an Elementary Flying School and who had failed to make the grade. Now, bitter and disillusioned, they had been remustered and were back in Levin for a further six weeks of ground study before leaving for Canada to complete their new training. We were a ready audience for their tales of woe and by the time we were ready to leave Levin most of us believed that our chances of survival depended on the luck of the draw. With some instructors we had a chance but others seemed only interested in seeing how many fledgling pilots they could ground and in a few cases there was some strong acceptance for this belief. The main reason for groundings was the assumption by 'Authority' that if a pupil did not solo in seven hours it was not worth spending any more flying training on him. The fact remained, however, that earlier on, some pilots who had taken ten or more hours to solo, turned out to be among our best. Another reason for the many failures was that, as the pressure increased, more and more instructors were required and there were just not enough old pilots from Aero clubs and such like around to fill the bill so Group adopted a policy of retaining top pilots from the courses and using them as instructors. It is easy to imagine the feelings of a young exceptional pilot who was being condemned to flying Tiger Moths when a pilot, with only a fraction of his ability, was passing rapidly through the system and into front-line squadron service which, after all, was what every pilot wants to achieve. All this led to frustration and impatience which had an adverse effect on their pupils. Far more would have been achieved, and there would have been far less waste, had Group said to these young instructors, 'Give it your best shot for six months and then you can forget about instructing'.

Among all these truths and half truths regarding instructors, there was one who was held in high regard by even the Grey Wolves and this was Johnny Nelson at Taieri (South Island), who had the reputation of never having 'washed out' a pupil. I was flying for almost a week before I realised that the pilot in the front seat was the famous Johnny Nelson and, strange as it may seem, he grounded my room mate, Hugh Smith after only about half an hour of flight training and he very nearly grounded me and this was after I had a number of hours solo flying! In Hugh's case the higher he flew the more urgent became his desire to leave it all behind and return to the ground. When he conveyed this message to his instructor, Johnny's reply was, 'Okay, out you go'. The joke became a little flat when Hugh tried to do just that having first undone his safety harness and parachute straps. For Johnny it was a case of arriving back on the ground before he had a tragedy on his hands.

In my case it was a little different. Feeling unwell, I reported to the camp Doctor, a recent medical student who possibly knew as much about sick people as I knew about flying, and had my condition diagnosed as some minor tummy upset. The cure was to send me on sick leave for a few days and then pass me fit for flying. The form then was to take me up for a check circuit, to make sure that I could get the old Tiger up and down safely, then send me off to do some solo flying. This turned out to be a disaster; I was worse than a first-day pupil. I, and my instructor, had to endure several more hours of dual flying which included a grounding check with the Chief Flying Instructor before I was allowed aloft again on my own. Forty years were to pass before I was again to have a repeat attack, which I now know is caused by a virus affecting the middle ear. The victim has a form of sea sickness and finds it most difficult to move about without losing his or her balance.

While at Taieri, Shale George, who was a member of a Wellington legal firm, drew a graph of a pupil's elementary efforts and it was quite revealing. We all started off on the same level and more or less kept pace for about four hours when the graph for about a third of the course continued its upward curve, a third started a downward slide and, in hindsight, it was obvious what the final result was going to be. For the rest, their graph just flattened out until just before the first solo when it took a sudden downward plunge but once this obstacle had been mastered the graph shot vertically upward and what was left of the course was on an even keel.

We idolised our flying instructors, and the fact that they could throw an old Tiger Moth about the sky and make it do all manner of things, cast them in the role of Supermen. How nice it was to have been so young and innocent!

Johnny Nelson and I were two of a kind and we eventually had none of the pupil instructor problems that so many fledgling pilots seemed to suffer from. Occasionally some act of mine would try his patience to the limit and beyond which would result in a torrent of abuse but as I could not make much sense from it all, the sanest thing was to remove the speaking tube! When, after a short interval, Johnny's unfailing good humour would return, he would look back at me with an expression which seemed to say, 'That was rather childish but some of your antics would try the patience of a Saint', then wafting back on the slipstream I would hear, 'Put that bloody tube back and let's get on with the war'.

After completing Elementary Flying, those of us who had elected to continue our training in Canada were sent on final leave and for me this very nearly proved a disaster. On completion of my leave I was supposed to be on a north-bound express which arrived at Auckland in the early hours of the morning on a pre-arranged date. By accident or design I did not arrive till the following morning to be greeted by two service policemen by whom I was taken into custody and charged with being absent without leave. I was escorted out to Whenuapia airfield and locked up in a defaulter's cell for what was left of the night. Later in the day I was ordered to appear before the Station Commander who, after listening to the sorry tale, considered it was far too serious a matter for him to deal with and decided to refer to Wellington for a decision. Once again my fate hung in the balance—army or air force.

Harewood, in the South Island, was not only an Elementary Flying School but also a base where the intakes of ground crew did their elementary training such as drill and learning to make their beds to the satisfaction of their instructors, and it was to Harewood that I was sent to do a spot of foot bashing while I awaited a decision on my future. In the early stages the only visible difference between ground and air crew was that the latter wore a white flash in their hat, so as I marched around amongst my new found friends it was obvious to all that here was an airman who had put up a 'black' and was now receiving his just desserts. Nothing goes on forever and eventually I was called into the Commanding Officer's office and told that I was going to be allowed to continue flying but I was left in no doubt as to my future should I offend again.

There were aspects of service life that never ceased to amaze me and in this case I was actually given a choice as to whether I would prefer to continue on to Canada or complete my service training in New Zealand. I chose Canada and was promptly sent to our own Woodbourne . . . But I was not too upset as all I wanted to do was fly.

CHAPTER II

ENGLAND

WHEN at Levin there were about one hundred and fifty trainee pilots, at least fifty at Taieri, plus at least a hundred or more at Woodbourne during my stay. Then after Woodbourne I travelled to England with a number of pilots and was posted at Hulavington, then Harden OTU. After completion of my training it was 485 (NZ) Spitfire Squadron, Number One Delivery Squadron at Croydon and finally to 486 (NZ) Squadron.

During my time in the air force, therefore, I must have met and known personally hundreds and hundreds of pilots yet in that five years of war, I met only two with whom I had trained. After I had been with 486 at Tangmere for several months Bruce Lawless[1] arrived. The last time I had seen Bruce was as we left Taieri, when he had been temporarily grounded and taken off the course due to a medical problem. The only other pilot was Colin McDonald who had been on my course at Levin and Taieri but with whom I had lost touch when he caught the boat to Canada and I had not. Colin had arrived at 485 just before me and after a very short stay had been posted to various squadrons and also training units as an instructor before being sent out to the Middle East. After completing a tour in the Desert and adjoining areas, Colin had returned to England and had joined 486. I have never lost touch with Colin and Bruce and we still correspond today although Bruce married an English girl and made his permanent home in England.

Woodbourne was to prove a very pleasant interlude. Harvards were a rather nice aeroplane to fly and apart from a nasty habit of being

---

[1] Flight Lieutenant F B Lawless DFC from Christchurch

difficult in spin recovery, a fault which was eliminated in later models, were a first-class trainer. While at Woodbourne I had a couple of problems of a minor nature, the first being when an instructor took me up for a stint of instrument flying. The form here was that the pupil, in the rear cockpit, pulled a hood over his head and could see only the instruments, while the instructor sat in the front from where he issued instructions and acted as safety pilot. What I was doing was landings and though I say it myself I was becoming quite efficient at this type of approach and let down. The instructor gives you various courses and altitudes to fly, then lines you up on the runway at a thousand feet and then it is the pupil's task to do a normal let down and landing by instruments. When the altimeter indicated that you were almost down you would hear over the intercom, 'All right I've got it', and it was quite a thrill to pull the hood back and to see the runway only a few feet below, certainly close enough to see the ground visually and carry out a normal landing in all but the most atrocious conditions.

After several attempted landings at base, where I had set the altimeter to read zero at ground level, he took us up to the Delta which was about three hundred feet higher than Woodbourne. He did not tell me about the change of landing area but even so all would have been well, providing he had kept his wits about him. The instructor must have been sitting there half asleep and I was happily going through my act in the rear cockpit with my eyes glued on the instrument which showed a height clearance of about three hundred feet, when—'bang', it was obvious that we had hit something fairly solid—the ground. I did not know how that instructor explained away the mangled aircraft, but I was to hear later that in a later accident both he and his pupil were killed.

My second problem was caused by the Morse Code which Group seemed to take fairly seriously. Strange as it may seem the trouble arose not because I was having problems in learning it, but because Morse was one of my favourite subjects and I was rather good at it. Long before entering the Service I had learned to receive Morse at a rate of over 30 words per minute, more than double the rate required, although I had not learned to transmit. Fortunately, we were only required to receive! During exercises with a light, the receiver watched the transmission and called out the letters to his marker who jotted them down. Once the gang found out that they could rely on me they would go through the motions of opening and shutting their mouths while their markers listened to me. The Morse instructor realised what was going on, but he never said anything. When it came to taking the Morse from the buzzer there was no way that the others

could beat the system, one just had to know it and if a pupil failed he
was held back until he could take the required fifteen words a minute
without making any mistakes. There was one pupil, Aundra Holmes,
who could just make the required speed in practice but in an exam he
used to panic. My solution was that we swap papers and if Aundra
made a mess of my paper what the hell, I could always plead that a
headache had been the cause and ask for a re-run the next day. Well
the worst happened and the instructor rubbed salt into my wounds by
saying that he had expected me to fail as I had never taken the Morse
lessons seriously! The instructor would not let me resit that cursed
exam until the day before we were due to go on final leave, and in the
meantime the course was paraded in their best blues and had their
'wings' presented by the Commanding Officer. It did not make me feel
very happy to have to stand on the side line and watch Aundra standing
proudly to attention while the wings were being pinned on his chest.
Later, after passing that wretched exam, I had to go down to the stores,
and sign for my 'wings' in the manner of drawing some equipment.

For me, the last hurdle was that dratted Morse, then it was final
leave for the second time and then off to Wellington to take passage
on the *Port Campbell*, the one ship that was going to have me aboard
when it left for 'Blighty'.

On the crossing to the North Island, by ferry, I was to meet a couple
of other sergeant pilots who I was to see much of during the next few
months and these two rascals' ability to get in and out of trouble made
my efforts look as if they were hardly worth a mention. We arrived
in Wellington about 7 am and after a heavy night at the bar we could
hardly have been described as being in top shape.

Our first assignment was to report aboard and after being signed on
as members of the ship's crew we were shown our cabins and then
granted shore leave till twenty hundred hours. We were warned that
the ship was due to depart about midnight and if we were not aboard
before that hour we could expect to be left behind. This bit of advice
was quite unnecessary as far as I was concerned. From civilians to
pilots, then to blue water seamen in less than six months, this was
climbing the ladder three rungs at a time! No doubt over indulgence
was partly to blame plus a fair amount of immaturity, but whatever
the cause we seemed to think we were God's gift to Wellington as we
swaggered from one Hotel bar to the next. Later, in a restaurant,
when some army types referred to us as 'Blue Orchids', we managed
to get ourselves engaged in a brawl but apart from smashing up a bit
of furniture and being thrown out by the proprietor and his bully boys
no great damage was done. Eventually we finished up at a dance of

sorts and my two mates got themselves involved with some girls but for me the safest course was to be aboard ship well before the appointed hour. Before departing Doug Gordon, a Christchurch lad, and Don Aldridge, who hailed from Darfield, made me promise to wake them at daylight as they wished to be on deck to see their beloved New Zealand disappear astern. I have no idea as to what time they came aboard or in what condition but there was no way that I could get a response as the ship moved away from the wharf and headed for the open sea. I wish I had tried a little harder as neither were to see their homeland again. Both were flying Wellingtons on 75 New Zealand Bomber Squadron, Doug failed to return from an operation and the last that was heard from Don was when, on a bombing mission to Italy, his radio operator reported that their 'plane was icing up while crossing the Alps.

About this time I had a secret fear that my hair was about to fall out and was foolish enough to believe a story that a nightly application of methylated spirits was just the treatment, so my last act, before going aboard, was to call at a chemist shop and buy a bottle of the foul smelling stuff. Until I had heard that it could be used as a hair restorer I had believed that the spirit had only two uses, starting fires and drinking when all other avenues failed to supply the craving for hard liquor. As I had no wish or desire to be suspected of either of these, I decided to conceal the bottle under my pillow and apply it at night when, hopefully, the stench would have disappeared before morning. So much for the best laid plans of man and beast. The cork somehow worked loose and Bill Keenan, who was occupying the bottom bunk, received a free application of 'hair restorer'. Unfortunately Bill's hair had long reached the stage where not even a miracle could have reversed the situation. I would have given a great deal to have been able to have observed Bill's reaction when he awoke to taste and smell the stuff and then realised where it was coming from. His advice to me was if you must drink the bloody stuff the toilet was the place and not being a gentle character, 'toilet' was not exactly the word he used.

For us a constant source of annoyance were the brand new Pilot Officers with whom we had been inflicted and who had an idea that it was their God given duty to deliver us in England in tip-top physical condition. With this thought in mind they initiated a program of pre-breakfast physical training. To have to crawl out of a warm bed during the early hours is torture enough but throw in a hangover, and life becomes a burden. Our two tormentors were no match for our sly cunning, such as over-sleeping with the cabin door securely locked;

there was no end to the acts we were able to dream up. Physical training moved from the compulsory to the voluntary and was then finally abandoned.

After passing through the Panama Canal, we had our first lesson of just how brutal war can be. In the evening, we saw a sailing ship. She approached with the sun astern of her sails—a sight long to be remembered. Next morning we were to hear, from the ship's radio operator, that some time during the night the ship, which was a neutral, had been the victim of one of Hitler's underwater butchers.

Our last port of call was Halifax, Nova Scotia where we were to spend a week and during that time we were billeted ashore in Canadian barracks where we found their central heating somewhat of a trial. The temperature was far too high and conditions generally very stuffy. Unfortunately there did not seem to be much that we could do to improve our lot as, no sooner had we turned the control down to what we considered normal, than one of our Canadian room mates would sneak out of bed and turn it up again. It was a case of we cooked or the Beavers froze and after all we were the intruders.

Unimpressed as we may have been by our new room mates, the same could not be said for their girls, the long-legged beauties! We were very impressed though I have no doubt that three months at sea could have coloured our judgement. The highlight of our stay was an invitation to attend a dance at a local girl's college. Bill's partner was an attractive lass and he set about bringing her sketchy knowledge of New Zealand up to date with tales of the fierce Maori warriors who lurked in the dark rain forests, their cannibalistic habits and their preference for the white people who lived along the country's coastal belt. At the rate the white inhabitants were disappearing into the Maori cooking pots, our brown brothers would shortly have to change their diet. Meanwhile, his lovely companion hung on every word, her eyes as round as saucers. Why could I not have seen her first and thought up those fantastic tales? Bill was one of those people, who once started, seem to be able to go for ever but even he had to pause occasionally. When he did it was the girl's turn. 'You know, William, those are the sort of tales we tell visitors about our Indians!' Poor Bill. What an actress that girl would have made.

After a week of ice skating, central heating, rye whisky from the drug store and Canadian girls, it was time to leave it all behind. Back to the *Port Campbell* and out into the North Atlantic which was no place to be in mid-winter. Great green seas sweeping aboard and leaving behind tons of ice which clung to the deck and superstructure; it seemed incredible that a ship could carry so much excess weight and still stay afloat, or at least the right way up!

We were assigned to watch-keeping duties, four hours on, then four off for the twenty-four hours of the day, fully clothed complete with life jacket at all times. The life jackets, though, were only useful as a source of warmth, for if our ship had been torpedoed or turned over in those gigantic seas it would not have been possible to survive in those icy waters for more than a few minutes. Well, the enemy let us slip through, maybe he had his own problems.

Our Captain, well past the normal retiring age, had a heart attack shortly after leaving the Convoy. Then, a plane was seen approaching at low level—a hostile act which could not be ignored. Don and Doug were on duty at the time and while Doug was swinging the Lewis machine gun in order to cover the approaching 'plane he somehow managed to hit Don a nasty blow across the head and several stitches were required to close the wound. This could have been an indication of things to come as the 'plane turned out to be a friendly Wellington and it was to be Wellingtons that both Don and Doug were flying when they lost their lives. Finally we reached our destination—England.

On our first night ashore we were billeted at an air force station where a Spitfire squadron was based and one of its pilots had that day shot down a German aircraft. What a tale he had to tell, greatly exaggerated, no doubt for our benefit. Next day we travelled by train across the West Country, our destination London, and what a depressing journey it was, bitterly cold with fog reducing visibility almost to zero. London, when we arrived, did little to cheer us up as it was in the grip of a pea-souper and in such conditions it was almost impossible to avoid becoming lost. It was akin to living in perpetual darkness. We were delighted when the time came to move to the aircrew reception centre at Bournemouth, on the south coast, which was to be our home for the next couple of months.

Pre-war Bournemouth must have been quite a place and a mecca for visitors, both British and from overseas but now, apart from a few permanent residents, the place was deserted, that is apart from the hundreds of aircrew who were billeted in the big private hotels. Here they awaited a posting to Operational Training Units which was the last leg of the journey before joining operational squadrons or to what other posting it was judged they could best serve the war effort.

Apart from a few Englishmen who had returned from training schools in Canada, most of the aircrew were from the Dominions, South Africa, Australia, Canada and New Zealand—they were all represented here.

With my two mates I joined this unemployed air force and with nothing to do but kill time, life became tedious. Limited finance, nowhere to go and less to see, the only diversion was when an occasional German bomber came over at night and dropped a few bombs around the place. The occasional delayed-action bomb could have been a problem but for some reason they all had twenty-four hour delays and exploded when their intended victims were in bed. At most times during the day, there was an inspection committee gathered around the previous night's bombing. It is not difficult to imagine the result if the big bomb, sulking beneath them, had chosen that time to detonate.

Finance, or the lack of it, was a problem for most but Don was a genius at raising the financial drought though some of his methods were a little questionable. Doug's conscience was a problem but it did not prevent him from borrowing some of our ill-gotten gains; under civilian law he could have been described as a receiver. Don's most productive racket was the poodle snatch. There were quite a few wealthy old ladies who refused to leave their mansions and were now forced to exercise their own dogs. In pre-war England, this task was carried out by servants but now these were hard to find and harder to keep. As the old ladies used to keep the animal on a fairly long lead, it was a simple matter to trail behind and when the opportunity occurred, pick up the little animal and unhitch it. These pampered pets were used to being handled by servants and seemed to enjoy the experience. To complete the deal it was only a matter of catching up and asking the victim if it was their dog, the assumption being that you had found it running free. The grateful owner never let us depart without a generous donation. Neither of us had the misfortune to pick on a previous victim for had we done so I am afraid some old lady would have had her faith in human nature rudely shattered.

Tiring of limited local entertainment, London was always an attraction but the cost of a return fare was our problem. However, it did not take Don long to produce a scheme which enabled us to travel back and forth as the unpaying guests of British Rail.

The first act in the chain of deceptions was to find a member of the orderly room staff who was open to bribery, which was not too difficult, as cigarettes opened most doors. With our issue from New Zealand House plus our English allotment, we were never short of this desirable commodity. As an added bonus, neither of my two mates smoked.

We would have our contact on the inside make us out a return ticket from a station south of Bournemouth and as it was permissible to call at any station along your intended route without having to surrender your ticket, on our return from London we had not completed our journey so the guard on the gate did not collect the ticket. Had British Rail clipped our ticket that would have been the end of our scheme. I am sure that some of the guards were awake to what was going on as occasionally one would give you a funny look and retain the much travelled ticket.

Don would have made a first-class Secret Service agent and his main asset was that he did not look the part. Short, with his hair brushed back to give him a kindly look, a hook in his nose, the result of a rugby mix up, and one eye that seemed to be permanently bloodshot. Most of us could produce a hangover to remind us of a night out but for Don a night on the town always seemed to affect at least one eye.

Nothing of interest seemed to escape Don's notice. Well, at least nothing that could be turned to his advantage, so it did not come as a surprise when Don suggested that the three of us spend three weeks as the guests of a Country Squire in Yorkshire! I was in no hurry to say yes, as in the past I had fallen for some of his schemes and had found them a rather costly exercise and it was obvious that this latest venture was going to cost somebody money and I did not need second sight to know who it was going to be.

According to Don a notice had appeared on the orderly room board that morning, inviting three New Zealanders to spend this holiday in the North and in order to give myself time to weigh up just what was involved I suggested that I go along and view the notice.

Don was not only up with my thinking, he was way ahead of it. He reached into a pocket and produced the document under discussion. The invitation sounded attractive, horse riding, shooting, strolls through the woodlands and much more. (The only item that was not mentioned was two very attractive maids who were to prove more than willing to accompany my mates on their nightly visit to the local pub.) The only problem—could we finance the trip?

During my time in the services I developed a trait which unfortunately did not survive the war and that was an ability to save money. I drank as much as the rest, perhaps more than most, was always a soft touch when one of the gang found themselves a bit short prior to payday and yet always seemed to have money in my wallet and Don seemed to think that I could handle that part of the venture. The major hurdle was to persuade pay accounts to advance each of us three weeks pay then a 'tarpaulin muster'[1] in order to find out how much my

---

[1] If a number of people decide to finance a venture but are short on cash, the form was to lay something on the ground, usually a tarpaulin, and everyone would throw on what they could afford.

mates could contribute, which was unfortunately very little. During three months at sea we had all been unable to spend our pay and had accumulated considerable nest eggs. Up till then I had been unable to spend mine but apparently that had been no problem for Don or his mate. A hefty contribution from my accumulated funds, and finance quickly ceased to be an immediate problem. It was easier to fall in with my mates, than argue against them and anyway I just couldn't resist a challenge.

Our plan was to spend a couple of days in London before continuing our journey North. This was not the brightest of ideas when travelling on a limited budget, as there was an attraction about London that was irresistible. It was the place where all the troops seemed to gather. If you wanted information regarding a friend, or a squadron, all you had to do was spend some time around the West End bars and sooner or later somebody would turn up who would be able to supply the required details. In addition to being the centre of the Universe, London had a terrific train service so that no matter in what direction a traveller intended to depart there would be a train leaving within the hour, so catching the next one could easily become a habit as day after day slipped pleasantly by. Later, when I joined 486 Squadron, I had a first-class example of just what a trap London could be. One of my room mates, Warrant Officer Jimmy Wilson, known to all as 'Woe', made numerous attempts to visit his mother's Welsh relations but never made it past the big smoke. I think I would be on fairly safe ground were I to say that he never made it to Wales, well not at least during the twelve months or more that we were together at Tangmere. Jim's mum corresponded with the Welsh side of the family and the much repeated question was, 'Have you seen my Jimmy yet?' They must have begun to wonder if there was a Jimmy.

I was not sure whether my role was banker, money lender or keeper of the family purse. The burden of seeing that we did not overspend, well at least until we had reached our destination, seemed to have descended on my shoulders and somehow I managed to get my charges onto a north-bound train after three nights in London. British Rail, in those early days, still had a diner attached and my mistake was in allowing us to stay behind when the steward (who we had befriended) cleared the car for the four of us to go on a whisky drinking binge. By the time we arrived at York station the only noticeable difference in Don's condition was that the white of one of his eyes was again a bright red and the other was beginning to colour up. As for Doug and the dining car steward, they were just plain drunk. There was no other way that their condition could be described. The only sad point was that we were paying for the whisky and our new found friend was helping us to drink it.

There is a thing about two drunks which is universal, they must either fight each other or they have to become blood brothers. The dining car steward must assist his friend to alight and, as anybody who has tried will know, assisting a drunk to alight from a train can be difficult. One drunk trying to assist another can be a disaster. Some-one had placed a large suitcase on the platform and Doug and his assistant fell over it. There was Doug in the middle of York station, flat on his back and on hand to witness the performance was our hospitable Squire and his assistant. I must say this for the English gentry, they are past masters at concealing their thoughts. From Squire Tyler's expression I could have gained the impression that was just how he had expected his guest to arrive!

I had heard and read of the stately homes of England but nothing that I had read or heard had prepared me for the vastness or splendour of the Tyler Mansion. It was surrounded by a vast area of lawns and flower gardens and all this set in the middle of about five hundred acres of beautiful park land. The inside of the house was just as impressive with a massive hall and dining room, with stairways leading up from both. The stairs were just as imposing as the rest of the set-up; I am sure that they were almost wide enough to have driven a car up. Don and Doug were allotted a double room. I am somewhat vague about the details although I well remember the single room in which I was to spend the next three weeks.

The most unusual thing in that most unusual room was the single four-poster bed which was larger than any double bed of my experience. The mattress was at least eighteen inches in depth and must have been feather-filled because as I sank down into it I had the feeling that I was sinking into a cloud. At each corner of the bed there was a seven-foot vertical upright and the top of the poles were connected by a rail from which hung drapes which descended to the floor. To sink into that delightful bed, then reach out and pull the drapes across was like disappearing into another world.

The next ordeal on that first night was dinner. This was the one meal of the day when all were expected to attend and by all, I mean family, house guests and any other bodies who happened to be on the guest list for that particular occasion. Dinner was always due to start at eight, preceded by a sort of happy hour, in the dining room, during which drinks were taken, introductions made and the affairs of the day discussed.

The Squire, no doubt, would be discreet and not mention the fiasco at the station but I could not be so sure of the estate worker. Nothing happened at the Big House which was not general knowledge almost before it happened. Our arrival had all the melodrama of a two-act play and now kitchen staff, gardeners, cowmen and the rest of the assembly would be waiting for a report on the second act. Well the two boys could make goats of themselves if they so desired and the way they were making the most of the happy hour this was more than a possibility. However, I was feeling my way in what for me was an entirely new situation and the first move was to go light on the drinks and keep a clear head and my wits about me. As I sipped slowly at my whisky and water, and made small talk, I could see a major problem in the making. What caught my attention was the quantity of cutlery that the table steward was setting out at each place. There had to be at least six courses with some requiring a tool in each hand and others only one. Awaiting a suitable moment I discreetly approached a member of the staff and asked him for advice. I would have given more than evens that I was not the first overseas visitor who had been confronted with a similar situation.

In order that the gentleman would have no doubts as to the seriousness of the situation I explained that up to now all that I had been used to was a tin plate, a knife and fork, plus a pannikan. The advice was so obvious that I should have had no problems in working out by myself, stay half a course behind the Squire and use the same utensils as he was using. Well at least if the Old Gentleman made a mistake I would have been in good company. During my four years in England I was, on several occasions, a guest at one of their Stately Homes and the advice, so freely given on that first night, served me well. Another mistake which I did not repeat, was to take anybody along with me!

The meal over, gentlemen stood while the ladies left, when it was cigars for those who smoked, after which we joined the ladies and sat around in comfortable armchairs while we drank coffee and discussed the day's events and made plans for the morrow. Now that ladies have taken up smoking and television has taken the centre of the stage the above is a delightful way of life which has mostly passed into history.

The two boys not only believed that Kiwi land was God's own they were also keen to compare it with other countries, including that of their host. From the gist of the conversation I gathered that 'God's Own Jack' was as good as his Master and there was no difference in the social standing between the have's and the have not's.

His Lordship waited for a lull in the conversation during which he introduced the subject of horse riding which, if we were agreeable, was one of the activities being planned for the morrow. What a lesson in diplomacy providing we were in a condition to appreciate it.

During the previous year there had been numerous parties of New Zealanders visiting the estate and not a single one had ever ridden a horse, a fact which rather mystified our English friends who somehow had gained the impression that most New Zealanders were expert horsemen. Well that was a situation which was about to be rectified as both my mates were excellent riders though, to me at least, it soon became obvious that they had gained most of their experience by watching cowboy films on Saturday afternoons.

It was just not possible that three horsemen could arrive at the same time so I kept off the subject even though I had learned to ride almost as soon as I had learned to walk. To me a horse just meant work. You had to run it in from the pasture, feed and groom the creature, then fit a saddle and bridle. After a day on your horse the above procedure would have to be reversed; it was not the sort of activity I was keen to undertake while on holiday.

Like an old soldier, I had every intention of seeing the adventurers off and being on hand to welcome them home but it was not to be. His Lordship manoeuvred me into a situation where I just had to go along. But there was no swinging into the saddle clad only in slacks and the rest of the casual garments which was the usual clothes in which I would turn out for work in far-away New Zealand. It was jodhpurs, knee-length riding boots, black coat and Homburg hat. So attired the Groom would lead the horse along-side a mounting block where the rider could step onto the saddle with the least amount of effort. From then on the picture changed.

There was no opening of gates, it was straight over the top and it was not too difficult to predict what was about to happen when our two city boys mounted a horse for the first time. At the first hurdle Don beat his horse over and somehow Doug's managed to get over without it's rider. Both had taken rather nasty spills so from then on it was a case of opening the gates. Both had been lucky to have come through the ordeal without serious damage and there was no way that I was going to take the chance of spoiling all our holidays by one or both breaking a limb or worse. The final straw for Don was when we came to a place where it was necessary to ride down a small bank which meant a drop of about three feet. When his mount stopped suddenly and just stood there, hind feet securely anchored on the bank above, Don slid out of the saddle and down the neck, finally coming to rest with his legs firmly clasped around the horse's neck while his head and hands were wedged in the muddy pool into which he had been thrust. That horse just stood there. The only thing preventing

Don becoming a muddy mess was the Squire's Homburger and gloves. The situation was not improved for the victim by the peals of girlish laughter from the Squire's daughter, a girl of about seventeen who was a member of the party and a magnificent horsewoman.

The two finally decided that riding was not for them but I was not to escape so lightly. Miss Tyler decided that she would like a companion on the early morning rides which she undertook and I was the obvious choice. As a matter of fact I was the only choice. That young lady was a proper Tomboy. If I had not put in an appearance by the time she was ready to take off she simply bowled into my bedroom, pulled back the drapes and tipped the contents of the bed, including myself, out onto the floor. Looking back I have to admit that I enjoyed those early morning gallops over, through or around obstacles; it was fun.

All this horse riding had a disastrous effect on my village social life. Most of the villagers, their fathers and grandfathers, had served a succession of Squires and all in all were a very close-knit community. There was no need to become involved outside as most activities were supplied by the estate including church, pub and also a cemetery. It was possible to be born on the place, live one's whole life there and to be buried there without having to leave the property. The result of this was that the Squire and his family were the centre of that little world and all that he or his family did was noted and talked about, including my early morning frolics with Young Missie, which was the way they addressed and referred to the young lady.

As I mentioned earlier the boys became friendly with a couple of local maids and the highlight of the day was for the foursome to go off to the local for the evening, with the result they soon became part of the local community and before long were on first name terms with all and sundry. On the odd occasions when I joined the party, it was not a success. I was treated as a member of the Big House and it was, 'Yes, young master, no young master.' There was no way that I could break through the social barrier, with the result that though always polite, it was evident that the assembly were ill at ease when I was around.

One evening when, as usual, I was at home with the family, Mrs Tyler brought up the subject of my lucky elephant. This had been carved out of teak and weighed five pounds.

This shiny black monster I had bought while passing through the Panama Canal and I believed that it was the good luck charm that was going to see me safely through the war. It went everywhere with me and always had a favoured position on my bedside table so he had moved into my life and had become a permanent part of it. My Hostess' problem was that her staff considered it evil and were reluctant to service my room with it standing on that table and glaring up at them. To me, the problem was the result of an old wives tale, the believers being of the opinion that if the elephant's trunk was curled up, the owner's luck was retained and nothing but good fortune would be the lot of that person, but should the trunk hang straight down, such as my animal's did, mis-fortune was all that I could expect. A senior member of the household staff had a sailor son on HMS *Hood*. He had refused to listen to his mother's warning and now he and his elephant, with its offending trunk, were gone forever. All my Hostess could get out of the lady was 'the Young Master will die if he keeps that elephant', and she obviously meant it. Well if it was going to help the situation I had no qualms about banishing the Old Boy to my trunk for the rest of our stay but I had a feeling that he gave me a funny look as I was closing the lid.

I was to meet Aundra Holmes in London on our return south, so I made a mental note to tell him the story as he had an identical elephant which he also had bought while passing through Panama. When eventually I arrived at the New Zealand Forces Club there was no sign or word of Aundra which was unusual since we had become firm friends since the day when I had put my flying future on the line in order to help him pass the Morse exam. Eventually, as always, someone was to turn up who was able to supply the reason for Aundra's absence. Apparently he had been night flying and had stayed too long in the 'Red' while attempting to land and had been killed. In flying language the term 'too long in the "Red"' means that he was using the glide path indicator which has three lights which are visible to the approaching pilot, but he can only see one, a blue indicates that the approach is too high and that the plane will overshoot the runway, a green indicates the correct angle of approach and a red that the angle is too steep and that if the pilot does not take corrective action his plane will crash well short of the field.

That bloody elephant! Fighting the Germans was a dangerous enough occupation without 'him' on their side. I collected him from my case and after making my way up to the highest point in the Club I opened a window and heaved the villain out onto the street below. No sooner had I disposed of that elephant than I realised the risk I had taken for at that time of day there could be a lot of people about and five pounds of teak landing on someone's head from three storey's up would have about the same result as a bomb exploding under your feet. When eventually I made my way down to the street there were no bodies lying around, and all there was to show for my rash action was a few pieces of teak.

There were quite a few embarrassing occasions during my stay at Long Hall, the worst being when the Squire caught the two boys playing poker with his nineteen-year-old son. What he took a dim view of was they they were dealing off the bottom of the pack and taking the son to the cleaners. In my opinion that boy was getting his just desserts as he obviously had learned a few smart tricks and had talked my two mates into the poker game in order to try them out. Once Don spotted what he was up to it was a case of a lamb amongst the wolves as his two opponents knew more tricks that he had even dreamt of. I was just idly watching the fleecing when I became aware that the Master had entered the room and by his face I realised he had seen what was going on. With a movement of his head he indicated that he would like to see me in his study, so I turned and followed him out of the room which would be one of the longest walks that I've ever had to make. To be caught cheating at cards while a guest in an Englishman's home would have to be about the greatest crime of all, and if I was about to hear that three New Zealanders were to catch the next train south it was no more than we deserved. 'Would I ask my friends not to play any more cards with his son.' That old gentleman must have been hurt by the way his hospitality had been abused but I left him in no doubt of my thoughts on the matter and the fact that they had been the culprits, all three of them, and that I was the one who had taken the bollocking!

Having some company on those pre-breakfast gallops was obviously being so much enjoyed by my fair companion that I did not have the heart to refuse but it was the afternoons that were so hard to fill in; London would have been a much more entertaining place.

Don and Doug were having a ball. They did not put in an appearance much before midday. I was sure that they were having breakfast in bed. Then as soon as their two girlfriends were off duty, the foursome disappeared in the direction of the Local and that was the last I was to see of them for the day. On one occasion, after their return, I was invited to join the midnight beano and while it was being prepared I spotted a cold chicken on a plate in the 'fridge' and helped myself to it. As I bolted across the living room with one of the girls in pursuit, I became aware of the Lady of the House standing at the bottom of the stairs. She must have heard the racket and come down stairs to investigate. I put on my brakes, the young lady cannoned into me, the chicken shot off the plate and finished up at Mrs Tyler's feet.

We have all heard the expression, 'You could have heard a pin drop', well on that occasion, even though it would have fallen on the carpet, I am sure we would have heard it.

'Having fun, children? I will see you all in the morning.' The good lady turned and disappeared up the stairs and as far as I was aware that was all that any of us heard of the incident.

The blue-bloods of England have been the butt of many unkind jokes, but they are ladies and gentlemen in the true sense of the word and when high death duties and taxes have disposed of the stately homes of England the world will be the poorer for it.

Back in Bournemouth nothing seemed to have changed so I decided to have an old football injury repaired. This meant spending a couple of weeks in hospital and when I was discharged it was to find that both Doug and Don had been posted in my absence and I was never to see either of them again. On my return to Bournemouth I was posted to Hullavington to do a refresher course on Masters before going to a Spitfire Operational Training Unit, then to a Spitfire squadron.

Flying conditions in New Zealand, when compared with those in England, were as different as chalk and cheese. In Kiwiland it was almost impossible for even a learner pilot to become lost because in conditions when this could happen, no fledgling would be allowed to fly. The country is long and narrow and like all areas close to the sea has more than its fair share of wind which disperses fog and low cloud, and this in turn enables the airman to obtain a clear picture of his surroundings in relation to coastline and the central mountain range which runs down the middle of both islands. How different it is in England, with never-ending small tree-lined fields and fogs which are unpredictable. At Hullavington the most notable feature was an old Roman road but even it was so camouflaged by it's attending trees that it was difficult to find. On my arrival at that field I had a few trips in a Miles Master, which was a twin-seat, low-wing monoplane, and then I set off in a Hurricane which was an experience that I was never likely to forget. The old training command Hurricane was not exactly the fastest plane around but it was a big improvement on anything that I had flown up to then. Also with its small cramped cockpit, it was rather daunting.

The Rolls-Royce motor ran sweetly enough but it was the swinging from side to side as I taxied out that took a lot of getting used to. There was a vast blind spot in front and it was not very difficult to visualise the result were the propeller to make contact with an aeroplane directly in my path which I had failed to see.

After flaps, magneto's, seat up, boost, straps and obtaining a clearance from the Tower, it was a quick look around, into wind and away. The procedure was to maintain fine pitch and full revs until safely off, wheels up, seat down and hood closed by which time enough height should have been obtained for the pilot to start adjusting revs and boost. This seems all so matter of fact as I tell it now but for a pupil pilot undertaking his first flight in an operational aircraft, by the time I had done all these things I was miles away from the airfield and completely lost. What does a new chum do? He is stuck up there in the limitless sky, with his frantic calls for someone to tell him where he is, unanswered. Looking over the side does not help as small tree-lined fields stretch in every direction and there is just no feature that will give an indication as to what direction home could be. In my case at least I had a full tank of petrol which delayed the time in which a decision had to be made and as a last resort I could jump out and make my way down by parachute while the old Hurricane found it's own way home! On that occasion I found the field eventually and knowing that the instructors would be awaiting my return and watching my landing with a critical eye, I happily managed what I considered a creditable approach and touchdown, only to discover that I was on the wrong airfield!

After a few trips at Hullavington, which were more or less to get us used to flying again, we transferred to a satellite to do further night flying. The name of this 'drome was Castle Combe and it was close to an old Roman village after which it had been named.

No new dwellings had been built in the village for a hundred years or more and it must have been almost as the Romans would have remembered it. As for the locals any of them who had moved more than a few miles from his or her birth place was regarded, by the others, much as the rest of the world regarded Scott after his dash to the South Pole! We did not understand the local dialect nor customs and when we visited the one and only tavern at the end of the day's flying, how were we to know that the seat we fancied was the undisputed property of a local by virtue of the fact that he had sat in that very spot, every night, for the last forty or perhaps fifty years. The stony silence when we entered the place would have daunted stouter hearts than ours. Like oil and water we did not mix.

CHAPTER III

FIGHTER PILOT

SPITFIRES, when I first saw them sitting out on the field at Harden, were smaller than I had imagined, slender dainty creatures but for me, like others before and after me, it was love at first sight. These were the aircraft that I wanted to fly and fight in. Although I was later to fly Typhoons and then Tempests, I still believe that the nicest aircraft to fly was a Spitfire, closely followed by the Tiger Moth. Neither aircraft had a single vice and if their pilot had sense enough not to interfere there were few situations from which they would not extricate him.

Impressed as I was with Spitfires, I was even more impressed by the instructors whose job it was to teach us to fly them. The instructor who had impressed me the most, up to this time, was Johnny Nelson, my instructor at Elementary Flying School. Johnny Nelson and the instructors at Harden had been cast in the same mould. The Harden chaps had all done a tour of operations either in France, over Dunkirk or during the Battle of Britain and what impressed us the most was that up till Harden we had become used to being talked down to by a lot of our instructors who seemed to think that they were God's gift to Pupil Pilots, the lowest form of life in the Air Force. Here it was different; we were accepted without reservation. Their attitude simply was—you fellows will be amongst them shortly, we have managed to stay alive possibly more by good fortune than by any superior effort on our part, if we can help you to do the same well that is what we are here for. They were a race apart with a dash and style that was exciting. Their top button left undone which indicated that the wearer of the tunic was a fighter pilot, Jimmy Edwards' style moustache, uniforms that seemed to indicate that they were in service twenty four hours in every day, all this plus hats with stiffeners removed and worn at a rakish angle gave the impression of a Buccaneer. A scruffy bunch they may have looked but they could do things with a Spitfire than even the designer would not have thought possible.

On our first morning our new flight commander, Flight Lieutenant Sanders delivered a lecture which was not the usual 'hats will be worn at all times, uniforms buttoned, said buttons to be kept bright and shiny, Officers to be saluted smartly wherever met'. As I recall it the pep talk went something like this. You intrepid birdmen have been taught a type of flying which is safe enough providing that you stay in friendly air but which will get you into a lot of trouble down South. When a wing returns from a sweep there could be sixty aircraft in the circuit all short on petrol and some of them shot up. There will be no time for fancy circuits, your job will be to get down in the shortest possible time and stay there. If you chaps are to survive you will have to be able to handle a Spitfire in any conditions. In fact, by the time you leave here, you just might be able to perform the circuit that I am about to show you without bending your aircraft or yourselves.

Our new teacher then climbed into a Spitfire and set off for the end of the runway in service, swinging the nose from side to side and taxying much too fast by our standards but this could be excusable. (Spitfires had a weakness in that the air intake was directly behind one of the Oleo legs and the engine would overheat if the aircraft was taxied too slowly or if parked for too long at the end of the runway while awaiting take off.)

The teacher must have kept a forward pressure on the control column thus keeping the wheels firmly on the ground, and at the same time selecting wheels up because when the machine became unstuck the wheels flicked up into the fuselage, a little hard on the hydraulics but very spectacular; well at least to a bunch of new chums who had not seen the act before. As the wheels came up, the aircraft started a climbing roll and by the time it was upside down it had completed a one hundred and eighty degree turn and was now directly down wind. The pilot then completed the roll and at the same time did another turn, losing height at the same time which brought his aircraft over the end of the runway. While this was going on the wheels had reappeared and the pilot did a perfect three-point landing. Just to prove his mastery of the aircraft, the Flight Commander then repeated the spectacular performance.

We had lived by the rule book and life had become a burden trying to memorise the things we should and the things we should not do. Now we had seen the book thrown out the window. For the first time our instructors were treating us as partners in a great adventure and we idolised them; to win their approval no effort on our part was too great.

Apart from my two room mates the rest of the course were locals consisting of Welsh, Scottish and English. The other three, of which I was one, were foreigners. Blackie was a very small Australian whose problem was that he could not keep away from women and, bless their fickle little hearts, they could not keep away from him. There were fathers and boy friends of girls that he had promised to marry. That boy had problems and all of them his own making. My other room mate, Charlie Ramsey, was an American and was one of the adventurous bunch who had crossed the Atlantic before their country entered the war, to fly and fight with the Royal Air Force's Fighter Command and who were later to form the three Eagle squadrons. Charlie had more problems than the rest of his countrymen. Twice the ships on which he was a passenger had been torpedoed and on each occasion he had been picked out of the water by a neutral ship and taken back to America.

At least Blackie's problems were his own and I was not involved. Charlie's were not so easy to sort out. He had a thing about black soldiers going around with white girls and to see a Negro fondling one was like the proverbial red flag to a bull. I had become very fond of Charlie and there was almost nothing that I would not do for my American friend but helping him to fight every black man who chose to go around with a white woman was not one of them. Charlie and I did not try to get into trouble, somehow it just seemed to follow us around, and the episode I am about to relate was the result of our being confined to camp for twenty four hours as the result of some misdemeanour on our part.

To make sure that we would stay on camp we had to visit the Officer's Mess every hour from seven till midnight and sign the Duty Officer's book. The Officer, whose job it was to see we signed the book, must have had other plans and so we were instructed to report to a rear door where a WAAF orderly would produce the book for our signatures. The young lady must have felt sorry for us because each time she also produced a more than generous whisky and then it was back to our Mess bar for another session of beer while awaiting our next trip to the Officer's Mess and more whisky.

We had become well known around the Station, mostly because of the problems Charlie generated, and of his feud with black men, and the general opinion seemed to be that whatever punishment we received it was well earned. That girl may have thought that she was

being kind to us but next morning we both had the father of all hangovers and both were down for line astern aerobatics. Someone must
have blown the whistle on us or perhaps the deterioration in our
signatures, as the night progressed, had given the game away, and our
instructors had decided to teach us a lesson.

Line astern formation requires the maximum amount of concentration. To add aerobatics creates an additional problem in that if
number two gets too far back it is almost impossible to regain position
without a period of straight and level flight. Get too close and it is
more than likely that you will nip the tail off number one's aircraft.
When I thought that I could take no more punishment I pulled the
throttle and the stick back and spun down into a cloud bank which
was directly below. Clear of the cloud and straight and level once
more I headed for home feeling rather pleased with my effort. I had
had plenty of practice in talking my way out of tight spots before—
and I had no doubt that I would think up a suitable excuse when my
instructor caught up with me.

Just as Base was appearing beneath, and I was rehearsing the story
that I was going to tell Charlie, a Spitfire ranged up alongside and
in it was my instructor with a grin I could almost see through his
oxygen mask! A pat on the back of his head was an indication that I
was to take up a position directly astern and this time there was no
cloud around.

Back on the ground my hangover had gone, the cure had been
rough but effective, Charlie had over choked his aircraft and had failed
to get off, now he was curled up in a chair, the picture of misery. I
could have almost found it in my heart to have felt sorry for him.
After leaving Harden the only time I was to see Charlie Ramsey
again was while on leave in London. His first words were, 'Jimmy!
The only difference between when I was with the firm you work for
and where I am now, is that when I put my hands in my pockets,
there is money there.' He was by then an Officer in the American
Army Air Force.

Apart from the odd occasion when fog blew in unexpectedly from
the Irish coast, our losses were while practicing tight squadron formation or while doing night landings. I can recall an occasion when a
Canadian was leading a squadron formation and a Scottish pilot,
flying directly behind, flew into his leader and the two pilots were
locked together in their aircraft, unable to escape and both were
killed. A moment's loss of concentration, why? In the Scottish pilot's
pocket was a telegram. His only sister had been killed the previous
night by a German bomb. His parents arrived the following day, an

old couple who had obviously married late in life; now fate had wiped out their children within two days. It was heartbreaking to see them trying to offer each other comfort. This was a side of war that we had to forget and whisky helped.

The other victim of the unfortunate accident had a most attractive English girlfriend and he had made no secret of his intention of taking her back to Canada after the war. Two of his friends went along to offer what comfort they could. That young lady could not have cared less—her problem was who was going to take her to the Sergeant's Mess dance the following week!

Every six weeks a new course of pilots arrived at Harden, associated with the local girls, some passing through, others being killed—and then the girls were on hand to welcome the next intake.

Most of my fellow trainees had entered the service straight from school and while I had no reason to doubt their flying ability it seemed to me a crime that some of them had been let loose amongst the public without their mothers around to look after them. Roy Barker, a young gullible lad, confided in me that he'd never drunk whisky. Well, providing he was prepared to pay for it, I was just the one to cure this defect in his education. By the time we had been thrown out of the pub, because Roy and whisky turned out to be a fighting combination, and I had dragged his body back to camp it was more than possible that my friend was off spirits for life.

Next morning my late drinking companion was restored to do local flying and the howl of the Rolls-Royce Merlin, as the Spitfire lumbered down the runway with the propeller in course pitch, alerted the airfield as to what was about to happen. There was just enough power available to lift the aircraft into the air and then things began to happen. The first obstacle, which happened to be the boundary fence, knocked the wheels off, then successive obstructions continued to remove parts of the aircraft until the Spitfire gave up the struggle and returned to earth. Apart from the complete destruction of one fighter there was not a great deal of damage done, Roy having escaped with a few minor cuts and we waited with baited breath for what the Station Commander was going to say. Surprisingly the main offender escaped with a baby lecture and a few pointed remarks regarding the need to carry out cockpit drill and also that whisky and flying did not mix!

Nothing ever happened around the Station as far as the pilots were concerned, which was not noticed and gossiped about. We were a never-ending source of amusement and amazement. So, over the loud hailer came, 'Sergeant Sheddan, report to the Commanding Officer'.

The only time we were ordered to report to that office was when we were about to receive a dressing down for something we had or had not done. However, on this occasion I could not recall any action of mine that would upset the Old Man enough for him to require a private interview. How wrong can one be. It seemed that I had taken a young pilot out and filled him up with whisky with the result that a Spitfire had been destroyed and no credit to me that the Royal Air Force had not lost a pilot on whom they had spent a lot of time and money. Any repetition and it was more than likely I would be spending the rest of the war in the army. That branch of the Armed Services was again stretching its greedy fingers in my direction. My instructor had been heard to remark that Ramsey and Sheddan were like goats, 'If they were not coming from trouble they were on their way to it!' It was just possible that there could have been a smattering of truth in his remarks.

Most service pilots believe that there is a Gremlin perched on their shoulder and ready to take advantage of a moment's lack of concentration. With the little green man in control anything could happen. On my last flight at Harden he must have had a few friends along to lend a hand; the result, one aircraft damaged beyond repair and one pilot so badly shaken that it was very nearly the end of flying for him. Had that happened it would have been the end of all my hopes and dreams.

My instructions were to do a height climb to thirty thousand feet which was about as high as Spitfire IIs could reach. My first mistake, as the aeroplane struggled up those last few thousand feet, was in winding the control column back with the tail trim instead of holding it back manually. The second was in not checking that all controls were in their proper place before rolling over and starting the homeward journey in a vertical aileron turn. In this manoeuvre the Spitfire built up speed very quickly and there must have been limited airflow over the elevator as I had no warning of impending disaster. As I centralised the control column, there was just not time for me to make the necessary adjustment as the 'plane started an upward surge and gravity took over. The usual procedure when the controls are being operated manually is for the pilot to ease forward on the 'stick' when the pressure is relieved, and the heart can pump sufficient blood to the eyes and brain but in my case there was just not time and I started to black out. Then as my brain was starved of oxygen I lost consciousness. What must have happened was that the Spitfire did a high speed stall because when again I began to take an interest in my surroundings, I was pretty much upside down and leafing around in more or less flat turns and losing height quite slowly. Strange as it may seem the engine was ticking over quite sweetly.

My first act was to wind the tail trim forward into a neutral position, then try all the approved procedure for regaining control. Stick, rudder, engine—nothing seemed to work and as there was no point in staying where I was, it was time to leave! It was at this point that the panic started. The hood had jammed and the automatic release would not function, nor, using my head as a battering ram could I force my way through the hood. I found myself cowering back as far as possible in what must have been a survival effort. Then, as I recall it, I seemed to settle down and accept the fact that death was only minutes away. It was as though I was observing the performance from the outside and was not actually involved. At five thousand feet the aircraft ceased its antics, everything appeared to work and I was again in control. Gremlins or 'finger trouble' had been the cause of the problem, but what happened next was just plain stupidity. To take an aircraft which had been subjected to the worst possible strain and one from which there was no escape, back to seven thousand feet and proceed to do a series of rolls and loops was stretching one's luck to the limit.

Back on the airfield the ground crew had to use a wrecking bar to force the hood open. The tail was a shambles with most of the fabric torn away and the fuselage was so twisted that this had been the cause of the hood jamming. The experts were of the opinion that the force required would have been far greater than the seven times gravity that is all the human body is capable of standing. They seemed to think that I should have burst open like a ripe melon!

At first it seemed as though I had escaped without any ill-effects, then the nightmares started, some sort of delayed shock, no doubt, for no sooner would I drop off to sleep than I would be trapped in an aircraft with the ground coming up at an alarming rate. It was terrifying. Sleep became impossible and I learned to survive in a twilight zone, like an animal. I was instantly awake at the slightest sound. I married after the war and by this time so permanent had my anti-sleeping habit become that I can recall my wife remarking that although we had been married for seven years, she had never seen me asleep. Before I learned to cope with my problem I tried to blot out the past with whisky but this did little to help.

I was never aware of any fear of flying when fully awake; it was when asleep that the nightmares began. It was always the same. I would be trapped in a spinning aircraft and just about to hit the ground when I'd awaken, usually covered in sweat and often on the floor.

I found I could survive without sleep which was one way of getting over it, although this was more or less behind me when I got to 486.

However the condition lasted long after I returned to civil life and became a habit. Initially they tried to cure me with drugs and then I had to overcome the drugs. It was something I shouldn't like to go through again.

It was now October 1942 and at last my posting came through. I was to join 485 NZ Squadron, flying Spitfires, which at the time was on rest and stationed at Kingscliffe which was a satellite of Wittering where Pat Jameson[1] was Wing Leader. Jamie, as he was affectionately known throughout Fighter Command, was a New Zealander and one of the pilots who had flown their Hurricanes from Norway onto the carrier HMS *Glorious* only to have their temporary base sunk under them and only Jamie and his CO survived. When I joined the squadron Reg Grant[2] was the Commanding Officer. He was later to lose his life while flying a Mustang and earlier, while on a fighter sweep, was to see his brother killed and not be in a position to help. It was small consolation that he was able to shoot down the German pilot.[3]

I was quite pleased with this posting. I had finally made the grade and was now a fighter pilot, although still effectively under training. My posting, however, did not turn out as hoped. I was pleased with them but they became far from pleased with me.

---

[1] Group Captain P G Jameson DSO, DFC and bar from Wellington
[2] Wing Commander R J C Grant DFC and bar, DFM from Woodville. Killed in action 28 Feb 1944 as OC 122 Wing
[3] Flying Officer I A C Grant from Woodville, killed in action 13 Feb 1943.

CHAPTER IV

WITH 485 NZ SQUADRON

AT this time 485 was not a happy squadron, especially for new pilots to come to. Its older members had been through a tour, and their dearest wish was to remain together as a unit and return to the fray; who could blame them. At that time Middle East squadrons were short of pilots and Fighter Command policy was to send out experienced ones from England of any nationality, so the arrival of a pilot from training command was usually followed, as far as the squadron was concerned, by the departure of an old friend. As a result it was no wonder that our arrival was not greeted with any great show of enthusiasm. There were only a certain number of pilots in any squadron, so my arrival meant an old chum leaving.

Into this mix-up I arrived, drinking too much and apparently scared at the thought of having to fly on operations. Scared I may have been, but it was not of the Germans; it was those dreadful nightmares and the knowledge that any pilot who arrived on a squadron and then reported sick, would not rate very high with the old hands, who had themselves been shot down, or worse, seen friends shot down and not been in a position to help.

The first Spitfire that I was to fly on 485 was George Moorhead's. George was a gentleman to his finger tips and it must have pained him greatly when I flew his pride and joy around, with its wheels down, because I had forgotten to lift them! Then, having remembered, tried to land with them still tucked up in the wings!! George was killed later when his Spitfire hit the water while returning at low-level from France. Next, Reg Baker, my new Flight Commander took me up for some practice formation flying and if I was not trying to climb over the top of his machine, I was so far away that the best that could be said was that Reg and I were flying in the same direction![1]

Lack of sleep, too much booze and punk flying, my career had reached rock bottom, so there was only one way for me to go and that was up. Worst of all was that I could not understand what was happening to me. At OTU I had been one of the top Formation and Aerobatic pilots and now I was performing worse than would have been expected from a new chum who was trying to fly his first Spitfire.

On 28 November, 1942, one of those inexplicable incidents occurred which seem to take place on squadrons from time to time. Bill Norris, a Sergeant Pilot[2], was assigned to fly a Rhubarb, which was a low-level sweep by two aircraft over enemy territory for the purpose of shooting up any targets which they might find. This type of operation was later discontinued because the losses were too high when weighed against the results. In the bar the night before, Bill was depressed, and was firmly convinced that he would be making his last flight the next day. We all laughed at his gloomy prediction and tried to cheer him up but it was useless. It did seem that the Bone had been pointed in Bill's direction, and sure enough, Bill did not return. This was the sort of thing that resulted in pilots flying with a Rabbit's foot in their pocket or a lucky scarf draped around their neck and having pinned his faith in a good luck charm; woe betide an airman rash enough to take off without it.

My brother Alex was the last of the Sheddan clan to be inflicted with that Christian name. For countless generations, extending back through our Scottish ancestry, there has not been an Alex who has survived his late teens or early twenties and all have died violently. The curse had followed the New Zealand descendants and my brother was the last. The night in December 1943 when Alex was killed, I had been out on a daylight fighter sweep over France and had spent the night at Manston because our home base was fog bound. When I arrived back at Tangmere there was a telegram from Air Ministry informing me that my brother was missing on an air operation and also a letter from Alex instructing me in what action to take in the event of his death. It would seem that he too knew that his time had come.[3]

I do not think his death affected me unduly; in hindsight I think the

[1] Wing Commander R W Baker DFC from Dunedin, CO 485 Squadron and CO 487 Squadron 1945. Killed in action 22 Feb 1945
[2] Sergeant F W Norris from Wellington, aged 21
[3] Flight Sergeant Alexander Bernard Sheddan, 166 Squadron RAF. Killed in action 20 December 1943

family expected it. When he'd said goodbye to Mother, his final words were, "Jim will come home but I won't", and she said his hand was so cold she knew she would never see him again.

Kingscliffe was a God forsaken place in the winter time and we spent our evenings in the Sergeant's Mess where the bar was the one and only attraction. I shall never forget one occasion when Les 'Chalky' White[1] and I were last to leave, not an infrequent occurrence, and made our way to the Nissen hut in which we slept. Having consumed a fair quantity of beer during the evening, Chalky decided to dispose of some of it before retiring indoors and it being a cold windy night, where better to do it than in the shade of the hut. Unfortunately the spot he chose was directly beneath a window. At the same time Allan Frewer had the same idea, the only difference being that Allan was inside the hut and in his hour of need he could find neither the light switch nor the door, so being a resourceful Kiwi he jumped up on his bed, pushed the window open and let drive. It was the window underneath which Chalky had parked himself. I was carrying on a stop/go conversation with my mate when all of a sudden there was an abrupt silence and then with a few muttered oaths, Chalky took off for the door-way. For a big, wide-shouldered man with hands and feet to match, it surprised me how quickly he could move. I made haste to follow and when I found and activated the light switch, there was Allan standing on his bed, as white as the proverbial ghost, with Chalky's big fist firmly clasped around his poor little 'spout', and the big man muttering, 'Piss on me will you, I will pull the bloody thing off.' About all I could see of the offending 'spout' was a couple of danglers! Just when it seemed that permanent damage was about to be done, Chalky's sense of humour returned.

I knew Leslie White as well as most of his service acquaintances and I never saw him loose his temper, though I could imagine that it would have been akin to a major volcanic eruption had he ever done so. Equally, I cannot say that I ever saw him burst into peals of laughter and yet he was a man who enjoyed life to the full and was always prepared to see the funny side of any situation. When he smiled, which he did often, a laughter line would start at the corner of his eyes and extend in a half circle down to the corner of his mouth. These wrinkles would work their way backwards as they were being replaced by new ones, until they almost reached his ears. His eyes would close until he was peering at you through slits and you heard a hearty chuckle which

---

[1] Flight Lieutenant L S McQ White DFC from Gore

was far more effective than laughter could ever be.

As we pass through life, we meet and associate with countless thousands of people and most leave no lasting impression but no-one who had the good fortune to know Chalky could ever forget him. He was a legend in his own lifetime and one of my greatest regrets was that I was later unable to attend his funeral, because by the time I heard about it there was no way that I could have made it.

Kingscliffe was an unhappy place for me. I was rarely asked to fly and was more or less ignored. There were a few like Chalky. George Moorhead, Max Sutherland[1], Marty Hume[2] and Norm Harrison, to mention a few, who seemed to sense that I had struck a rough patch and went out of their way to try and make me feel that I was wanted, but their efforts were sabotaged by the Squadron Adjutant who never missed an opportunity of getting on my back; how I hated and detested that man.

Just before the Squadron was to leave for Ireland, to practice deck landings, a telegram arrived from Group with instructions that a pilot was to be sent to Matlaske to do an air firing course. A heaven-sent opportunity of disposing with a problem child.

Issued with a Spitfire in late October, I was ordered to fly to Matlaske and stay there until the squadron returned to Kingscliffe. Away from the squadron and the unhappy atmosphere, my confidence returned and with it, my flying skill. All that was required of me was to do a couple of half-hour periods daily, shooting at a towed drogue and on occasion I would accompany the towing aircraft as it made its way out to the firing range, which was several miles out to sea, and amuse myself by doing barrel rolls around the slow old Lysander.

This passion for aerobatics very nearly proved my undoing. To barrel roll around another aircraft needs a lot of concentration and I did not notice the approaching cloud which was soon to surround my Spitfire like a blanket and turn day into night. In a situation such as this, a pilot thinks he knows the position of his aircraft in relation to the ground or, as in my case, the sea, but unless there had been a change in the way that gravity worked my aircraft had to be the wrong way up as odd bits of rubbish were leaving the floor and sailing up past my head. Instruments temporarily out of action, upside down in cloud and the sea less than two thousand feet below, I had a problem! Of course, a moment's hesitation or the wrong option taken and a

---

[1] Flight Lieutenant M G Sutherland from Otago Head. POW 22 August 1943
[2] Squadron Leader M R D Hume DFC from Martinborough. CO 485, Squadron Sept 1943—Feb 1944

pilot and his aircraft are quickly past the point of no return. There is, naturally, the option of using the parachute but this most pilots are loath to do, while there is a chance of saving their aircraft, and, unfortunately when it becomes obvious that to jump is their only chance, it is sometimes too late.

What I did was to centralise the control column, while the aircraft must have been in a vertical dive, then slowly move it back as the speed built up. This action gradually flattened the angle of dive and also allowed the artificial horizon on the instrument panel to return to normal. When I eventually broke cloud, my machine was more or less on an even keel and about three hundred feet above the sea.

Flying only took up a very small portion of those three weeks and as keeping out of trouble was not one of my strong points, it was not long before I was on the carpet.

I had teamed up with a Canadian pilot who had been flying one of the drogue-towing aircraft and having got himself grounded, was awaiting a posting back to Canada. It was a bad combination.

Our first act was to be caught poaching pheasants that had increased in number as a result of the Lord of the Manor and his wealthy friends giving up hunting the poor little birds as they were away shooting at Germans. The tenant farmers guarded the Master's property zealously and reported us to the Commanding Officer with the result that we received a proper wigging. The last straw for us was when my friend and myself were steering an unsteady course for home one evening and met a large horse wandering along the highway and decided to take the animal with us. On the way back to base we had to pass the WAAF billets and we decided to introduce our friend to the girls. The girls were not in the least upset by our late call but would have nothing to do with 'Dobbin' so we left and took him with us.

At Matlaske we were billetted in a large country mansion, Matlaske Hall. A Typhoon squadron, who were flying from the field, used for their sleeping quarters a large sun-room, access to which was from a large outside landing, through massive swinging doors. We persuaded the horse to clamber up the concrete stairs which connected the ground and the landing, then ushered him into the sun-room after which we securely fastened the doors. Deep in the arms of Morpheus, not a pilot stirred. It would not be too difficult to imagine the panic when the first sleeper half awoke and found a horse peering down at him, especially if he were a city lad. It is more than likely that he thought it was Hitler's secret weapon. Big as that animal was, he must have been a dainty mover as he had changed position several times during the night without knocking over a camp bed or disturbing a sleeper. Like all living things there is no doubt that our horse would have problems but constipation was not one of them! His sleeping partners were not amused and as he could not have entered that room unaided and locked the doors behind him,the hunt was on for his associates.

Girls are sometimes not to be trusted for keeping secrets, well at least not one like that. They well and truly pointed the finger at us and it was back into the Old Man's office for us both.

That Squadron Leader must have thought that commanding an Air Firing School was going to be a pleasant and safe way of conducting a war. Well we had news for him. In his restricted little world, I expect that he had not heard about the Dominions. The verdict—I was to return to my squadron immediately. My Spitfire was undergoing an inspection and would not be available for several days but this did not save me. The Station Adjutant had been in touch with 485 and they promised to send the Squadron Tiger over to collect me. What a tale that man must have told to have prompted such action on my behalf. In due course Chalky White and the Tiger arrived; his big grin left me in no doubt that he had already heard a greatly exaggerated account of my misdeeds.

Why I agreed to fly the Tiger on the return journey to Kingscliffe I just do not know as it is a well accepted part of service life that you do not volunteer for anything. The next mistake was to agree with Chalky's suggestion that we refuel on the way home. There was Tiger's milk available at Matlaske so why complicate the issue by involving another landing, possibly more, before we found a field with the required grade of fuel?

Airborne and half the journey over, the time had arrived when a refuelling stop was a must, so selecting a field with lots of small aircraft around, down we went. No brakes and taxying far too fast, I was relying on the slipstream for steerage. On emerging from the shelter of a hangar a tail wind neutralised the slipstream and my Tiger was temporarily out of control and rushing towards a large ditch which had appeared ahead. There was no time to kill the motor and hope.

The obvious course of action was to push the throttle wide open and trust that the increased slipstream would force that rampaging Tiger to answer the helm and swing away from the ditch which was getting closer by the second. I am afraid that it was not to be my day as the old Tiger went charging into the ditch. Up went the tail, the nose going in the opposite direction, to be followed by a loud splintering kind of noise as the wooden propeller broke up and bits of it flew in all directions. This little diversion was followed by complete silence.

The silence did not last for long. There was much muttering and swearing and peering over the back of the front seat from my lofty perch. There was my mate trying to disentangle himself from the instrument panel but from the noise he was making he had received no permanent injury. Bodies were beginning to arrive from various directions and as it was not the most desirable of positions, perched up there and being stared at, we made haste to dismount. Chalky's attitude was, 'You got us into this mess, now see if you can do as good a job of getting us out of it.'

Our destination, Kingscliffe, had no aircraft available to fly us there so the only other means of transport was a train of doubtful reliability. The first problem was to obtain two travel warrants, then arrange transport to the railway station. With the trouble I had in obtaining those warrants, it would not have been too difficult to have believed that we were a couple of German saboteurs trying to obtain first-class passages back to our homeland.

Next, transport. The chap in charge of that department was a corporal and he seemed to have the idea that part of his duties were to be as difficult as possible. The indications were that it was going to be a very long war.

The station, when we eventually arrived, seemed like a whistle stop in the middle of nowhere. The arrival of a train, if and when, seemed somewhat of a mystery to both locals and railway staff. One eventually puffed its way in and so began the long, slow, weary journey to home base and the explanations which would have to be made. As that old train hooted its way from station to station, fellow passengers kept looking at our parachutes and building up romantic pictures, no doubt, of the two intrepid birdmen. If they had only known.

For me the journey held no pleasure. At the end of it would be a hostile reception committee led by the Squadron Adjutant, eagerly awaiting my arrival. Normally the sidelining of the Squadron's Tiger would hardly have been noticed, but it was my misfortune to put on my little act a couple of days before Christmas, just when arrangements had been made for a pick up of some guests who had been invited to spend the festive season with 485.

For me at least the path was becoming clear. I could safely say that in whatever direction my future lay it was not going to be with 485.

Next morning it was the Adjutant's office for both of us. Chalky, being the senior member, was asked to supply the sordid details while I stood with lowered head as my part in the affair unfolded. I have to admit that, like any defending council, Chalky brought out any points that would help to minimise my crime but my performance since joining 485 had not left him much room for manoeuvre. The Adjutant did not want to hear my version, for as far as he was concerned it was an open and shut case. I had been tried and convicted long before I entered his office. He thought the only way to ensure 485's survival was to have me posted. For him it must have been beyond his some-what limited understanding that one Sergeant Pilot was capable of causing so much disaster. My departure was his immediate war effort, perhaps, by far his greatest.

Chalky was okay. A rough diamond maybe but a good fellow to have around in an emergency. With his big hand on my bowed shoulders he muttered 'Don't take it too badly, Jim, it will come out all right,' which helped me at a time when my spirits were at their lowest ebb.

The next time I saw Chalky was after he had been shot down over occupied France, escaping after capture and making his way back to England. While in France his commission had come through and now he was an officer and a gentleman but still the same old Chalky despite his fine feathers.[1]

My dearest wish was to take my place beside my comrades in the air battles over France but fate and one Adjutant had decided otherwise. Now I would be grounded or spend the rest of the war at some sole-destroying job like flying a drogue-towing aircraft. Another summons came to the flight office in January 1943, happily my last. A posting had come through, I was to report to Number One Delivery Flight at Croydon. I was to get a clearance and leave immediately. This did not cause me any pain as nothing the future held could be worse than what I had just been through. The Adj was in one big hurry to see me on my way before somebody had time to change their mind or maybe before further damage could be done.

Delivery Flight; it sounded as if I would be delivering bodies or freight around the place, possibly in a Tiger Moth! Well, at least I was still flying and in spite of past misfortunes, some day, somehow, I would fly on operations.

---

[1] White was shot down on 22 August 1943, in the same action in which Max Suther-land became a prisoner of war. White shot down an Fw190 but had then to crash land in France. He evaded capture and returned to England.

CHAPTER V

DELIVERY PILOT

LONDON was a place where I did not linger. I could just imagine trying to explain to old friends that I had failed to make the grade on 485 and was now about to take on the dangerous role of flying 'Tiger-schmitts'. At Croydon I reported to the Commanding Officer of my new unit, No. 1 ADF, Squadron Leader R W Wallens[1], who introduced me to his second in command, a fellow New Zealander, Flight Lieutenant Gordon Grant. Then it was out to the crew room to meet the rest of the team, ranging from Flight Lieutenants to Sergeants. Britain and her Allies were well represented there, Poles, Czechs, Australians, Canadians, Rhodesians and South Africans, it was a glorious mix-up. A cheerful bunch they appeared to be. There were no long faces that I could see.

So much for Tigers. My first assignment was to collect a Spitfire Nine from a MU and deliver to an Eleven Group squadron. These were the very latest in the Spitfire family. The boys at 485 could talk of nothing else and eagerly looked forward to the day when their Spit Fives would be replaced with these super aircraft. My next job was to take a Typhoon down to 193 Squadron at Harrowbeer on the south-west coast. No dithering about or, 'do you think that you can do it?' I was given an assignment and it seemed to be taken for granted that the task was well within my capabilities.

I did not undertake my first trip in a Typhoon with any degree of confidence. I had never seen one of these aircraft, few pilots had. It was the latest Hawker creation and had a Napier Sabre twenty-four

---

[1] Ronald Wallens had been wounded during the Battle of Britain. He later flew on Air Sea Rescue work and won the DFC

cylinder, twenty three-hundred horse power sleeve valve motor, which was more or less still in the experimental stage. It was a case of being thrown in at the deep end. The form was: first read through the Pilot's Notes in the flight office, then at the MU where there were no flying personnel, get a mechanic to show you how to start the monster. From then it was up to you to get the Typhoon up in the air to its destination and down again. Quite an assignment for a new chum when, at that time, the pilots, who had been taught to fly them by instructors, were scared stiff until they had done a considerable number of hours without coming to grief. It would be safe to say that when Typhoons first came into service they were preceded by a terrifying reputation simply because both motor and airframe were still at the experimental stage and it was literally at least two years before most of the snags were eliminated, during which time they had to be flying operationally.

What a terrific aeroplane that Typhoon was. Big and fast, and with its four cannon nothing on either side of the Channel could match it. This was not operational flying but the next thing to it and I felt that providing I could keep my nose clean and not put up any major 'blacks' it should not be too difficult to arrange a posting back to an operational squadron. If and when that happened, for me it would be Typhoons; I would consider nothing else.

Most deliveries were made by civilian pilots from the ATA—a lot of them girls. Their organisation had forbidden them to fly in uncertain weather so to keep the squadrons flying, the delivery flight had been formed and was staffed by service pilots. When No 11 Group squadrons were suddenly short of aircraft, and civilian deliveries were suspended, the problem would drop in our lap. Literally we were expected to fly even when the birds were walking. Often we would arrive by road or rail to collect a machine only to find, because of bad weather, all take-offs and landings had been suspended. To cover this eventuality we carried an authority from Fighter Command which gave us the doubtful privilege of authorising our own cross-country flights. We were a law unto ourselves and on occasions conditions were so marginal that we had to do an instrument take-off, yet I cannot recall a single accident while I was at Croydon that was caused by bad weather.

There was a Boulton Paul Defiant night-fighter squadron stationed at Croydon. These were single-engine aircraft which carried, in addition to the pilot, a gunner who operated a rear-firing machine-gun turret. One of the gunners attached to the squadron was a New Zealander who was known to one and all as Count Dolman or simply as 'The Count'. Our Count, running his fingers lovingly through his

Jimmy Edwards moustache, would enthuse about his vast cattle empire in far away New Zealand; the girls loved it. He was always the most popular member of any party. Much later, back home, I was to meet the Count in a Christchurch hotel. To my, 'Hello, Count', he whispered in my ear, 'Lay off the Count stuff, Jimmy. I am plain Jack these days'. It seemed that the title and the cattle empire had not survived the war.

As service pay would not support our life-style the Count and I formed a money-raising partnership. What the Count's racket was he never divulged but it must have been a good one because I never knew an occasion when he could not produce money. My additional source of income was ice skates and then shoes.

The Purley Ice Skating Rink was only a short distance away and all that was needed were a few attractive assistants to contaminate new arrivals with the ice skating bug and my prospective victim would pay the world for a pair of ice skates. I was the only supplier of skates so when a pilot was deserted by his lady love or posted I was always on hand to repurchase the skates, at a token price of course! The only snag was that my assistants had a fair idea as to my profit margin and demanded a fairly steep price for their services. It was a case of the biter being bitten.

As for the shoe fiddle, New Zealand personnel of all ranks were entitled to shoes as a Royal Air Force issue, the reason being that in New Zealand they were part of service dress. In England this item of footwear was scarce, expensive and required a large number of precious ration coupons. Providing a prospective customer could produce an old pair of similar design, we were in business. I was not actually giving the commodity away but nothing stimulates demand like scarcity. Again I had to have an assistant on the inside, this time a senior Flight Sergeant in stores as it would have been difficult to explain how I was managing to wear out a pair of shoes a week, sometimes more depending on the amount of trade available. The middle man greatly reduced my income. If only I could have dealt directly with the customer I would have been on easy street.

My fellow pilots were a carefree bunch, as for them operational flying was over. Most were ex-Battle of France or Britain and now had medical categories which limited their flying to no more than a thousand feet. The main problem was damaged ear drums, mostly caused by having to come 'downstairs' in a hurry while flying with a head cold. Carefree they may have been but how most of them mistrusted Typhoons. Some refused to fly them and others did so under protest; for these brave souls it was a continuing nightmare from the time they received their delivery instructions until switching off at journeys end. There were two exceptions, a Flight Lieutenant Raffer, a Czech, and myself. Given the opportunity we would have flown nothing else and as a result we shifted all the Typhoons, the only exception being when there were too many for us to cope with, then it was panic stations.

Typhoons were big. At seven tons they were nearly twice the weight of a Spitfire which, with its Rolls-Royce motor, had been around for a long time while the Typhoon with its Napier Sabre motor was a new creation having been rushed into service to help counter the Fw190 which had started their tip-and-run raids on the English south coast. This crash program had left little time to detect and correct development and construction faults. Now engine and airframe were being plagued with the sort of troubles that would have been ironed out in the more leisurely days of peace. The main difference between the Spitfire and Typhoon was normal cruising and maximum speeds, for while a Spitfire cruised well below its top speed a Typhoon cruised at a speed that was not much below its maximum, and this high speed made it a difficult aircraft to intercept. This difference in speeds was mainly brought about by the difference in revolutions of the two motors. Whereas a Rolls-Royce cruised at about eighteen hundred revs per minute and had a maximum of twenty eight hundred, a Sabre ambled along at a rev setting of three thousand, four hundred which was only three hundred and fifty below what the engine was capable of producing. As fighter aircraft produced their best efforts at their top speed the quicker they could attain high revs in an emergency, such as trying to escape when being bounced by superior numbers or when pursuing an opponent, the more a Typhoon had a decided advantage over the much slower Spitfire.

In saying this I am not decrying the efforts of the Spitfire which was a superb aircraft for aerial fighting. As for Typhoons, with all that power available they took off like a rocket, and had a vicious swing on take-off if you didn't counteract it quickly enough with a kick on the rudder. The early model had problems that other aircraft never had, plus a lot more. For example, oxygen 'on' at all times both while manoeuvring on the ground as well as when in the air, and tails breaking off while diving and in level flight. Only on very rare occasions did a pilot survive a ditching, so it was little wonder that they were feared by most pilots whose lot it was to fly them. As the saying goes, 'there is so much good in the worst of us and so much bad in the best of us' and so it was with Typhoons. They were not all bad. For instance, in a forced landing the big motor could and did flatten all in its path which gave the pilot, and the rest of the aircraft following closely behind, an armchair ride.

One of my first Typhoon deliveries was on 11 March 1943 to 486 Squadron which was stationed at Tangmere on the south coast. With the high cruising speed, and its clean lines, one of the initial problems I experienced with the aircraft was how to reduce speed to a level where it was safe to lower the wheels and flaps, and not having been told otherwise I was using the same approach as I had been taught on Spitfires which was to come low over the field, close the throttle and pull straight up in an almost vertical climb. As the speed falls off you put down the flaps and undercarriage, then lose height in a side slipping turn which keeps the nose and wing out of the way and gives an interrupted view of the runway until you straighten up just prior to touching down.

A small, dapper New Zealand Flight Lieutenant, named Umbers, was waiting for me as I taxied into 486's dispersal.[1]

'Sergeant, who taught you to land a Typhoon like that? Watching your performance just now, I nearly had a heart attack. You just do not know how close you came to killing yourself. The squadron are due back any time now. My pilots are experts at landing Typhoons, so if you are interested in staying alive, hang around and watch how they do it'.

Presently there was the sound of an aeroplane approaching the field at almost tree-top level, wheels and flaps down and being held in the air by the use of a ton of motor. For me this was an unimpressive performance. What an ordeal it must have been for the pilot, blinded by that big motor and trying to maintain direction by peering along its side. By the time that I joined 486 Des Scott was commanding the Squadron and all the pilots were using the method of landing which had so upset Flight Lieutenant Umbers, with the result they were putting twelve aircraft on the runway in about the time it had taken to land one aircraft in those early Typhoon days.

The incident above was my first meeting with 'Spike' Umbers, who later became 486's Commanding Officer, and later I was destined to see him killed as we were attacking a barge on the Dortmund–Ems canal. The barge happened to be a flak trap, a form of warfare at which the Germans were experts (see Chapter 13).

---

[1] Later Squadron Leader A E Umbers DFC and bar, from Dunedin, CO 486 Squadron Dec 1944. Killed in action 14 Feb 1945

Problem aircraft Typhoons might have been, but for me it was love at first sight or it would be more correct to say, from the first time I pushed the throttle open and felt the surge of power from the big Napier motor, pinning me back against the seat. When we could arrange it, Flight Lieutenant Raffer and I flew together and while one watched, the other put his aircraft through its paces. We compared notes later; loops, rolls, spins, those big beauties held no terrors for us even though there was a warning, in Pilot's Notes, that recovery from spins might be difficult. What a roasting we would have received if our Commanding Officer or the CO of the Squadron to which we were delivering the aircraft, had found out what we were up to. Flight Lieutenant Raffer and myself were regarded, by the rest of the Delivery Flight, as suicidal lunatics because of our love affair with Typhoons. Nevertheless it was a fact that the German pilots who encountered the Typhoon hated it because of its speed and impressive fire power.

Andy, one of our Polish pilots, was a real character. If rostered to deliver an aircraft which involved a night away from base, his girl-friend would carry the day. The mere sight of a cloud on the horizon would convince him that the weather was unsafe for flying. No threat or inducement would persuade him to leave the ground. Reverse the situation, Andy away, and the weather so clamped that the balloons that surrounded Croydon were not visible from the 'drome, and the girlfriend was always patiently waiting. You would hear the buzz of a motor up there in the overcast and out of the mirk would emerge a Spitfire, with all the precision of a homing pigeon, with Andy at the controls. It was true love.

We had two Canadians on the field; Evine who was attached to the Delivery Flight and known to all and sundry as Big Beaver, and Cowan who was a pilot on the night-fighter squadron and was known as Little Beaver. These two Canadians once suggested that I spend a day with them in London. I should have known better.

Our first call was at Canada House where Little Beaver collected a parcel; you know the sort of thing, comforts for our brave boys. This particular comfort happened to be a pair of pyjamas. That piece of night attire caused us all sorts of problems as we made our way from one West End club to the next. Never has a piece of clothing been lost and found so often on the same day. Eventually the new owner decided that the only way that they were going to remain permanently in his possession was for him to put them on and this he proceeded to do—over his uniform, of course! What a sight, the pyjamas were at least three sizes too big and with the legs and arms rolled up he looked like a pre-war advertisement for Michelin Tyres! In each club or bar visited we were objects for derision and our little friend, instead of accepting it all in good part, displayed an aggressive side of his nature we had not hitherto suspected.

Although greatly outnumbered we managed to create a reasonable amount of havoc before being thrown out of each night club that we visited. At last a friendly policeman took us under his wing and we spent what was left of the night in a cell. Next morning some fatherly advice from the Desk Sergeant—'Boys, do yourselves and us a favour, go back to your unit and stay there. The Germans are doing this place enough damage without any assistance from the Royal Air Force.' Next day when we reported for duty, with black eyes and other evidence of a rough night, the Old Man took it all in his stride, 'So you characters have been at it again. Tell me the worst, how much trouble have you managed to get into this time?'

Life at Croydon in the Spring of 1943 drifted along pleasantly enough with a dance every pay night in the Aerodrome Hotel which was now the Sergeant's Mess and sleeping quarters, to which all the local beauties were invited. In addition London was close enough to slip into for a night's entertainment, when we tired of the local fare, and Croydon was a refuge for any of our friends who were visiting the 'Big Smoke' and who required a night's lodgings. Few were the nights when the old Aerodrome Hotel did not have a star boarder.

An added attraction as far as our guests were concerned, was that we could lay on air transport to almost any part of the country to which they might wish to return. My brother, Altitude Alex, called on me soon after arriving from Canada and we spent a happy evening at the bar bringing each other up to date and drinking whisky. Alex surprised me by the amount of whisky he seemed able to dispose of without any obvious effect and when, later in my room, we continued our whisky session on a bottle of rye whisky, I could not cope and took a tumble.

Next morning my brother showed little sign of the previous night's binge but not so me. Later in the day while trying to deliver a Hurricane I went around the field against the circuit then tried to land with the wheels up. It was just not my day! Flying was dicey enough without a hangover. We had no wireless contact with the ground because this would require landing and having the crystals changed for each group we were flying over, and we were quite often flying in the very worst kind of weather. There should have been a high casualty rate but this was not actually the case. Ordinarily, delivery pilots were methodical, had quite a few flying hours behind them, and possibly a little older and more careful than operational pilots.

Turnhouse, a Scottish aerodrome (Edinburgh), had more of its share of non-flying weather and often we had to use our authority to override any attempt to delay our departure. Sometimes we took off and remained on instruments for two or three hundred miles before the cloud cleared enough for the ground to be seen, and as we flew south there was always the added risk of becoming entangled in a balloon barrage while flying blind. On one occasion it was not weather but serviceability that was the problem. We had planned to be back at Croydon that evening and were prepared to accept almost any risk. If the need is great enough almost anything is possible but this does not include getting a couple of Spitfires into the air without their engines!

There was a Beaufighter to go down south; we could take that. Neither my South African associate nor myself had ever flown a twin-engined aircraft let alone a Beaufighter and here we were considering a Beau without even a pilot to fill in the 'do and do nots'. It was sheer madness. These aircraft had a worse reputation than Typhoons, if that were possible. Typhoons had a surplus of power but that was one commodity that this particular model of Beaufighter lacked. They were eventually taken out of service because of their high accident rate, mostly at the training schools. Most of the accidents were while taking off and landing which is the stage when under-powered aircraft are most likely to come to grief. Most pilots are fatalists—what will be will be, so a flip of the coin decided who was going to sit in the driver's seat was one toss that I was not unhappy about losing. Each went our separate ways, my companion to see if he could coax the engines to fire up while I signed for the monster and collected its log books. Providing we could persuade that old Beaufighter to take us safely into the air we had lots of time to become familiar with its innards, (it had dual controls), between Turnhouse and our landing at Croydon.

Problems have a habit of duplicating and so it was to prove on this occasion. While making my way out to the aircraft I was intercepted by a very large Wing Commander Padre. 'You boys are taking a Beau-fighter down to Croydon'. At least he had his facts right. 'Would you be good enough to drop me off at Coltishall?' Two take-offs and landings, with a lot of excess weight for part of the journey we could well do without. What was I to say to the man apart from nothing? If he had suicidal tendencies well at least he was in good company. I agreed.

Safely on the ground at Coltishall it was suggested that I take over and fly the second leg but that was a duty that I wanted no part of. There is only a limited number of times that you can stick your neck out, in any one day, and I had a feeling that I had used up most of my rations. It would have to wait for somebody else.

During wartime there always seemed to be bodies hanging around airfields, hoping for an airlift, and when a spare seat is available it is rarely unoccupied for long. One day in March I had to fly the little Maggie to Henlow, deliver a Typhoon to Harrowbeer, bring another back, then return to Croydon in the little aircraft. Providing there were no hang ups I should be back at base while there was still plenty of daylight left. When about to commence the final leg, I was asked to drop off a pilot at Cranwell. The prospective passenger was one of the fair weather fraternity, a girl of about twenty who had just delivered a Typhoon. Something must have gone astray with her pickup arrangements. Even in working kit she looked a real smasher. I parked the young lady in the rear seat and then for some obscure reason, it was neither old age nor lack of attraction, I forgot all about her. It was not until I was approaching Croydon and preparing to land that I realised that I still had my passenger. The Maggie had dual controls so all she would have needed to have done was to have given her stick a nudge or reach forward and tap me on the shoulder. No transport pilot could fly past Cranwell without seeing it. She had sat there like a dummy while her airfield slowly disappeared astern and now with the shadows beginning to lengthen what was I to do? Perhaps she had planned a night out with the boys. Well, I had to make up my mind in a hurry as darkness was approaching rapidly and was not going to wait. I also knew there were no night-landing facilities at Croydon. If I landed she became my responsibility. I could not just dump her at the mess and slope off, besides, I had promised to take a girl out that night and to produce another was like flying in the Beaufighter—it would be asking for trouble! I decided that flying back to Cranwell was going to involve me in a night landing at Croydon but it was the lesser of the two evils!

I was happy at Croydon and could have spent the rest of the war there. Like a man with a mistress who knows he is going to get his fingers burnt but cannot keep away so it was with me and operational flying. I just could not think about anything else. Well, at least I could ask our CO what my chances were of getting a posting to an operational squadron. Nothing ventured, nothing gained. The first essential was to do a spot of research on the Old Man. It would be pointless asking for a favour when he was suffering from the effects of a hangover.

'What is the trouble, Sergeant? Aren't you happy with us?' The Squadron Leader looked upset.

'Sir, I have come twelve thousand miles to get into this fight. The way things are going, it is likely that I am not going to get a chance to fire a shot in anger.'

'Well, if that is what you want, make an application and I will send it on to Fighter Command with a suitable recommendation. You must have more time on Typhoons than most of the squadron pilots. By the way, have you any particular squadron in mind that you would like to join?'

'I do not mind, Sir, as long as it is not a New Zealand one. I would much rather serve on a mixed squadron.'

My experience with the New Zealand Spitfire Squadron had left me with a hang-up. However, it was not to work out as I wanted. During the time that I had been delivering Typhoons to 486, Des Scott had taken over command of that squadron.[1] Des had every confidence in Typhoons and the rest of the squadron pilots were beginning to follow his lead. Under Scotty's inspired leadership, 486 was to become one of 11 Group's top squadrons.

Some time later the orderly room corporal broke up our card game with the announcement that a posting had come through for me and that I was to report to the Commanding Officer.

'Well, Sheddan, you have not got all that you asked but at least it is Typhoons. You are to report to 486 at Tangmere. Good luck and when you finish your tour I would like to have you back.'

When the gang heard what I had volunteered for, they not only thought that I was crazy, they said so. We had a farewell party which was like an Irish wake, the only difference—the corpse was walking around amongst the guests and drinking beer instead of being propped up in a corner. Our Australian pilot, Cocks, who was known by all and sundry as 'King Kong' after some pre-war Australian wrestler, solemnly shook my hand.

'Not Typhoons Jimmy. It grieves me to see a mate about to commit suicide. Well at least it was nice knowing you.'

The two Beavers were sure that they were saying farewell to an old friend for the last time, and they were right. Three months later I paid

---

[1] Later Group Captain D J Scott DSO, OBE, DFC and bar, from Ashburton; CO 486 Squadron April–Sept 1943. OC Tangmere Wing 1943-44 and 123 Wing 2 TAF, 1944-45

a fleeting visit to Croydon which was a mistake. Nothing is ever the same. The pilots there were strangers. King Kong had finished up in an ammunition dump while trying to roll a Spitfire at low level. Big Beaver, hurrying home to a new wife late at night, ran out of daylight and did not make it. Little Beaver had misjudged a night landing with fatal results. The list of brave comrades who had not lasted the journey was becoming endless.

After my cheerful farewell at Croydon, I set off for Tangmere. This was mid-May, 1943. Up till now my only contact with 486 had been when I had been delivering aircraft and my 485 experiences were still fresh in my mind. Would I be accepted? Was I making a mistake? Should I not have applied to have the posting changed? I was being given another chance and if I blew it this time I would not be given another.

CHAPTER VI

WITH 486 NZ SQUADRON

THE 486 transport was at the local station to meet me. So at least my arrival had not gone unnoticed. I reported to the Squadron Orderly Room and the Adjutant took me over to the Sergeant's billets and I was introduced to my two room mates. Froggatt known to all as 'Froggie' and Jimmy Wilson, known as 'Woe' by virtue of his being the senior Warrant Officer on the station, though never did such responsibility sit so lightly on its wearer's shoulders. Wilson was the spokesman.

'When you have organised your bits and pieces come over to the Mess and meet the boys.' Then as if an afterthought, 'I hope that you are a sound sleeper because Froggie snores.' Hiding behind a toothbrush, Froggie looked the type who might indulge in a spot of gentle snoring; however, he hotly denied the insinuation.

Arriving at the Sergeant's Mess, I was approached by a character with a pint in his hand and a grin on his face.

'You must be Jimmy Sheddan, the latest member of our team? I am Frank Murphy, commonly known as Murph by all those horrible types that I fly with.' [1] Murphy grabbed my hand and seemed pleased to see me. 'Come over to the bar and I will buy you a pint and introduce you to the rest of my gang.' Murphy was of medium height, his hair normally dark, was turning prematurely grey. Behind the gaiety was a look of strain as though he could have suffered a lot. His scraggy moustache gave him the look of a buccaneer and he limped noticeably. I was later to learn that he had been the victim

---

[1] Later Squadron Leader F Murphy DFC from Bolton, Lancashire. Joined RNZAF in 1941. Test Pilot at Hawkers and after the war, Chief Production Test Pilot

of infantile paralysis which had left him partially crippled in a hand and a foot. Now, as I sipped Murph's pint, a lot of New Zealand pilots gathered around and he made the introductions.

The first of these was Fitzgibbon, in whom I was to have a special interest. Hundreds of airmen had entered camp as prospective pilots and finished as air gunners. Fitz and myself, as far as I know, were the only two airmen to reverse the procedure, in as air gunners, out as pilots. Happy, cheerful Fitz, so pleasant to everyone, pilot extraordinary and always ready and willing to help. He was killed when the tail of his Typhoon broke off while he was diving on German shipping near the French coast.[1]

Norman Preston was another cheerful character. Fitz and Norm had been together a long time and were rarely seen apart; this could be a mistake. The day Fitz was killed was one of the rare occasions when they were not flying together. When Norm heard the news he was shattered. Norm and Flight Sergeant Bennett, who was Preston's number two on this occasion, failed to return from a shipping strike a few mornings later.[2]

Taylor-Cannon, known as 'Hyphen' completed a tour with 486, then returned for a second, to be killed while attacking German road transport. Leo Walker, Tyerman, Arty Sames, Rangi who was to be shot down and finish the war as a prisoner, Froggatt, Jimmy Wilson, a big snowy headed boy with a smile which would have charmed the birds out of the trees. These were some of the 486 pilots that gathered around me. It was like coming home and being greeted by old friends.

'That's a nice tie you have there, James.' What Murphy thought so special about it I couldn't imagine. The only thing special, as far as I was concerned, was that it was the only one that I possessed. For some obscure reason it seemed to hold a special interest for Murph, as he ran it lovingly through his fingers.

The villain then proceeded to bite pieces off it and was half way to the knot before I realised what he was up to. With portions of my mutilated tie intermingled with his moustache, Murph was obviously quite a performer. His companions were patently enjoying the act and hooted with laughter.

'You bloody saboteur!' I grabbed Murphy's tie with my teeth, intending to remove at least half of it while I had the opportunity, but that tie was tougher than I had anticipated or perhaps there was some

---

[1] Pilot Officer R H Fitzgibbon, from Rangiora. Killed in action 6 Sept 1943
[2] Pilot Officer N E Preston, killed in action 16 Sept 1943

special technique. Be that as it may, all I managed was to remove some of my front teeth. How that merry band laughed. The indications were that the party was going to be a success. On the bar there was a large knife, which I later discovered was used by Warrant Officer Wilson for cutting up the cheese and onions during his nightly crib sessions. Armed with this and starting with Murphy, I chopped off any tie I could manage to get close enough to. Confronted with a wild-eyed pilot wielding a huge knife, my victims just stood and offered little resistance. Having to fly Typhoons might have had a depressing effect on some squadron pilots, but there was no evidence of it here. Any doubts I might have had about joining a New Zealand squadron quickly vanished, never to return.

The camp dentist and the equipment officer having repaired Murphy's attack, I was in reasonable shape to meet the rest of the squadron. The first was Flying Officer Jim McCaw, known to pilots and ground staff as 'Black Mac'. It wasn't because of his hair or face colouring but because of the antics that he managed to become involved in while on the squadron and also while on leave.

A trip to London with Black Mac was one that would have been difficult to forget and one that only the very brave would undertake a second time.

Mac would cheerfully take on a dozen soldiers but when a London Bobby waved a finger in his direction and said, 'Come along with me Kiwi', he became as docile as the proverbial lamb. One of the best stories regarding Mac, was when he had been invited to spend a night as a 'guest of our London friends'. Our hosts never bothered to turn the key on the cell door, so on this occasion Mac decided to sneak out and rejoin the London night life. The desk sergeant watched his charge crawl stealthily out and then immediately make an equally silent return. The police officer must have reasoned that a Kiwi who had lost his sense of direction was a menace both to London and himself so he turned the key in the lock. Mac's version was that once outside he discovered that he had left his hat behind and it was while trying to retrieve it that the mix-up had occurred!

A letter from his uncle Frank was appreciated by us all as we listened to Mac quoting the various tit bits. Uncle Frank's story about the Wellington virgins who held a meeting in a telephone box was his way of telling his nephew that the Yanks had taken the place over!

Other pilots that I was to meet the following morning were Sweetman, Cook, Waddy, Smith[1] and Jimmy Cullen[2]. The first casualty that I recollect was Flying Officer Brown whose Typhoon's motor had cut out during a return from a Channel sweep on 16 May and he had tried unsuccessfully to ditch. This Officer had recently married one of the loveliest girls in England and it didn't seem possible that now he had gone. Somebody had to break the sad news and I did not envy Scottie his task of telling that raven-haired beauty that the husband she was so much in love with would not be coming back. The war that had brought them together, had now torn them apart.

Much later than night, accompanied by my two room mates, Froggie and Woe, I made my way unsteadily to our billet. During the night my slumbers were disturbed by a particular noise as though a tap had been left partially on. Switching on the bedside lamp I was to see Froggie standing in the middle of the room, eyes closed, obviously sound asleep and snoring gently.

Sleep walking was no novelty to me but the most amazing thing was that Froggie was piddling into a shoe, which he held in one of his hands and it was the liquid escaping through a hole in the toe and falling onto the floor which had awakened me. His nightly ablution completed, Froggie dropped the shoe, which made a considerable amount of noise. Then he returned to his bed still snoring and quite unaware that the light had been on and that his antics had been observed. In the morning when I gleefully told Woe about Froggie's performance he was not amused. 'A bloody fine mate you turned out to be. That was my shoe that old Froggie was pissing into and you just lay there and did nothing about it!'

Next morning, on my way to breakfast, I noticed a ladies bicycle in a fire tank or swimming pool—it served both purposes—and later Fitz, who had been a witness to its arrival there, told us the story. After the party Norm Preston had set off with his WAAF girlfriend under one arm and her bicycle under the other. A navigational error had resulted in all three finishing up in the water tank. Ties, shoes, water tanks; on my new squadron the indications were that I was not going to be short of entertainment.

Froggie would in due course become a station master in Dunedin. Many, many times he repeated that if any of his old buddies visited

---

[1] Later Squadron Leader A H Smith DFC and bar from Auckland, CO of 197 Squadron, POW 31 Dec 1944
[2] Later Squadron Leader J R Cullen DFC and bar, from Waihi, CO 183 Squadron 1945

the village he would be most disappointed if they did not stay with him. 'I'll have the local band on the station to welcome you and the coppers in case things get out of hand.' Froggatt was possessed of a natural wit and was a great entertainer. He would be the one person who we all looked forward to seeing on our return to New Zealand.

Several years after my return from overseas I received an invitation to an aircrew reunion in Dunedin. As it would be attended mostly by ex-Bomber squadron personnel and the chances of my meeting old associates was doubtful, I was not particularly interested but it was a heaven-sent opportunity of once again meeting up with Froggie and catching up with all that had happened since we had been together at Tangmere. We had been mates together for some considerable time and in addition had managed to get into and out of quite a few scrapes. War-wise, I considered him one of my oldest and dearest friends. I persuaded another friend, Gavin Law, who had been on Sunderlands out on the Gold Coast, to join me on the venture which incidentally would involve us in a four-hour motor journey both ways. Gavin also didn't expect to meet any of his old flying mates but at least we were making a journey into Froggatt country and knowing the old warrior, anything was likely to happen.

I brought Gavin up to date. 'There is an old mate of mine who is a station master in Dunedin. You will enjoy meeting him.' I rambled on. 'We will not bother about booking in at a hotel. I know that Froggie will be upset if we do not stay with him.' Gavin very tactfully tried to point out that the war was over and that people changed, especially important people like station masters, but I would have none of it. 'Not Old Froggie. You'll see.'

About 3.30 p.m. we were installed at the bar in a Dunedin hotel and more by good luck than good management it was Froggie's favourite pub. He was well known to the bar staff and we were told to expect him to arrive shortly after five. It was a case of curbing my impatience which was not easy. I had looked forward to this moment for many years now. It was all about to happen.

'Hullo chaps.' Froggie stood before us, a little older, a little greyer, but still Froggie as I remembered him.

'Hullo chaps.' Froggie ignored my outstretched hand and no sooner had I introduced my friend than Froggie excused himself to greet a crony who had just arrived and together they moved to the other side of the room.

'I'd better book us in, then at least we will be sure of a bed for the night,' Gavin seemed concerned.

'Don't worry. Froggie would appear to have a very important discussion on his hands at the moment. He'll be back. He won't let an old mate down. I know Froggie.'

'You're just as big a larrikin as you were when we met in London but face facts, Jim, people change. Your old mate is a big shot now and he won't take kindly to you reminding him of his wartime antics.'

Six o'clock and at last Froggie was heading in our direction. My old friend hadn't forgotten me.

'Well, chaps, it was nice to have met you and if either of you are down this way again look me up. It's after six o'clock and I mustn't keep the wife waiting.'

The disappointment must have shown massively. Gavin did his best to ease the hurt. 'We've all changed, Jim, some of us more than others. A lot of water has passed under the bridge since you and Froggie knew each other at Tangmere, so don't take it too badly.'

This was not my first disappointment and it did not take me long to forget all about Froggie and his important position in the local community as we mingled with the rest of the ex-airmen who had assembled for the reunion. Later at the dinner, I was seated next to an ex-bomber pilot and what a tale he had to tell. Before we had finished the first course he had left the controls of his beloved Lancaster and was down at the tail helping his deadloss gunner to shoot down an attacking fighter. This little act successfully completed, he then had to sort out his navigator and other members of his crew. It was difficult to understand why this superman had bothered to take along all these extra bodies on his nightly jaunts over Germany. It seemed to me that his crew were only excess ballast and that was one commodity he could well have done without.

A few years later the wisdom of Froggie's reluctance to renew wartime associations was demonstrated to me. I was spending Christmas Eve in Invercargill. On my way out from West Arm, I met an old friend who had been an armourer on 486 while we were stationed at Tangmere. I was booked in at Desslers, the Hotel that most of the West Arm personnel stayed at when returned to civilisation after a spell up the lake. For us the bar never closed. About midnight, after both of us had drunk more than was wise, my friend suggested that I go home with him and spend the night at his place.

'Come out and meet my wife, Jim. I have often talked about you and I know she'll be pleased to see you.'

If that good lady received any pleasure from my visit she certainly did not show it. When we entered the house, my friend's wife was sitting in an armchair and her eyes seemed to be fastened on some obscure object on the far wall. The only time she moved during the entire period I was under her roof was when my pal introduced me and I attempted what I thought was going to be a gracious bow, but which turned out more like Colin Meeds charging into a rugby scrum. If that poor woman had not made a quick move I would have landed in her lap.

It did not take us long to forget the unfriendly reception as we set about the Christmas hamper which apparently had arrived that day and at the same time entertained each other with bawdy wartime stories. The wife must have wondered how her husband had managed to win the war with me on his side. Indeed, she might even have begun to have had doubts as to which side I was on! By the time we had cleared the liquor cupboard, daylight had arrived so it was a case of my ringing a taxi and quietly stealing away. My poor old friend. I'll wager that was one Christmas Eve he would remember for a long time for it is a fair assumption that after my departure, the storm broke about his ears.

The first duty of a new arrival was to report to the flight office which is the domain of the squadron adjutant. Then the next step is to report to the Commanding Officer. This interview is all important for if the budding operational pilot fails to make a suitable impression, his future, as far as that squadron is concerned, could start and finish right there. I had already paid a high price, on a previous occasion, because I had failed to pass this all important test. My dress uniform had been through two nights of debauchery—my Croydon farewell and my Tangmere welcome, so it was beginning to look like well used night attire. Replacement ties were not available. The tie-chewing act must have been the 'in thing' and any pilot whose tie had been attacked by Murph and his henchmen had no chance of borrowing a new one. In spite of Wilson and Froggatt's efforts to fit and adjust Murphy's handiwork their failure was painfully obvious. This, coupled with my mangled uniform, broken teeth and bloodshot eyes gave me a sinister look. Not the sort of chap you would take home and introduce to your favourite sister.

As I followed the Adjutant into that office I was quite resigned to my fate. All that I had asked for was a second chance—and had worked hard to get it. Then in a moment of madness I had thrown it all away.

I felt no bitterness towards my new Commanding Officer. Had I been in his position and confronted with the task of trying to assess a new pilot's potential, I would have had a fair idea just what decision I would have made.

'Good morning, Sergeant.' Scottie stood up and extended a hand. He was tall with wide shoulders and the build of an athlete, a mop of fair hair and blue eyes, set wide apart, which seemed to look right through me. Irrespective of what his decision was going to be, I instantly liked the man.

'Welcome to 486. We are pleased to have you with us. I see you have quite a lot of time on Typhoons which is unusual for a new pilot. Also I see by your last CO's report that you volunteered for this posting. You and I must be about the only two friends the Typhoons have. You'll be in A Flight with Flight Sergeant Murphy who is in charge while Flight Lieutenant Umbers is on leave. Murphy is a good chap and will show you the ropes.'

I could have said that it was Murphy's showing me the ropes that was more or less responsible for my present condition. I had a shrewd idea that Scottie already knew and approved of his Deputy Flight Commander's actions.

'I was visiting 485 a few nights ago and when I mentioned that one of their old pilots was joining us I gathered that you were not exactly one of their white haired boys.'

Oh dear, I might have guessed that my unsavoury past would not take long to catch up with me.

'Your past is your own affair. We all have our rough patches from time to time. It is your performance while you are with us that we are interested in. Frankly, after the reports by your last two commanding officers I find it difficult to believe that they are talking about the same pilot. You look as though you could have had a fairly rough night. Spend the day finding your way around the place and we will see you tomorrow morning.'

I had gone into that office with a hang dog look. Now I'd been given a chance to redeem my past. From that day, for me at least, Scottie could do no wrong. The day was not far distant when I would be sitting in Scottie's chair and when that day did arrive and I had a difficult decision to make, it was comforting to try and picture Scottie in a similar position and to speculate on how he would have handled it.

Scottie and I were to tread similar paths. Earlier in the war he did all in his power, as an NCO, to convince the powers that be that he was not officer material. When he kept out of trouble long enough to get a commission, he bounded to the top. Trouble seemed to follow me around also. While at Tangmere I was commissioned, reduced to the ranks and was not recommissioned till after the squadron arrived in Holland at least twelve months later. When later I took my Warrant Officer's dress uniform into the camp tailor to have the crowns removed and replaced by the thin blue line which announced that I was a Pilot Officer and now the holder of the King's commission, I had it returned to me with the two broad rings with a thin one between which was the rank insignia of a Squadron Leader.

The only time I was to see Scottie shaken was in May when he delayed his return from France until all the squadron aircraft were running dangerously low on petrol. It was a near thing, quite a few did not make it back to base and there were several forced landings. I can still see Scottie glued to the phone, his hands shaking as he puffed nervously at one cigarette after another. He did not leave that phone until the very last pilot had been accounted for. Luck was with us and all the pilots eventually made it back to Tangmere.

The problem during a squadron sweep was that the pilots spent so much time searching the sky above and behind that should the leader make even a slight alteration of course, a pilot on the outside of the turn could be left behind and would have to use full throttle to regain position. During this critical time a pilot who had been left behind would be fair game for any enemy fighters lurking above. An added worry was that Typhoons cruised at a speed that was not far short of their maximum which involved a straggler with a long and exhausting chase before he could regain position. A pilot who found himself in this situation would be using up his precious fuel at three gallons a minute, instead of the usual one and it was not unusual for a Typhoon to run out of fuel shortly after landing and have to be refuelled before it could taxi into its dispersal. Nor was it unusual for the fuel situation to be so critical that a couple of turns at full throttle could have made the difference between making it home or having to force land on the other side of the Channel.

Later, on 19 June 1945, history was to repeat itself. This time it was my hand that was shaking as I nervously puffed at a succession of cigarettes. I had many close calls during the years I spent as an operational pilot but was never unduly disturbed. It was when a mistake on my part very nearly cost a friend his life that, like Scotty, I had my one and only bout of the shakes.

We were practising close squadron formation for our support role in the forthcoming airshow over Kastrup airfield at Copenhagen. Our brief was to stay over the airfield in tight formation in order to entertain the sightseers during periods when there was a lull in the various flying displays being staged.

The form was to fly over the airfield in tight formation then make a one hundred and eighty degree turn, whence we were in position to repeat the performance. In order that we remained in view of our audience we were doing cross-over turns, which were very spectacular but also very dangerous. I would say over the intercom, 'Music Leader turning one hundred and eighty degrees in ten seconds', and after counting to ten, do a reasonably tight turn during which the three members of my section would follow me in tight line astern formation. While myself and the rest of my section were completing this manoeuvre, the inside section of four aircraft would drop down allowing my section to pass over the top. At the same time the outside section of four would drop back and by cutting the corner as they passed over the top, take up the inside position. By the time the two outside sections had exchanged positions, my aircraft and section would have completed ninety degrees. Then, when I had completed the remaining ninety, the two sections would have again completed another cross-over turn and be back in their original positions.

We had practiced our act for days and the performance was as near perfect as it was possible for us to get it. Then, a mistake on my part and trouble struck. In a mix-up everything happens so quickly that it is difficult later to give an accurate account of what actually took place. Later, while mentally trying to sort out the how and why, the only conclusion that I could come to was that after announcing the one hundred and eighty degree turn I had omitted to add in 'ten seconds'. This being so, Eagelson would assume that the squadron was about to do a normal turn and that being the case the normal procedure would have been for him to have stayed where he was. During this squadron formation, Eagelson was leading the port section of four aircraft and McDonald was leading the starboard section. During the turn Eagelson remained on the inside and gradually tightened his turn up as my aircraft turned towards him. Half way round the turn and I was becoming concerned as Eagelson was where he should not have been! His starboard wing was tucked in behind my port one with only about twelve inches between them. As I watched I saw 'Eagle's' aircraft begin what appeared to be a flick roll in my direction but what was actually a high speed stall. The only way that I could avoid Eagle's aircraft rolling on top of mine was by side slipping to starboard. Fortunately, McDonald and his section had dropped back and commenced their turn, otherwise two thirds of the squadron would have been involved in the mix-up. Even to this day, I get the shudders when I think of what could have happened.

From the time that the aircraft started to stall to when it eventually dived in the water, I never had my eyes off it, not even for one second. As I remember it, the 'plane flicked onto its back, then the nose gradually dropped until it was diving vertically. From where I was watching, it was obvious that there was no way that the pilot was going to regain control of his aircraft, there just wasn't enough height. I found myself shouting over the radio telephone, 'Get out Eagle, for God's sake, get out'. By that time, however, if he was not already on his way, he wasn't going to make it!

It seemed an eternity before the pilot tumbled out and the 'chute blossomed. From where I was watching, the plane and parachute seemed to hit the water almost at the same time. Eagelson treated the incident as a big joke but it was no joke as far as I was concerned. I felt that it was possible that I was responsible and I knew just how Scotty must have felt that day at Tangmere.[1]

---

[1] Flying Officer O D Eagelson DFC from Auckland

CHAPTER VII

'ALL IN A DAY'S WORK'

FLYING Typhoons on operations was a new venture for, until joining an operational squadron, all I had been called to do was deliver them from one airfield to another. No pushing the motor to its limit and beyond, never more than an hour in the air at any one time (and that was always over land), no enemy fighters or hostile flak. True, the complicated piece of machinery under the cowling would not have won any prizes for reliability but should the worst have occurred a forced landing ashore would not have been too difficult. As has been said so often, the worst of their many faults was, to date, no pilot had managed to land on the water and live.

Flying had become a much more serious business. It was now a case of immediate readiness which involved hours of cockpit duty during which it was a matter of sitting on that rock hard parachute and dinghy pack, straps firmly fixed, helmet and all it entailed, such as oxygen and radio telephone, clamped into position. After endless days of such duty, when nothing seemed to happen, the Tannoy would suddenly bellow, 'Scramble Red Section!' It was then a mad panic to start up, and with throttle wide open, take off straight ahead, regardless of the direction of the wind, then head out to sea at full revs and boost while awaiting instructions from Control. When this information arrived we hoped that it would enable us to intercept or overtake an intruder. More often than not it was some sea bird which had somehow become involved on the plot, which was responsible for the flap. Just occasionally we were rewarded by the sight of a hostile aircraft, high-tailing it for home, but this made the long hours of cockpit duty all worthwhile.

The next step in the operational development of the Typhoon was in standing patrols which involved long hours flying over the restless sea, at low level in order to confuse enemy radar, which resulted in our vision being restricted by the gradual coating of a salt film on the windscreen and side panels. As a Number Two, it was a case of trying to stay in formation and, at the same time, avoid hitting the sea with a wing tip during turns. In such a position we would have been easy prey for any enemy fighter which might have been in the area.

An even greater cause for concern was the temperamental Napier Sabre engine which was most unhappy with it's diet of one hundred and fifty octane fuel and which kept banging and spluttering. The man in the hot seat was acutely aware that if the 'fan' up front stopped turning, there was no way that he was going to get that seven-ton aeroplane up high enough for him to bail out. A successful landing at sea was also impossible.

A lot of the problems with the engine were caused by Napier farming out the construction of various parts to small firms who were amateurs as far as this type of construction was concerned. Once this was realised and Napier undertook the construction of all components, most of the problems passed into history. Unfortunately, during what best could be described as an experimental period, a lot of valuable lives were lost.

In the early days of the Typhoon, an engine that stayed in service more than a few hours before being replaced and returned to its maker in order to be stripped down and have defective parts replaced, was an exception, but occasionally an airframe and engine would remain together until both were due for a 'major'. Jimmy Wilson's SA-B and it's engine were one such combination. When the time arrived for Jimmy's beloved 'B' to be replaced, his next two aircraft each failed to return. After the second loss we suggested to Jimmy that he put the letter into cold storage for a while. Operational flying was dicey enough without taking that letter along to ensure the failure of the mission. Our unkind remarks were a blow to 'Woe's' ego. He had been in the habit of boasting about his first plane's performance as though he personally had been responsible for it's run of good fortune.

Long after the enemy had discontinued the hit-and-run raids, we were still committed to those low-level sea patrols which, although the danger of engine failure was a real as ever, were boring in the extreme, for the enemy just did not show up. Occasionally an air-sea rescue patrol would turn up to break the monotony as happened to me on 3 September when we ended up searching the water ten miles off Le Havre. To the layman this would seem a piece of cake, just a matter of stooging around until an airman and his dinghy were spotted below and after reporting one's find, then a matter of keeping an eye on the downed airmen until a fast launch or seaplane turned up. Unfortunately it was never that simple. Low down flying was problematic enough and gave little opportunity for searching the sea. Higher up, a small dinghy became difficult to see and one had only to take one's eyes off it for a moment and it vanished. The sea does not give up it's victims easily and it was massively frustrating to know that some-where below was an airman who was depending on you for his rescue, and you could no longer find him. In this case he was found, though not by me.

Another dicey task was shooting up coastal shipping. Taking pot shots at small boats with airborne cannon would seem like money for old rope but not so. Not only did they carry their own defensive flak but also they stayed close enough inshore for their land-based brethren to get in on the act. The combination of land and sea-based artillery always assured us of an unfriendly welcome.

The form generally was this—we'd fly a sighting patrol, 'either at sea level or around five thousand feet', spot our intended victim from afar, then attack at maximum speed. The intention was to do as much damage as possible during the few seconds that it took to sweep across the target, then up and away, as there was little future in returning for a second pass, for on a second run, they would be waiting for you.

A weak spot in the high level attack was that there was a possibility that your Typhoon's tail would break off while diving at speed. When this happened the aircraft or what was left of it, became unstable and its pilot would be thrown around and battered unconscious in seconds. To see this happen to a comrade was shock enough, but then your thought was, 'how much more will *my* aircraft take before it begins to fall apart?

Our war was a gigantic game of hide and seek, and no sooner had we mastered a problem than another took its place. So it was with coastal shipping when all daylight sailings were abandoned and the only movement was then at night. Our only hope of an interception was to patrol near their home port as daylight was breaking in the hope that any arrivals had been delayed and were still beyond the protection of shore batteries, or had sailed early in the evening and it was still light enough to spot them.

So the war slowly ground its way to an obvious conclusion, the task of the hunter becoming more difficult as we ranged further and further from our island base.

Gradually our Napier Sabres were becoming more reliable but nothing could be done to a Typhoon's ditching performance and always there was the never-ending sea waiting for its next victim. From shipping strikes it was intruder patrols and escorts over the Low Countries with the occasional low-level sweep by a pair of aircraft when the weather was unsuitable for any other type of operational flying. These intruder missions were known by the code name of 'Rhubarb' and it was a fool-hardy pilot who volunteered a second time. My own ditching came in October 1943, of which, more later.

In a normal sweep we would either climb above light flak altitude, soon after leaving base or, in order to fox the enemy radar, remain as low as possible until just out of range of the coastal flak at which point we would climb to over five thousand feet before crossing the coast. When two aircraft set out on a Rhubarb, cloud base was never over five hundred feet, usually much lower, the thinking being that if attacked by superior numbers of enemy aircraft the pilots could quickly hide in cloud. This was alright in theory but an airman would be flying blind and with a ceiling so low it was a difficult business when the time came for the pilot to try to descend to a height at which he would again have visual contact with the ground.

When commencing a Rhubarb it was essential that the two airmen be able to see what was ahead and this in turn meant crossing the enemy coast as low as possible, but coastal flak could hear aircraft approaching and had only to maintain a constant stream of shells and wait for their victim to fly into it. Once safely through the first flak obstacle the pilots would be fully occupied trying to position them-selves in relation to their map, in order to bypass known pockets of flak, and at the same time watch out for obstacles in their path and hope that a suitable target would not be bypassed before they were in a position to attack.

With the fixed guns on fighter aircraft the pilot had to see his target in time to enable him to pull up and then depress the nose and virtually point his aircraft at the intended target. Once the aircraft left the safety of the ground it was a sitting target for any light flak guns in the area.

Eventually the 'Top Brass' had to face the fact that losses far out-weighed the results and this type of aerial warfare was largely discon-tinued. But, obviously, the unfortunate thing was that while this obvious conclusion was filtering through to the higher-ups, a good many pilots were to be lost and at the height these sorties were carried out very few pilots survived any resultant crash.

None of us were sorry to see the last of the Rhubarb patrols but it was not long before we were planning the next saga in the Typhoon cycle, with the aircraft being employed as fighter bombers, attacking targets with a five hundred pound bomb under each wing.

Our instructions on missions were that if we could not positively identify a target we were to drop our bombs in the Channel on the way home, as it was unlikely that a Typhoon's undercarriage was strong enough to stand the extra weight of bombs on board and would possibly collapse. What was likely to happen if a pilot had a 'hang-up' (the bomb does not release) and seven tons of aircraft landed on top of its lethal friend, was a personal problem as far as the pilot was concerned.

Like long-range petrol tanks, bombs were an afterthought for the designers and often refused to leave the aircraft, especially when enemy fighters turned up and it was imperative that they be discarded, as they increased the wing loading and drastically reduced an aircraft's performance. As in the law of the jungle, both sides were experts at sorting out a lame duck.

On one occasion I well remember, our next Commanding Officer, Squadron Leader Ian Waddy, had a hang-up which dropped off as he landed and after bouncing about fifty feet in the air proceeded to chase the aircraft along the runway and appeared to be gaining ground as Wad's aircraft lost speed. To watch the performance was nerve racking enough, and it did not take much imagination to realise that next time you landed, your aircraft could have one or possibly two hang-ups and that instead of bouncing on impact they just might explode.[1]

Dog fights, bombing, shooting up aircraft on the ground, transport, railway engines—it was all part of a day's work with life becoming more uncertain as the enemy increased his flak cover of vital targets.

It was at this stage of the war, autumn 1943, that the enemy introduced the flak-trap, the one weapon we could not successfully attack or defend ourselves against and it would be safe to say, the one weapon that we feared most.

To the layman the word 'trap' would suggest that we were being lured in to an inescapable cage, whence the door was locked securely behind us. For any pilot unfortunate enough to be lured into it's web, a flak-trap was a little more permanent than a temporary lockup.

The bait was usually a train in the middle of a small wood or a barge moored at the side of a canal or possibly a collection of lorries with enough camouflage to suggest that they were attempting to hide. Around these 'Jezebeles' possibly in an acre of well camouflaged flak, there would be 88mm, 20mm's, light machine guns, rocket flak, you

---

[1] Squadron Leader I D Waddy DFC, from Belheim took over 486 Squadron from Des Scott in September 1943. Later CO of 164 Squadron, POW 25 August 1944

name it and it was there, and at the touch of a single button up it came. Where you had been, where you were and the area through which you were about to pass. The form, when attacking ground targets, was to get in and out before the enemy knew you were there. However, this method of attack was made to order as far as the operator of a flak-trap was concerned. With a squadron of aircraft in the middle of the pattern, when he pressed the button his guns just had to hit something.

For those of us who had survived the first few attempts at shortening our life span, we developed a sixth sense if there was something that did not fit. Perhaps a stationary engine was putting up too much smoke, the camouflage on some transport was underdone or a moored barge gave the impression that it had been in it's present position for too long a time.

The last straw for us was being ordered to dive bomb the 'no-ball' (codename for the V1 rocket sites) targets. These were the German V1 rocket launching sites that sprang up in the Pas de Calais. Nobody had indicated to us that they were Hitler's latest secret weapon. We were merely given a map reference and all we could see from aloft was a small building in the centre of an equally small wood which in it's turn was surrounded by a hell of a lot of guns, into which we were expected to dive vertically and let our two bombs go.

As we crossed the French coast on these ops, and started to climb to our operational height of ten thousand feet, we would see the sky in the target area turn into a solid bank of flak which indicated that another squadron was already attacking and that the welcoming-committee were ready and out in force.

When flying Number Two I used to try and keep my leader's aircraft between me and the flak hosing up from below, hoping that this would help but I was fooling myself. A shell could miss my Number One by a few inches and burst at my level.

There was a typical pattern. A shell bursting at a distance produced a black smudge, not unlike a small cloud; closer and a red flash would be visible in the centre of the smudge. Closer still, when about lethal distance, and the pilot would hear and feel the cockpit hood buckle. Any nearer, 'one of our aircraft did not return, the pilot missing, believed killed'.

I will never forget the trip in January 1944 on which Jacko Holmes, the popular Commanding Officer of 197 Squadron, was killed.[1] Jacko had crashed in flames in a Fairey Battle bomber during the Battle of

---

[1] Squadron Leader M P C Holmes DFC, killed in action 24 Jan 1944

France. Badly burned and temporarily blinded, he had crawled for nearly an hour before his cries for help had been heard. Returning to the fray, Jacko was a character who just did not seem capable of taking the job seriously. Although I was on a different squadron and only a Flight Sergeant, I knew Jacko personally. He had been leading his squadron when it had assisted in my rescue from the English Channel (see Chapter 8).

'Sir, how do you keep your mind off all that flak as we fly and dive through it?'

It was a reasonable question and I found it hard to believe that Jacko could retain the big grin during such an ordeal. Jacko replied to my question, 'Jim, I fire the cannon on the way down. It doesn't do much good but they make a racket and helps to take my mind off that bloody flak'.

On this trip 486 was following Jacko's squadron and as I rolled my 'plane over and started the dive there was a flash in the target area which could only be caused by an aircraft exploding. Over the radio telephone I heard, 'Red One has gone straight in!' It could only have been Jacko; we were a sad bunch as we headed for home.

Why did it have to happen to Jacko? We were fighter pilots and this dive bombing lark was not our thing although by this stage the Typhoon was becoming well established as a low-attack aircraft and would continue to be so before and after the invasion of Europe.

Nevertheless, it seemed to us that we were being asked to pay a high price for the small amount of damage that we appeared to be doing.

Tangmere was a large airfield, it's squadrons widely dispersed which added to the transport difficulties for pilots on standby or on readiness. It was possible to draw a bicycle from the equipment store but unfortunately, this mode of transport had an irresistible attraction for our ground crews. These loyal 'slaves' would be upset at any suggestion that they would steal a pilot's bicycle and to my mind, 'borrowing' might minimise the crime but the end result was the same. I announced my intention of drawing a bicycle. The news was not received with any degree of enthusiasm.

'Murph', who seemed to have taken a special interest in my welfare, said, 'Don't waste your time, Jim, the Erks will use it more than you will and it will not be long until all you will have to show for your efforts will be one bicycle listed on your clothing card. You can take my word for it, bicycles are costly items'. There was a touch of sadness in Murph's voice. Maybe he had already been down the same road.

'Borrowed' or lent, did it matter, the end results would be the same. Records would show that Flight Sergeant Sheddan was the guardian of one RAF bicycle. Fail to return the above-mentioned equipment to stores and the unfortunate Flight Sergeant would have to pay.

The follies of youth! We tend to ignore the advice of our elders, a trait which no doubt is as old as mankind itself. However, I had a little scheme up my sleeve and was not deterred by the negative advice of the stores officer. 'Flight Sergeant, from the moment you sign for that bicycle until you return it and have it taken off your card, the RAF will hold you responsible for it's welfare. Fail to produce and it is going to cost you quite a fair amount of money!' I was undeterred! In any event, I could be dead tomorrow!!

My first call was the station paint shop where the 'chiefy' and I dreamed up a foolproof colour scheme which would leave Tangmere in no doubt as to whose bicycle it was, no matter where it's wanderings would take it, or who was in the driver's seat. Pink frame, red wheels, purple handlebars, blue and white spokes, such an apparition could not fail to attract attention. My final act was to take the bicycle along to the guard room and issue instructions that if it was seen in the company of anybody, apart from myself, it was to be taken in protective custody.

That piece of gaudy machinery must have been a challenge to one of those Highwaymen masquerading as a 486 airman for it took the paint shop longer to do their paint job than it took some villain to lift it! Within twenty four hours, it had gone. I kept my ear close to the ground; there was not much happening around the station that I did not hear about. But how that bicycle was smuggled off the station would have to be one of 486's most closely guarded secrets. Even at this late hour I would dearly love to know how I was swindled and by whom.

I guess it was stripped down and repainted in short order to quickly blend in with all other station bicycles, which, upon reflection, was the only problem with my 'fool proof' scheme.

Air Ministry, in their wisdom, decided to issue operational pilots with a monthly ration of petrol. The idea behind the scheme was that it would encourage them to leave the station when not on duty (or perhaps for them not to steal it!) Generally, of course, pilots did not own a car until Group decided to issue this petrol. Obtaining cars was not a problem as the civilian population could not obtain fuel, so as a result they were only too happy to offload their vehicles. Being the only buyers it was almost cheaper for us to purchase a car than it was to buy a bicycle. What a laugh, a gallon a week was barely enough to tune the motor. However, there was a solution to the petrol problem. As I once heard a very rough character remark, 'Once you get your foot in the door, you can spit a long way up the passage'.

Our old Tiger Moth rarely left the ground but when it did the grade of petrol it used was the same as that used by a motor car. From the time motor cars became essential equipment for pilots, the Tiger's fuel bill increased in leaps and bounds. It's makers had fitted the Moth with a small fuel tank which held enough petrol to keep it airborne for about four hours. At the rate our old Tiger used fuel, the tank would have held hardly enough to start up, certainly not enough to have enabled it to have taxied out and become airborne. For us, therefore petrol was no problem, for ten cigarettes one of our Erks would top the tank up and throw a couple of four gallon jerry cans into the boot.

Scotty, as befitted a Commanding Officer, bought a 1936 Austin which, I expect, would have cost him in the region of thirty five pounds sterling. Such a princely sum was well beyond our limited resources, so Joe Helleen, Sandy Powell, Bruce Lawless and I formed a syndicate, the idea being to raise the necessary in order to purchase a vehicle. Before a suitable machine could be found Joe had been shot down over France, and Sandy had become so entangled in the web that his thirst and girl friends had spun around him, that he had to withdraw. The loss of our two partners left Bruce and myself with the problem of financing the deal, providing that a suitable car could be found within our price range; our combined liquid assets were eighteen pounds! Looking around proved to be thirsty work and soon the pool had shrunk to seven pounds and fifteen shillings.

One evening while in the bar of a Chichester hotel, we were telling a civilian friend of our problems. Wonders will never cease! Not only did he own the car that we were looking for but seven pounds and fifteen shillings was the price he wanted for it. After last orders we went along to have a look at the 'bomb'—at that price what else could it have been. It turned out to be an old Austin Seven of 1927 vintage parked in what must have been an old hen house. It was covered in dust and a collection of junk. After removing the 'camouflage', we helped to push the relic outside and discovered that not only was there air in all the tyres—but that the tank actually had petrol in it. The motor burst into life without much persuasion on it's owners part, so, on the strength of the demonstration, we decided to buy the old girl. On later reflection, events had gone too smoothly, it must have been a plant. We had been set up and it was our good fortune that we had only this limited amount of finance available.

After completing the deal we headed for Tangmere, but had not gone far before we began to realise that with ownership went problems. Our first was a large policeman waving a torch. It was a dark night and we had no lights, but with the black-out we had a genuine excuse. No brakes, as the man behind the wheel soon discovered, and the law seemed to think that I should also have a driver's licence! Also, with no registration or ownership papers and after a quick look around, by torch light, he discovered that there wasn't a vestige of thread on any of the tyres. After listening to our story, that policeman's opinion was that we had been grossly overcharged. His advice was to get the thing to Tangmere, even if it involved pushing it most of the way, and keep it there until it was road-worthy, though he seemed to think that this was a very remote possibility.

The battery was on it's last legs but where in all England were we to find a six-volt replacement and how were we to pay for one providing it could be found? The battery crisis we solved by removing the rear seat and installing a twenty-four-volt Spitfire battery. The high voltage we solved by using a quarter of the battery at a time. The Spitfire trolley accumulator had the same size tyres as our car so a few cigarettes changed hands and soon the old Austin was sporting a set of new tyres and that included the spare. If the tyres on the trolley accumulator were any indication of the age of the Spitfires, they must have been around since World War One.

Bruce and I decided to draw up a set of rules. My partner insisted that girls were out and apart from lending our gem, there was not much more to add. The big battery took up all the back seat so there was no problem with destitute friends bludging a ride. Like Russia and her Allies the path ahead seemed clear of obstructions!

Cars of various shapes, sizes and vintage began to appear on the squadron. Murphy, Taylor-Cannon and Black Mac became the joint owners of a high priced English car which, pre-war, must have been someone's pride and joy. When Murph and 'Hyphen' departed, tour expired, the disposal of the car was left in their partner's hands. Eventually Mac sold it for less than we had paid for our Austin. I would have liked to have been around when his ex partners received their share of the sale.

Brian O'Connor's car seemed to spend most of its time parked outside the Sergeant's billets, a large stone substituting for the front wheel assembly. The back seat of 'Oc's' buggy was a favourite spot for his mates and their girl friends. Several times I watched hopefully as the car developed a dangerous rock and appeared to be about to tumble off it's precarious perch.

The makers of Sid Short's car were so confident of it's starting ability that they had not provided it with a starting handle. Unfortunately it had not lived up to the maker's expectations. Hills in and around Tangmere being nonexistent, the only solution was for Sid to have a girl friend big and strong enough to push the car until the engine burst into life. Looks and an attractive 'chassie' were only of secondary importance to Sid. As the pair motored around the countryside the girl friend seemed to take up most of the front seat while Sid peered around a corner and did his best to keep the monster under control.

The highlight of Christmas Day 1943 was a car race around the airfield, most drivers taking a co-driver along to observe and advise. Bruce and I were an early casualty when some villain put a revolver bullet through a front tyre! Sandy Powell helped us to repair the damage and as a reward we allowed him to drive our pride and joy up to the Mess. Sandy's driving ability was not up to his tyre changing and he collided with the building and in the process broke a large window. Replacement windows not being readily available, the gales which seem to blow up from the Antarctic at that time of the year, made the Sergeant's Mess a most unpleasant place. The day a new window was finally fitted Sandy put his head through it and this was the last straw for the equipment officer. He directed the Station 'chippie' to nail some lumber over the opening.

Later, while stationed at Newchurch on the Romney Marshes, the poor quality of our Austin's breaking system was nearly the cause of an accident. While returning from Hastings to Newchurch, I picked up a hitch-hiker along the Hastings–Rye section. The road in this area was narrow, had many sharp bends and at places was dangerously close to the edge with the sea hundreds of feet below.

While passing an army convoy around a corner, ahead appeared an army lorry which was travelling much too quickly considering the nature of the road. The lorry was too close for comfort and literally the Austin's brakes were almost non-existent. We were on a collision course and there was no way we were going to offer any resistance to the lorry. The Austin and its passengers would have been annihilated. Unfortunately the road, at that point, was close to the top of the cliff but fortunately there were several trees in the area and though my sudden right turn caused the Austin to start a roll, a tree intervened and prevented what would have been a plunge over the top and down onto the sea and rocks below. The army driver pulled up and after a remark which sounded like, 'Flying a bit low today Kiwi', he and his

troopers hauled my car back onto the highway. There was no sign of
my passenger who must have baled out and taken off. A little further
along I again overtook the hitch-hiker but all I received for my invitation to rejoin was a heap of abuse. The gist of his advice was that there
might be surer ways of committing suicide than riding with me in that
heap of junk which I chose to call a car but off hand he could not
think of any.

CHAPTER VIII

DITCHED

ON 3 October, 1943 we were detailed to meet a formation of Bostons from 88 Squadron, on their way out, and escort them back to base. On reaching our allotted position there was no visible sign of the Bostons so Des Scott, who was leading the Squadron, called the Boston Leader, who reported that they had just passed beneath us. Conditions were such that there was no way we could sight our charges who were blending with the ground cover they were flying above, so Scottie brought the squadron down to almost ground level in order that we could pick up the Bostons against the skyline. The result of this was that by the time we reached the French coast we were much lower than we should have been and well within the height range of the light coastal flak.

Just as we crossed out there was a bang, bits and pieces flew around the cockpit and my motor stopped. Although I called up and reported my situation my first impression was that I had not made contact as my 'plane just seemed to hang in the air as the rest of the squadron flew serenely on and as a matter of interest, that was the last I was to see of 486.

In the distance I could just distinguish what appeared to be a cloud on the horizon but that must have been the French coast. When the engine stopped and a blade of the big propeller was stuck up in front of me like the finger of doom, I had two options, either attempt to bale out and take my chances with the light coastal flak and the offshore mine fields, or continue out to sea and attempt to ditch which was something all Typhoon pilots dreaded as these aircraft were considered unditchable. On my first flight over the English Channel, I had watched Flying Officer Peters attempt to land his damaged Typhoon on the water and although he appeared to make a perfect landing on a relatively calm sea, there was a cloud of spray and we did not see either the 'plane or the pilot again. The Typhoon's big airscoop was blamed for this aircraft's poor ditching performance yet later, the Tempest which had the same airscoop and engine, would alight on the water and float while its pilot had all the time in the world to inflate his dinghy, cast it onto the water and step into it. The only difference between the aircraft was that the Tempest had a much thinner wing.

At the time it would seem that I was taking the line of action less likely to succeed but with the decision made I followed an instruction from the fighter pilot's bible—make up your mind instantly and never change it. There just was not time at the speed we lived. The first course of action was to get rid of the hood, make sure that the straps were tight and knock the switches off. Nothing is more disastrous than the engine giving a feeble splutter just when you are about to touch down. With all the wide Channel stretching out before me there was no fear of overshooting and hitting an obstruction. I was able to come in fast and level off about a foot above the sea and maintained that height by keeping a constant backward pressure on the control column which had the effect of retaining lift as the speed dropped off. Fortunately the sea was calm and by keeping the 'plane airborne to the last possible moment, the tail was the first part to make contact with the water.

At that stage the Typhoon was planing along on its tail, at high speed, rather a pleasant sensation, and all fear of landing it on the water vanished. It was old hat; a piece of cake! Like waves moving up on a beach on a calm day the little rivulets of water moved gently along the fuselage until they reached the trailing edge of the wing. While this was taking place I was undoing the safety harness in readiness to leave in a hurry, and they reappeared at the leading edge.

No sooner did the ripples appear at the leading edge than bang; it was like hitting a concrete wall and with no straps to restrain my forward progress I was pitched head first onto the gun sight and for me the lights went out. Whatever caused that sudden breaking between seventy and eighty miles an hour to virtually a dead stop?; it was not the little airscoop which produced so much resistance because at that stage it was hardly touching the water, it had to be the thick high lift wing section. When the buffoons did the ditching trials with models of Typhoons in the tanks, they predicted that the aircraft would be difficult to land on the water and equally that a Tempest would create no problems. With scant regard for what happened to pilot or 'plane the boffins were eagerly awaiting the day when a Tempest was forced to alight on the water.

Strangely it was my best friend and also my best man, when I was married in London just after the war, who had the doubtful honour, that is if my memory serves me correctly. While in pursuit of flying bombs, Bruce Lawless was forced to ditch somewhere off Hastings while the tide was receding and his aircraft stayed afloat, sinking gently as the tide went out and Bruce was able to wade ashore. But back to the story.

So violent was the force with which I hit the gun sight that although my scalp was protected by a thick leather flying helmet it was split open, right down to the bone. Also, although my face was protected by an oxygen mask, half way between my nose and my top lip there was a gash which went through to my gum and there was an equally large gash about half an inch below my bottom lip, which also went through to the gum. Had I tried to fly the aircraft onto the water or had I let it drop onto the water instead of keeping the pressure on in order to put it in tail first, or had I overdone the backward pressure and caused the aircraft to have lifted even as little as a couple of feet, there is no way that I could have survived a flat drop into the water. Had there also been a slight swell which would have made the wings make contact before the tail, I am sure the results would have been equally disastrous.

After making contact with the bracket of the gun sight I cannot recall leaving the aircraft. My first recollection was being dragged head first, which was being caused by the cord from my headphones which was still securely plugged into its socket in the aircraft. To remove an oxygen mask and flying helmet while under water when both were firmly secured, especially as I still had my thick flying gloves on, was no easy task. A moment of panic and I would have had my time. At this stage I could not have been very far below the surface as I seemed to come up immediately.

Once on the surface the first act was to inflate the dinghy by activating the small CO_2 bottle which was attached. What amazed me was that such a small bottle could contain such a large amount of gas, although we had been warned that they could malfunction and the inflating dinghy generate so much pressure that the pilot would be unable to leave the aircraft or be able to pull the stick back. If this were to happen near the ground there was nothing a pilot could do to save himself. It was as a precaution against such a thing happening that we always had a long bladed knife, the size of a small dagger, pushed down inside one of our flying boots. In theory it was hoped that a pilot faced with such an emergency would have time to grab the knife and deflate the dinghy. Once the control column was pushed against the instrument panel it did not take long to get rid of a thousand feet so the unfortunate pilot could not afford to have any hang-ups.

As far as I can recall we had no practical tuition on how to operate a parachute or a dinghy. As far as I was aware all one had to do was inflate the thing, then walk up the canvas ladder which hung down from one end and you were home and housed, it was just as simple as that, or so I had been led to believe. Oh, how different it all was when I tried to put it into practice.

With my clothes saturated and my flying boots full of water and feet, I weighed the proverbial ton and no sooner did I attempt to climb the ladder than I tipped the little boat over on top of myself. Then I was faced with the task of struggling out from underneath and turning the thing back into its intended position, while, I might add, swallowing a quantity of salt water during the process. The top of the dinghy was on a level with my chin and as far as I was concerned getting safely aboard was on a par with my trying to climb Everest on a Sunday afternoon. I was almost crying with frustration. There had to be a way of getting into that dinghy, other pilots had managed it but we had never heard about the ones who had failed.

The solution was so obvious that it was almost laughable. All that was required was to push a portion of the boat down low enough for water to enter and the more water the dinghy held the easier it became, once half full it became as solid as the rock of Gibraltar, and it then became a simple matter to climb the ladder provided, then by using the attached baler, empty the water over the side. For the first hour all I could do was to try and relax. What the time was or how long I had been there was a matter of guess work as my watch had been put out of action but eventually I became aware of Typhoons searching an area in the far distance and I could only hope that they were searching for me; but at the time I was not aware that I had any means of attracting attention and at the distance they were, I might as well have been the invisible man. Later I was to learn that it was in fact 197 Squadron who had been sent out to look for me. Group in their wisdom had detailed 197, who had been high cover and would not have had a clue where I was, out to look for me, while 486 who could have come straight to my position was ordered to direct Air Sea Rescue to some Boston survivors.

Darkness comes early in October and it soon became obvious that if I was to be rescued at all it was not going to be that day and as the light began to fade the wind started to get up and with it the sea. Just before dusk two Spitfires in line abreast appeared from the direction of France and they were so low that the one who flew directly over me could not have come any lower without hitting the water with his propeller. He was so low in fact that I crouched down. Had I sat up I would have been clobbered. It was just as well that I was not aware that I had signal rockets as all that I would have achieved would have been to have alerted the enemy.

Darkness set in and with it the sea began to perform. Wind and tide had been pushing me steadily towards the shore and from the noise I could only guess that it was the waves breaking on shore, and at any moment I would find myself floating amongst the mines which were liberally scattered along the coast. The sea was making a racket, the temperature had dropped, I was wet and cold and dinghies are so designed that by throwing out the sea anchor the occupant is drifting with his back to wind and sea. Also, there is a cape which can be pulled up around the shoulders and this should divide the attacking waves which would then shoot off each side. All right in theory, but in practice that is not the way it worked. The water, when it hit the middle of my back just simply planed up and over the top and somehow managed to find its way inside my clothes, then descended till it reached my waist, where it spilt out into the dinghy. The result of all this was that I was being continually doused in ice cold water.

When it tired of that little lark the sea had another trick up its sleeve which was even more diabolical. My clothes by this time, through the action of salt and water, were quite stiff, so in periods of relative calm the portions of contact with my skin would begin to warm up; then the sea would suddenly get rough and give the dinghy a shake causing the cold portions of my clothes to come in contact with half warm skin. The result was as though someone had turned your warm shower off and thrown a bucket of ice water at you. When this happened I was so cold that I could not stop my teeth from chattering on and on.

I had long since through exhaustion given up trying to empty the water over the side and this added to another of my discomforts. Mae Wests have a packet of dye lightly sewn to them and the form is for the stranded pilot to detach this and throw it over the side. It is attached by a lanyard so it cannot drift away and dyes an area of the surrounding water a colour which can be seen by searching aircraft for a considerable distance. An over-energetic parachute packer had made such a thorough job of attaching the dye container that there was no way that I could detach it and I spent the night soaking in the concentrated bath of heavily dyed water.

In the morning my skin was so brown I could have passed for a native and what was more, there was no way that I could remove it.

Like a poor sun tan I had to endure the off-white colour for ages later on until it eventually decided to leave me. Worse still were my finger and toe nails which were a brilliant shade of green and there was no way that the colour could be removed. Well, at least I found out that my finger nails grew much quicker than my toe nails.

Without any fear of contradiction, that was the longest night of my life. Every time the moon found a hole in the clouds and shed a little bit of light I thought that daylight was coming only to have my hopes dashed as the hole closed up and darkness descended once again. One of the pleasures of life is that nothing lasts forever and so it proved. When the light became strong enough for me to see I was surrounded by water and there was no sign of land; and it was while cleaning up the dinghy and emptying water over the side that I discovered the signal rockets.

It was at this time too that an event occurred for which I have never been able to find a suitable explanation. There was and had hitherto been, no sign of bird life about but a small bird which was about the size of a pigeon, but which looked more like a penguin, shot up out of the water, sat on the side of the dinghy for a few moments while it stared at me through cold fishy eyes, then turned and dived back into the water. I never saw that bird again or any others that looked remotely like it.

About this time I can recall thinking that if 486 were coming out to look for me they should be here any time and as I glanced over my shoulder there were seven white spinners which swept directly over me and started to do a climbing turn.

To make sure that I had been seen I grabbed a signal rocket and fired off the charge which soared skyward and which on reaching its maximum height, burst into a red glow and began to fall slowly back towards the sea. I was so occupied with watching the signal and the orbiting aircraft that I forgot about the signal container which, unbeknown to me, contained a second charge programmed to ignite about ten seconds after the first.

My hand containing this lethal bomb was resting on the top of the dinghy and the muzzle of the signal container was so placed that the second signal skidded across the rubber tube and plunged into the sea only a few yards from where I was sitting.

Had that missile punched a hole in the tube or through the rubber sheeting, which covered the bottom of the tyre, I would have been in the water supported by the life jacket and there would have been no way the Air Sea Rescue boys would have relocated me in the conditions that existed at that time. Sitting there, the aircraft were plainly visible to me and I thought the pilots would have no problem in keeping me under observation, thus I was not unduly disturbed when they began to drift further and further away.

What I did not realise was that it was not because they were afraid of alerting watchers on the French coast that they were drifting further and further out to sea, but that they had lost sight of the dinghy and knowing that I had a number of rockets which I was making no attempt to use, Des was beginning to believe that they had arrived too late and that I had passed out from exhaustion or that the waves had tipped the dinghy upside down and drowned its occupant.

When the Walrus arrived Des was unable to produce a customer so the alternative was to abort the mission, as they could not keep a squadron of aircraft and a Walrus milling around so close to the enemy coast without creating a hostile reaction. However, the Walrus pilot decided to make a sweep towards the French coast and no doubt being much lower than the Typhoons and much more experienced at identifying floatage, he spotted me bobbing about the waves.

The landing did not appear too difficult. However, it was when trying to get near enough to collect me that the real problem emerged. One moment I was down in a trough with the big machine towering above, next the position was reversed and I had a real fear that I was about to crash down onto the aircraft.

After a lot of expert manoeuvring we were both on the same level and close enough for the number two to reach out with a long pole, snag its hook into the top of my life jacket and drag me in through the hatch. Once safely aboard, my rescuer produced a knife and used it to cut the lanyard by which I was attached to the dinghy and let it drift away. The feel of a solid deck under my feet was terrific, I could almost believe that I was back on good old England's terra firma. The Old Walrus shook itself free of the surging water, then a much bigger wave than its comrades charged at the port float and swept it away, at the same time causing the 'plane to lose flying speed. We were back on the water and there was no way it could ever become air-borne again.

The Gods of War seemed to have made up their minds that I was going to be their next victim. Without the float the lower port wing was dragging in the water and before long the ship was going to turn turtle. The only answer was to apply a counter balance by applying weight to the tip of the starboard wings and that weight was the air gunner and myself. The gunner gave me a practical demonstration crawling out on to the root of the port wing, grasping the leading edge in his hands and hooking his toes over the trailing edge; thus anchored he slowly worked his way out to the far end.

I would have loved to have stayed in that warm cabin and having watched the air gunner make his precarious journey out along that wildly bucking wing, frankly I was terrified. But they had risked their lives to save me and by now I was part of the show so there was no way that I could flunk it. Once in position it was a case of hang on for dear life while the 'plane charged down one side of a wave and up the face of the next. Both of us knew that were we to lose our grip, whether hands or toes, there was no way that we were going to be found once swept into that swirling mass of water.

We must have been in that position for at least an hour before the two Air Sea Rescue boats appeared and all the time we could see the pilot talking into his microphone but could not hear the message that he was trying to pass because of the noise of wind and water, so really we did not have a clue just what was happening or how long it would be before we could expect assistance. One thing that I am sure of, I would not recommend that way of being rescued. From here on my mind is a complete blank as to how I was transferred from wing tip to boat. The wing was so fragile that to bring a boat alongside would risk crushing it and tipping its occupants into the water and as far as I was concerned my hands were so cold that they were fastened over the leading edge like claws. But rescue me they did and with my wet clothes removed, wrapped in warm blankets plus a generous tot of spirits, I slept most of the way home.

The crews of the two boats and the aircraft had a fairly torrid time as there was a short sea running, and those launches motor at least forty knots and when at speed in that sort of seaway they shoot off the top of one wave and crash down onto the top of the next with a resounding thump, which seems to shake the whole boat. When not doing this they are rolling and yawing viciously with tons of green water sweeping their decks.

Those Air Sea Rescue boys were the real heroes of World War Two. Out in all sorts of weather and conditions, month after month. Nobley did they live up to their motto, 'The Sea Shall Not Have Them'.[1]

When I eventually arrived at the Southampton Naval Hospital the doctors had to sew my scalp and face back into position and therein lies a tale. There was no doubt that we pilots fancied ourselves a little

---

[1] It was not until 1989, when I was contacted by the aviation author Norman Franks, that I discovered who had actually rescued me. He then put me in touch with them, Flight Lieutenant's Tom Fletcher DFC DFM and bar, and Len Healey DFC DFM

bit and the hallmark of the successful fighter pilot was leaving the top button of his tunic undone and possibly a moustache, of which an observer could stand behind the man and see both ends protruding at the same time! My facial hair is very brittle and insists on growing straight down so soon after I first arrived in England, I would go each day to the camp barber and he attacked my embryo moustache with his curling tongs. In the initial stages it was horrible, the smell of singed hair parked under my nose and a moustache which felt and looked like a piece of over-burnt toast. However I persisted and the finished product was not too bad. The only problem being that I had to take in a couple of reefs before it would fit into the oxygen mask and with it in residence there was not much room for the rest of me.

However, after the medics had seen to me and I began to take an interest in my surroundings I found that they had cut my beautiful moustache off in order to sew my lip up and I just could not face enduring all that agony again in order to replace it.

CHAPTER IX

WOMEN AND OTHER TROUBLES

'WOE', 'FROGGIE' and myself along with a few other 486 pilots, when not rostered for early morning flying, had developed the habit of staying in bed till long after breakfast was officially over. The girls looked after us, however. It was a case of meals at all hours as far as 486 was concerned.

One of the girls, Dolly, an attractive young lass of about seventeen, must have been warned by her mother to keep away from men and was well on her way to becoming a man hater. After a lot of persuasion, she promised to come to the camp pictures with me but when the big night arrived, I became involved in a drinking session in the Mess and forgot all about my fair companion. Poor girl; so her mother had been right after all. She had the sympathy and support of her work mates and next morning down went the hatch in our faces. Late breakfasts were off as far as 486 were concerned. Our two diplomats, Wilson and Frogatt, were given the task of finding out the reason for our sudden unpopularity and if possible pour oil on the troubled waters. They were left in no doubt as to the cause of the upset but somehow managed to smooth the ruffled feathers. Consequently I was threatened with all kinds of mediaeval torture if ever I pulled the act again.

All went smoothly for a while, then to make amends, I asked Dolly to come out with me again, promising faithfully that there would be no re-occurrence of the last time. Being a cheerful young lass and not being capable of bearing a grudge for long, she said yes. It was not my custom to become involved in after dinner drinking bouts so I have no logical explanation why this should happen on the only two nights that I had planned to visit the pictures during the entire time that I was at Tangmere. Next morning the slide went down again and this time there was no reprieve.

Outside the main gate at Tangmere was a country store with a small dining room attached where breakfast could be had, at a price. The taste of mildly cured bacon was a pleasant surprise after the over-salted variety that had been served up in the Mess and there was always an egg. Eggs were a luxury that we had not seen for a long time. When they had appeared they were of the dried variety and any resemblance to an egg was entirely imaginary.

No longer able to bludge a breakfast at the Mess, we developed the habit of obtaining a late one at the roadside store and in time we became almost like one of the family, or so we thought.

Their son, a prisoner of war, was in bad shape and about to be repatriated. Strolling around the store was a very large rooster which we had watched grow to maturity. If that bird had known what was in store for him he would have had little to crow about. On the first Saturday after the son's return, there was to be a family reunion and the rooster was to provide the main course.

When in January 1944, the storekeeper heard that 486 were to leave Tangmere he insisted that we turn up for a farewell breakfast and what a breakfast, with a double ration of bacon and a couple of eggs. Very generous, or so we believed, until we were handed the bill. That slap-up breakfast possibly did not cost the world but not far off it when weighed against our slender financial resources. We were unhappy. To put it in plain language we had the feeling that we had been swindled. Our solution? Next morning when we flew out at first light, we would take the rooster with us.

That night, instead of returning directly to our billets, we detoured and collected our rooster. It looked so easy. The chicken house was unlocked and just inside, on a low perch, there was our victim, ready and waiting. I had the idea that despatching a fowl would be money for old rope but I was to be badly mistaken. It was to take the combined efforts of three airmen before he gave up the ghost, and was bundled into the cockpit of my aircraft for the flight to our new base at Beaulieu.

To celebrate my arrival at the new station I flew low over the field and pulled up in a vertical climb in what was to be the start of a loop and roll off the top. Just when I was at the top and about to roll out, my passenger, whom I thought dead, started to crow. There was little enough room in the cockpit for me and if that fowl started flapping around I could have been in all sorts of trouble. The obvious answer was to open the hood and let it find it's own way home! A moment of panic, then I realised that there was no visible movement. 'Clang!' as the penny dropped. The cause of the disturbance was our sudden ascent into a low pressure area, and it had been the air under pressure in the bird's lungs escaping which had been responsible for that horrible 'noise'.

We handed our prize over to the station cooks for processing but their report was not encouraging. As one of the waiters put it, what we had asked them to cook must have been the father of all birds as it was one big lump of sinew and gristle. This could not be, we said, we knew that bird's history. It was practically an old friend and we had watched it progress from chick to adult. However, the mystery deepened. True enough, when we came to eat it, the bird had to be the toughest thing that any of us had ever tried to wrestle with and after we had given it our best, even the camp dogs were no more successful. Had the returning soldier tried to gnaw his way through that rooster it would have made prisoner of war meals seem like dining out at the Ritz.

Later, a pilot, who had stayed behind to collect an aircraft, told us the full story. That morning, after our departure, he had arrived for breakfast to find the family in a state of shock. The previous night some villain had entered the chicken house and stolen an old family pet and from the amount of feathers left lying around they were left in no doubt as to what it's fate had been. If the story was to be believed the rooster had been with the family for many years and was so old that he could no longer make it up to the perch so a low one had been provided. Nobody had told us that 'our' rooster had a great grand-father who was still around!

We had our girl friends on the station but seeing them every day in uniform seemed to rob them of some of the glamour. Somehow it seemed like going out with your sister. So, the civilian girls outside seemed to offer an irresistible attraction and, of course, for them, even the married ones, pilots had an equal attraction. If a girl had a husband it was a secret that was not readily disclosed and as a service husband sometimes had the knack of turning up unexpectedly, this could be dangerous as some of those commando types were not the gentlest of characters.

One night, or early morning, one of our airfield guards intercepted a prowler who was trying to sneak onto the 'drome and took him into protective custody. Although dressed in what appeared to be a Flight Sergeant's uniform, complete with an RAF flying badge, the service police thought it strange that their prisoner was without footwear and the condition of his socks indicated that he had travelled a consider-able distance so clad. Just what might be expected of a German airman

who, having baled out and lost his boots during the descent, was now
trying to hijack an aircraft and head for home. The nocturnal visitor
insisted that he was one of Scotty's mob but this did not fool anybody.
German intelligence had an astounding amount of knowledge, not
only of squadron dispositions but also the names of their personnel.

Most Squadron Commanders would have taken a dim view of
having their slumbers disturbed at an early hour in order to identify a
Sergeant Pilot who had somehow got himself into trouble with the
service police. Most would have issued instructions that he be kept
under lock and key for what was left of the night. That was not Scotty's
way. We were like one big family and no effort on his part was too
much trouble to get us off the hook. Later, however, he would want
to know the true story, with no reservations, and we found that there
was no point in trying to pull the wool over his eyes.

As an NCO, Des must have been quite a character. Our antics were
merely minor repetitions of some of his former days. Having stood
between us and our accusers, Scotty was quite capable of handing out
his own brand of rough and ready justice if he considered the crime
warranted it. In such a course of action he was always scrupulously
fair and we respected him for it. On this occasion it was our own Norm
Preston. Who else could it have been?

Norm's story was that while escorting his girlfriend home he had
fallen into a pond or static water tank; I cannot recall the exact details.
The upshot was that he had been invited in to sit in front of a heater
and dry off. If our pilot's story was to be believed he had dozed off
and when he woke he was all on his lonesome. It would seem that the
lady had retired to bed and left him to it. Well it had a ring of truth
as an escort snoring off was most unlikely to impress any girl. We were
unkind enough to suggest that Norm had made an exit through a
window as the husband came in through the front door. Be that as it
may, when Norm had last seen his shoes they were sadly in need of
repair but later, when they were handed in at the guard room, that
had been taken care of.

Upsetting senior officers was a squadron speciality. When we were at
Volkel in Holland, later in the war, our Group captain was a favourite
with both flying and ground personnel. As a top fighter pilot and a
Kiwi to boot he was one of us. Not only did he know us all personally
but also he would frequently join in our nightly frolics at the bar. He
was, of course, Pat Jameson, who had been the Wing Leader at
Wittering when I joined 485 Squadron.

Slowly we began to realise that Jamie was not around as often as had been his custom and when he did show up he seemed to be favouring the company of the more sober types such as the ground officers. Perhaps it was that we were drinking too much and this was his way of indicating his disapproval. The final straw was when he had our bar redecorated. To us it did not seem like home any more. For the war we were prepared to tolerate any indignity but this was too much. Jamie was absent for about a week, possibly on leave in Blighty and we had a ball. The final act was to black lead a pilot's feet and then support him while he marched in the door, up the wall, across the ceiling and down the far wall. It was all good fun but next day after viewing our handiwork we began to have second thoughts as we awaited the Groupie's return. There was a deadly silence as Jamie quietly stood and looked at the decorations, then he announced his decision. The bar was closed for a week as far as 486 were concerned. This was not to be the only occasion when 486 pilots were to suffer the indignity of having to undergo a 'health' week.

In December 1944 when Squadron Leader Iremonger[1] had just departed and we were awaiting the arrival of our new Commanding Officer, Squadron Leader 'Spike' Umbers, the squadron officer pilots celebrating a successful day's shooting had decided to visit the Sergeant's Mess and we over-indulged in the liquors, of which they had a plentiful supply. On that day we had established a record for the number of enemy aircraft shot down by any one squadron and continuing our run of success we managed to write off every bit of transport in the Wing, with the exception of the Group Captain's jeep.

We had started celebrating in our Mess, then went to the Sergeant's Mess where they had an abundance of liquor which on top of what we'd already consumed, was disastrous.

I recall the Wing Commander's Opel car was burnt out, and there were several head-on crashes in trucks, while others were left in bomb craters. A party of German saboteurs could not have inflicted more damage in so short a space of time. Fortunately for me, I had found an empty bed and came to in the morning in full marching order but with the father of all hangovers.

To complete the devastation Pilot Officer Eagelson, the following night, helped himself to the jeep and it also joined the casualty list. All 486 pilot officers and NCOs were ordered to report to the Groupie's office and please explain.

---

[1] Squadron Leader J H Iremonger DFC, from Wiltshire, England later Wing Commander

Jamie asked who was responsible for the running of the squadron; Flight Lieutenant's Appleton and Miller both claimed the distinction. Jamie had been around Fighter Command for most of the war but this was the first time that he had heard of a squadron having two COs at the same time.

'Eagle's' effort the previous night earned him a discipline course at Sheffield which had been established specifically for the purpose of punishing aircrew who had stepped out of line. I was an Old Boy of this school. My crime back when we were at Tangmere was not for wrecking Wing transport. I had been much more successful in that I had managed to write off two Typhoons!

While Eagle had earned his trip to Sheffield, I considered myself unjustly treated. We had been on a bombing trip to a rocket sight and as the squadron swept into the Tangmere circuit and prepared to land, I was feeling mighty pleased with my effort. A moment's lack of concentration and I levelled out a fraction high. As the 'plane stalled, it hit the runway, wheels first and bounced. This was not unusual and the correct procedure was to put on full power and go around again and have another try. With the long East/West runway stretching out in front, I decided to arrest the bounce with a burst of motor and set it down again.

In a squadron landing, once safely down, the form was to continue onto the far end of the runway in use, almost at flying speed, thus clearing the way for the 'plane coming in directly behind. With twelve aircraft landing on the same runway in under a minute there is no margin for error. Jimmy Wilson, flying the aircraft directly in front, had made an exceptionally short landing and with my aircraft further down the runway than was normal, it was a case of an accident waiting to happen. Wilson had many close calls during his operational career but none, I'll wager, was closer than that and one he escaped from with barely a scratch.

Next day, for me, it was a visit to the Station Commander's office and while I nervously stood outside and awaited a summons to enter, the Group Captain was called away as there had been another landing accident out on the field. There were only two squadrons of Spitfire XIIs in existence and both were based at Tangmere. During a squadron landing, two Spitfires had collided on the runway and five more had hit the mix-up while landing, thus more or less wiping out a complete squadron. By the time Group Captain Paddy Chisholm had returned to his office he was in a rare mood and not prepared to listen to any explanations that I might have to offer.

'Flight Sergeant, what you did was bad enough but what happened out there this morning was just plain sabotage! I am sending you to discip. camp at Sheffield for six weeks and cancelling your commission'.

I had that morning been notified that I had been granted a commission and was now a Pilot Officer but Pilot Officers are on probation for six months during which time the commission can be cancelled. At the end of that period, providing the holder has conducted himself as befits an officer holding the King's Commission, he receives automatic promotion to Flying Officer. Normally a pilot who had received the savage sentence which had been handed out to me, would have his logbook endorsed accordingly and either permanently grounded or remustered to some task. The fact that there was no endorsement and that I remained with 486 would suggest that someone must have had second thoughts probably because there was no way that a mere NCO could be allowed to show that he had been the victim of a Group Captain's ill-temper. When I heard Scotty rampaging on as to what a terrific chap Paddy Chisholm was, I ask myself what he would have said if he had been on the receiving end of the raw deal his hero had handed out to me.

There was no point in crying over spilt milk—the only course was to go along with the system. There is a lot of truth in the saying, 'Every cloud has a silver lining'.

The first morning at Sheffield, I, with about a couple of dozen prisoners, for that was how we were treated, stood rigidly to attention as discip. Sergeant reeled off a list of 'do and do nots'.

'Is there a barber amongst you misfits?'

'Yes, Sir', I replied.

'Is there something wrong with your eyesight, Flight Sergeant. I am a Sergeant and that is how I expect to be addressed when you are speaking to me. Report to me after parade'.

Up to now my experience of hair cutting had been sitting in a barber's shop and patiently waiting while he waded through a number of customers who always seemed to have arrived ahead of me. However, acting as camp barber was preferable to the 'bull ring' and as long as you left the roots and ears behind there were no complaints from higher up! The drill sergeant was unkind enough to hint later that my cutting style would suggest that I had spent more time shearing sheep than I had cutting hair! Then he confided, 'A lot of these misguided souls are going to try and bribe you with cigarettes. I will expect my share. Double-cross me and you are going to wish that you had never been born'.

It would seem that I had fallen amongst thieves. Amongst my fellow culprits were a Sunderland crew who had somehow omitted to anchor their flying boat and it must have drifted out into the Atlantic; and the bomber crew, who had lost their way back from Germany, force landed, set fire to their aircraft, hidden up when daylight came, only to discover they were just a few miles from their airfield!

Bending or ignoring the rules drawn up for the safety of aircraft and their occupants was a trait of which most operational pilots were guilty, and I was no exception. Here are a couple of examples. RAF safety orders stated that when an aircraft had a non-flying passenger in the front or rear seat, the control column was to be removed from that cockpit before take off. When Neville Parks, one of our New Zealand armourers, suggested that I fly him to Croydon in the Squadron's Tiger Moth, I said okay. I also agreed to leave the front control column in and give him a spot of dual on the way. The old Tiger was a gentle aircraft and it did not seem possible that we could come to any harm. All went well as the Tiger, under my control, lumbered down the runway and climbed to about a thousand feet, whence I leaned forward and touching my pupil on the shoulder, indicated that he was now in charge.

With no idea when a plane was straight and level, Neville's first reaction was to pull his control column back. Without any way of communicating, my only option was to apply forward pressure on my control column. As far as I was concerned it was a no-win situation as I had to be careful as to how much pressure I applied, for if my controls ceased to function it was curtains for both of us. With Neville pulling and me pushing, we were much too close to the ground to indulge in the sort of antics in which my pupil was involving us. Even Tigers have a limit as to the amount of abuse that they will put up with and a deadly silence began to descend around us which always tends to happen when a Tiger Moth is on the point of stall. My frantic shouts of, 'Let that bloody stick go', seemed to have no effect on the lunatic occupying the front seat but the law of self preservation must have begun to operate, for a couple of hands shot into view. Not a moment too soon as by then we were on our way down. Another lesson learned. Rules are there for your protection, ignore them at your peril! Another misdemeanour along my thorny path was not so much the fact of disobeying regulations, but a failure to carry out a procedure that by that time should have been almost automatic. This one was the obvious 'gun button switched to fire' after crossing the coast on the way out and returned to 'safe' when approaching the coast on the way home. My second mistake on the same journey back in the

summer of 1943 was to get too close to the aircraft in front when
landing, which resulted in mine being caught in it's slipstream which
had the effect of throwing my 'plane almost on its side. While I was
attempting to straighten the machine, I squeezed the gun button and
four cannons, which were pointing directly at a hangar, promptly burst
into life. Well at least the airmen working in the hangar could feel that
they were taking an active part in the war. The aircraft ahead of me,
in which sat Des Scott, also had a near miss, as Scotty later remarked!

At least Sandy Powell waited until he had landed his aircraft one
day and had safely parked it in it's bay before setting his cannon off,
which he did by hanging his flying helmet over the top of the control
column. It, too, was quite a performance.

Bruce Lawless and myself could not, for the life of us, picture Sandy
as the kind of individual who would cause a girl's heart to flutter but,
to the opposite sex, he had a charm that was irresistible. It was always
Sandy who marched off with the most attractive girl leaving Bruce and
I wallowing in his wake. Only once was I to have the chance of putting
one over on our 'Casanova' and like most successful operations, it was
not planned.

On this evening, Lawless being on leave, I had planned a quiet
evening in Chichester so, before leaving the station, called at our
Mess with the intention of having a couple of drinks before setting
out on my journey. Who should I find at the bar but Sandy, all
togged up. There could only be one reason and it had to be a woman.
At that time he was squiring a most attractive young lady. I would
have given a fortnight's pay to have her look at me the way she
used to look at Sandy. I knew the girl and had been in her company
on numerous occasions but I was only tolerated because I was
Sandy's friend and he was around. As I was passing the Mess telephone, it started ringing and when I answered it I recognised the
young lady's voice.

'Hello, Pam, Jim here. I expect you would like to speak to Sandy?'

'Jim, will you speak up, I can barely hear you?'

As a matter of fact I could barely hear myself, Sandy was not very
far away and he might hear and catch on.

'Sorry, the phone has been on the blink lately. Sandy has been
rostered for night flying. He asked me to answer your call and
explain'. There was a big sigh over the phone and I could sense
her disappointment. 'When you have a pilot for a boyfriend you
must expect this sort of thing,' I continued, 'but don't let it spoil
your evening. I have nothing planned and the car all to myself.

Top: Myself as a humble Leading Aircraftsman, April 1941, about to start pilot training. The journey had begun.

Middle: With my Dad and brothers, Dave (left), who had to stay and work our farm, and Alex (right) who also joined the airforce.

Left: With 485 Spitfire Squadron, 1942; (left to right): Brown, M G Sutherland, -?-, F/Lt M R D Hume, S/Ldr R J C Grant DFC DFM, F/Lt R W Baker -?-, G Moorhead, self, L S Mc White.

Top: With my Flight in 485 Squadron; (left to right): Sgt Chalky White, PO George Moorhead, F/Lt Reg Baker DFC, F/Lt Max Sutherland, self, PO I P J Maskill and Sgt Gordon.

Middle: Hawker Typhoon lb (JP853) of 486 Squadron, Oct 1943, flown by Frank Murphy.

Bottom: 486 Squadron B Flight dispersal, RAF Tangmere. In the foreground are Allan Smith, Frank Murphy, Ian Waddy and the CO, Des Scott.

Left: Some of the boys in 486 Squadron; (rear): Rangi Swinton, J R Cullen, Vaughan Fittall, Taylor-Cannon; (front): G Thompson and Bluey Dall.

Middle: Me, (left) looking typically dishevelled, with brother Alex (far right), outside a bar, naturally.

Bottom: My CO, Des Scott DFC, in front of a Typhoon, with Gp Capt W J Chris (left) Station Commander at Tangmere, Ian Waddy, a future CO, and Allan Smith.

Top: 486 (NZ) Squadron 1943. (left to right): PO Rod Fitzgibbon, PO Noel Fair Faircloth, F/Lt Ian Waddy, FO H N Thomas (IO), S/Ldr D J Scott DFC, FO Allan Smith, FO Frank Murphy, FO Norm Gall, FO J R Cullen, PO Happy Appleton, Doc Jones (MO), PO Norm Preston; in front: FO Bluey Dall and PO Arty Sames.

Middle: Jim Black Mac McCaw, Allan Smith and FO Andy Brown. Brownie was killed on 16 May 1943 when his engine failed during a shipping strike, flying as No.2 to Allan. Jim McCaw later shot down 19 $\frac{1}{2}$ V1s. Allan Smith later commanded a Typhoon squadron.

Above: The old and the new - in early 1944 we begin to re-equip with Tempests. Here is one of our old Typhoons and a new Tempest (*IWM*).

Top and Middle: Tempest chasing a V1 over the English countryside.

Above: Close up of the V1, its rocket flame clearly visible, and even more so at dusk.

Top: We usually tried to get the V1s over the sea. This one is heading for the English coast across the Channel.

Middle: Based at Beaulieu in the New Forest we liberated this sign as a trophy. While Bruce Lawless and I hold the board, Wackie Kalka holds the dog, with Sandy Powell and Eagleson looking suspicious.

Left: Back from a sortie: Stafford, Taylor-Cannon, Eagleson and Evans.

Left: Eagle Eagleson line-shooting for the press, with a press-ganged audience. Another V1 in the bag - but he did get 21 of 'em! (*IWM*)

Middle: Our two V1 aces, Eagle Eagleson and Ray Cammock, who got 21 and 20 respectively. They look as if they are discussing another way of shooting down the buzz bombs! (*RNZAF*)

Bottom: Tempest V (JN766). Dusty Miller bagged two V1s in this aircraft on 23 June 1944. (*RNZAF*)

Top: The boys at Newchurch 1944. The CO, James Iremonger, is standing 2nd from the right, and Taylor-Cannon is 3rd. Jim McCaw sits behind the cockpit, 4th from the right. Woe Wilson stands 8th from the right.

Middle: While this snap-shot has seen better days, it shows how rugged we looked in 1944! Standing left to right: Sandy Powell, Bailey, S J Short, Joe Wright, Oc O'Connor, and Kalka; seated: Butch Steedman (checking how good he looks), Eagle and Jack Stafford. This lot claimed 60 doodlebugs between them. Not bad for a bunch of scruffs. But the V1s got one too - Joe.

Above: The armourers load a Tempest of 501 Squadron with 20mm ammo. (*RAF Museum*)

Top left: Yours truly by the tail of my Tempest.

Top right: Joan, my English nurse - and later my wife.

Above: Noni Wright of the BBC interviewing some of the gang. Norm Gall and Bluey Dall in front, Spike Umbers and Sergeant M O Jorgenson behind. The sad thing is that none of these four survived the war. *(RNZAF)*

Top left: My pal Bruce Lawless on a sunny day. Not sure if he's looking at his V1 kills or the picture of a pint of bitter! *(FB Lawless)*

Top right: Another pal, Harvey Sweetman, who still lives in Auckland today. *(RNZAF)*

Above: Eagle Eagleson in a Tempest with 26 V1 kills marked - could have been JN770 or JN803, each of which scored more than 20 buzz bombs destroyed.

Top: Tempest SA-N (NV763) with its hard-working ground crew. *(via C Thomas)*

Middle: Harvey Sweetman, Spike Umbers and Hyphen Taylor-Cannon with the centre board from an airborne life-boat, which had been acquired. It was used as a Squadron score board and is now in the RNZAF Museum at Wigram, Christchurch. *(RNZAF)*

Above: Y-Yorker taxies out at Volkel. We had to have an airman on the wing to direct us about on the ground as we couldn't see over the engine cowling. Note external drop tanks. Ralph Evans baled out of it on 15 April 1945. *(RNZAF)*

Top left: Three of the boys pose for the camera again, with the spinner from an Me l09G. Johnny Wood, Taylor-Cannon and Bill Bailey. *(A R Evans, via C Thomas)*

Top right: Me and Tubby Ross in front of SA-Z.

Above left: Bruce Lawless DFC, a good pal of mine who decided to settle in the UK but we keep in touch. *(F B Lawless)*

Above right: Dave Thomson (on his wedding day). He and I shot down a huge flying boat on 2 May 1945. Note 486 Squadron badge on pocket.

Top: In the snow at Volkel: (left to right): Self, Bill Trott, Brian O'Connor, Spike Umbers, now our CO, Wood, Colin McDonald and Miller …

Middle: … and some more; W J Campbell, K A Smith, Appleton, Harold Longley (an N-Zedder in 3 Squadron) and Ike Fenton.

Left: Still frame from a camera gun of a truck being strafed on a Dutch road.

Top left: My four predecessors, and therefore four of my COs. Johnny Iremonger DFC, from England … *(J H Iremonger)*

Top right: … Spike Umbers DFC, from Dunedin, killed in action 14 February 1945 …

Above left: … Hyphen Taylor-Cannon DFC & bar, from Oamaru, killed in action 13 April 1945 …

Above right: … Smokey Schrader DFC & bar, from Wellington; survived. *(via C Thomas)*

Top: Our 122 Wing CO, Group Captain Pat Jameson DSO DFC, with his staff (left to right): S/Ldr E D Mackie DSO DFC & bar, (CO 80 Sqdn and soon to be 122 Wing Leader); S/Ldr K F Thiele DSO DFC & 2 bars, (CO 3 Squadron); Pat Jameson, S/Ldr A E Umbers DFC & bar, (486 Sqdn). Note that all four are from New Zealand: Otorohanga, Christchurch, Wellington and Dunedin.

Middle: My Tempest - SA-M (SN129), with squadron leader's pennant and a few swastikas. What's good enough for Bruce and Eagle is good enough for me!

Above: Tubby Ross seated in my Tempest; his line-shoot, not mine.

Top left: Group Captain Johnnie Johnson DSO & 2 bars, DFC & bar; commanded 1 Wing in 1945, 486 Squadron being on its strength. We sometimes went duck shooting together. *(G Anthony)*

Top right: Bob Spurdle DFC & bar. When Rosie Mackie became 122 Wing's Wingco Flying, Bob took over 80 Squadron. Yet another New Zealander, he came from Wanganui.

Above: Back home from the war, with my sister Francis. It had been quite a journey.

Come out with me'. A period of silence as my unselfish offer was being considered, then,

'Do you think Sandy will mind?'

'Not at all. He will be pleased. You know how much he hates it when he is the cause of spoiling your evening'.

I happened to know that on a previous occasion Sandy had become involved in a Mess drinking session and had failed to keep an appointment. Also on that night he had been night flying. It was a good standby and one that was hard for a civilian girlfriend to disapprove.

'Don't worry your pretty little head. I'll pick you up in half an hour'.

'Thanks, Jim. I will be waiting and report that phone, I can just about hear you and that is about all. It sounds as if you are whispering'.

After a most enjoyable evening I returned to the station only to discover that the Sergeant's Mess and it's bar was still open with Sandy almost in the identical position in which I had last seen him at least five hours previously. Bob, our bar steward, was a terrific chap and providing the senior member present gave the okay he would keep the bar open all night. Sandy being the only person present, and being almost incapable of giving the order which would authorise Bob to drop the shutters, it was a case of waiting until his money ran out or when he reached saturation point. Sandy had reached the stage where he was almost crying drunk and kept muttering, 'The bitch. She promised to ring. Women, I've had them'. All that I could do was sympathise with my good friend and offer a number of reasons as to why she had been unable to keep her promise. I was becoming an expert at consoling heart-broken lovers. For at least a couple of hours, since the closure of the hotel, I'd endured Sandy's girlfriend draped around my neck and weeping on my shoulder but I was not kidding myself that the sudden shift of affection was because of Sandy's standing her up, it was more than likely to have been caused by the amount of gin that she had consumed during the evening at my expense. She had been all over me, like a rash, but I was not complaining.

The following night: 'Sergeant Powell, telephone'. I had only to see Sandy's red face and hear his high pitched, 'And you bloody well believed him?' to know who was on the other end of the phone. Sandy could be violent if provoked so it was time to steal away.

Sandy was incapable of holding a grudge, however, and in a couple of days, relations were back to normal. But I was only half way home and the time could not be long delayed when I would have to face the girlfriend and I had an idea that she would not be quite so forgiving.

There was another incident not long after which also caused Sandy trouble, and as usual the basic cause was a woman. In a hotel in Chichester, Sandy and I had met and been befriended by a wealthy business man and his delightful daughter. To me the father was a proper drip and it was a puzzle how one so stupid had been able to amass the vast amount of money he obviously had. For us, the daughter was the attraction. About nineteen, good looking with a lovely figure and in addition to being highly intelligent, she also had a terrific sense of humour. As was to be expected, the moment the girl clapped her lovely eyes on Sandy, that was it. As far as she was concerned there was no-one else in the room. I can recall remarking to the old dad that it was obvious who his son-in-law was going to be, but although he had initially been quite happy about his daughter's interest in Sandy, it seemed to me that he had now suddenly gone cold on the idea.

Whatever or whoever had been the cause, Sandy, for the first time since I'd known him, was in love and the girl obviously returned his feelings. Sandy, and I being his friend, had been guests in their spacious home on more than one occasion, and when we did not have to fly the next day, spent the night there. Things then got to the stage where Sandy spent his days off and most of the nights in the girl's company. It was at this time that a local, who had been a silent observer, tipped me off to the fact that the girl, who we thought was a daughter, was in fact the man's wife! I found it hard to believe what I was hearing. What could a girl like her see in that nondescript individual, except his money, of course. It seemed that the husband received some sort of satisfaction in introducing his wife as his daughter and then sitting back and watching the RAF wolves trying to do a line with her. An even bigger surprise was in store, for when I told Sandy what I had heard, he told me that he already knew!

To have your wife's lover living in your house almost continually, day and night, and not wake up to what was going on beggars belief. The man was even more stupid than I thought in the first place.

As far as the squadron was concerned, Sandy had become a passenger. All he seemed capable of thinking about was this girl and when our Commanding Officer realised what was going on, his answer was to post Sandy to a close army support unit which would take him as far away from Chichester as possible and hopefully break up the unhealthy association. From then on it is not known, and perhaps never will be known, precisely what happened. But the facts are these. The husband joined the RAF ground crew and on his first leave brought a Tommy gun home with him. Somebody used a knife on the girl and almost cut her head off; the Tommy gun had been used to smash in the husband's head; and Sandy's aircraft had failed to pull out of a dive and he was still in it when the Typhoon ploughed into the ground.

CHAPTER X

THE TEMPEST V

AT the beginning of 1944, our squadron began to be re-equipped with another Hawker creation, the Tempest. This new aircraft was an improvement on the Typhoon, for although it had the same motor, a fin had been added along the top of the fuselage which gave the tail section the appearance of belonging to it. Also the depth of wing had been drastically reduced. This fining down of the high lift wing section gave the new aeroplane an increase in speed as well as greater manoeuvrability. As usual, for every step forward there is a price to pay. The narrowing of the wing section reduced the space available for cannon to be fitted, so existing armaments had to be redesigned. The resultant smaller, slimmer 20mm cannon were reluctant to fire and when they did, quite often continued until they ran out of ammunition.

No sooner had this problem been sorted out than it was decided to replace the three-bladed propeller with a four-bladed one. This last modification gave the aircraft increased acceleration and rate of climb, but quite frequently the pitch control would lock into fully fine and the resultant overspeed would cause the motor to seize in a matter of seconds. So common did this become that forced landings with a defunct motor became almost like pulling into the curb with the family car. At the time we were doing a lot of night flying, in preparation for beach-head support on D-Day, and it is no bed of roses when your one and only motor packs up at night and you are not high enough to bale out. This was how Alf Turner was killed.

Before the squadron left Tangmere, in January 1944, five sergeant pilots had joined it. All five had been more or less together since joining the Royal New Zealand Air Force and now had reached the final stage together. Four out of the five were to lose their lives while serving with 486 and Alf Turner was the first to go. Alf, a pilot of above average ability, took off in a Tempest at night to do a spot of local flying and shortly after take-off lost contact with the ground. For a pilot of Alf's ability it should just have been a routine flight and when someone of his calibre disappears, irrespective of how or where, the effect on the late arrivals is devastating. Two days were to pass before Alf and his aircraft were found, not far from the airfield and beside a busy highway near Oxford. The population had become immune to crashed aircraft; for us it was just the tragedy of it all that was so hard to take.

In hindsight, we now know that the sudden interruption in the Tempest building program had been caused by the decision to change the three-bladed airscrew to four blades and with this modification came the overspeed nightmare. Undoubtedly, Alf had taken off and no sooner airborne than the propeller of his aircraft had locked into fine pitch, the resultant overspeed had caused the motor to seize and too low to use his parachute, Alf had attempted to land in the dark and had not made it.

The back room boys, after ditching trials with models, (carried out in water tanks), expressed an opinion that unlike a Typhoon, a Tempest could be safely landed on the water. This we received with a fair amount of disbelief. We had been told by the same people that it was the big propeller and air scoop that was the Typhoon's problem, now they had been duplicated in the Tempest. Who could blame us for asking how many more pilots would have to die before it was accepted that a combination of propeller, airscoop and water was fatal.

Later, in May, we were doing sweeps over occupied France and, as we had done with Typhoons, we flew out almost at wave top height until within sighting distance of the French coast, then, made an almost vertical climb, in order to cross in above light flak range. We waited on each occasion with bated breath for a motor to pack in on the way across or a pilot to run out of altitude while trying to make it home with a crippled Tempest. Fortunately, it did not happen, and it was not until he was on a flying bomb patrol, on 10 June that Bruce Lawless was faced with the problem of attempting to land his damaged Tempest in the Channel. The upshot was that not only did Bruce's aircraft alight smoothly on the water but it continued to float for a considerable time!

Though we received our initial Tempests in January 1944 at Tangmere, just when we were beginning to congratulate ourselves that we were about to exchange our Typhoons for the RAF's newest and fastest fighters, there was a delay in the Tempest production and the move was put on hold. Our Tempests went to 3 Squadron and we continued with Typhoons until April.

In March 1944 we moved from Beaulieu in Hampshire, north to Drem in Scotland for what we believed was going to be an overdue rest period. The aircraft were flown to our new base but as there were not enough aircraft for us all, the rest of the aircrew were faced with a long weary journey by train.

Our first stop was London, then after a few hours in the West End it was all aboard for Scotland. During our temporary stop we had taken the precaution of purchasing enough beer to last the journey. It was suggested by a member of British Rail that we retire to the guards van and continue our noisy party there but what he had neglected to mention was that the van was full of 'posh' furniture. With a war to fight and win this was only a minor problem. We managed to open a small door on the side of the van and after reducing it to a manageable size we despatched the furniture through the opening. Arriving at Edinburgh, maps protruding from the tops of flying boots, thirty eights dangling from our hips, unshaven and red-, eyed from the effects of beer and lack of sleep, the locals could not have been blamed for thinking, 'If these are our friends and allies what must the enemy look like?'

The officer in charge of that band of pirates was 'Happy Appleton'. With his red whiskers he could have been mistaken for Long John Silver. All that was required to have completed the picture was a parrot on his shoulder and a patch over one of his blood shot eyes.

No sooner had we arrived at Drem than another movement order arrived. The squadron was to move back south to Castle Camps (March 1944), an airfield near the university town of Oxford, to re-equip with Tempests. How we managed to win the war must have been a mystery to a lot of people.

It was at Castle Camps that 'Eagle' first displayed his undoubted ability as a cook, his speciality being bacon and fried eggs. Supplies of this choice commodity presented no problem to our 'chef', he simply raided the pantry in the Officer's Mess. Our nightly beanos came to an abrupt end when Eagle, with his battle dress tunic stuffed full of eggs, left a trail, which gave no doubt as to the reason why there was a chronic shortage of some foodstuffs in the 'Gentlemens' Mess.

Soon after arriving at Castle Camps the squadron flew up to Ayr, an airfield situation on the west coast of Scotland, to do a short training course which involved shooting towed aerial targets. This was a coal mining area and a few young miners had a mistaken idea that they were tough. A lot of these youngsters were known as Bevin Boys after the Cabinet Minister who had been responsible for drafting them into the mines instead of the forces. We were warned to keep away from the local towns and it was even considered unsafe to leave the airfield for there was no love for the Royal Air Force hereabout. It was a local sport for the young louts to beat up aircrew. They might have bluffed our predecessors but this time their victims would be no push over.

The first night all the 486 NCO pilots headed into the local village; no bunch of self-styled rough necks were going to tell us what we could or could not do. We made it obvious that nothing would give us greater pleasure than a brawl, however, the brave coal scratchers kept their heads down. It was one thing to beat up boys but a different ball game to take on a tough bunch of sheep herders and cowcockies from the other side of the world.

After a boisterous night around the local bars we headed back to camp and on the way had to pass a hall where a dance was in progress. We decided to pay a call but found the door securely locked. Obviously there was no intention of allowing uninvited guests to mingle with the local girls. A few hefty kicks of 'Butch' Steedman's big foot soon removed the door and we followed him into the hall amidst a silence you could almost hear. However, this did not last for long. Brian O'Connor, in his efforts to assist the drummer, somehow managed to put a stick through the end of the drum, and the accordian, after having a bottle of beer tipped into it's innards, ceased to take any further part in the evening.

In that part of the world it seemed the custom for the mothers to go along to the dances. I expect the idea was to see their young ladies associated with people whom their parents approved. On this occasion they grabbed their daughters and took off. It was not long before we had the dance floor to ourselves, so we had no option other than to call it a night and head for home.

We were heading towards the airfield, quietly minding our own business when along came what must have been one of the local tough guys on a bicycle and, making no attempt to avoid a collision, he charged through the middle of us and in the effort became unseated and both him and his bicycle finished up in a heap on the footpath. Sandy Powell, ever the gentleman, was helping the rider to his feet and at the same time apologising profusely, though Sandy had nothing to feel sorry about, when 'whang', Sandy collected a fist in an eye which resulted in a shiner which was visible for days. That young

miner could not have made a bigger mistake or picked on a tougher
opponent. A swing of Sandy's foot and the young fellow was back on
the pavement, face downward. No sooner had he arrived than Sandy
was on top with a couple of hands full hair. There was a sickening
crunch as a face made contact with the footpath.

'Take that you bastard and tell me when you've had enough'.

'Whang', more rough treatment. It was becoming clear that Sandy's
victim was fast becoming incapable of knowing when he'd had enough
and was unable of saying so even if he did. It was time for us to attempt
to smooth Sandy's ruffled feathers and carry out a rescue mission.
Again on his feet, the young hoodlum grabbed his wrecked bicycle,
Sandy having kicked the spokes out of both wheels for good measure,
and took off. We had no further problems with the miners but we took
the precaution of never going out alone, it was a case of all or none.

After the air flying course was completed we returned to Castle Camps
where we were told that when the troops went ashore in France in
June 1944, our possible role would be beach-head cover which could
involve flying out, or returning, in the dark. It was expected that the
German fighters would react in considerable numbers so, in order that
we arrive on our patrol line as a squadron it would be essential that
the squadron be able to form up and fly tight formation in the dark.
The use of wing tip or elevator lighting was out as this would make
us easy prey for the enemy night fighters. Our first task, therefore,
was to become efficient at flying the Tempests at night, then to
practice taking off and forming up as a squadron at night with the least
possible delay.

Apart from 'Eagle's' nightly fry-ups an event that sticks in my mind
at this time was 'Bev' Hall's reaction after consuming a small quantity
of beer. Bev was a gentle farmer and an excellent pilot, who up to this
time, I had never seen partake of alcohol. Indeed, he obviously
realised grog would affect him and he had refused to touch it thus far.
His one love was dancing and he had a host of lay friends who were
willing to partner him. Bev had a wife and infant son back in New
Zealand and he made no secret of the fact that he missed them greatly
and was longing for the day when the shooting would be over and he
could return to his homeland.[1]

This pilot was of a serious frame of mind. He looked much older
than his years and was never known to lose his temper or raise his

---

[1] Flying Officer B M Hall, from Dannevirke. Killed in action 27 Dec 1944

voice. This made his reaction to alcohol all the more difficult to understand. He began by losing his temper over the most trivial things,
starting to rave and shout. It would appear that taking part in dances
was being unfaithful to his wife, it was immoral and that his dancing
partners were the cause of his downfall. Having come to that conclusion the next step was to write abusive letters to all his dancing
partners accusing them of trying to break up his marriage. There must
have been at least a dozen ladies involved, quite a few of them happily
married. The only thing they had in common with Bev was that they
liked dancing. He made no secret as to the contents of the letters and
when sealed and made ready for despatching he insisted that Butch
Steedman do the posting immediately. Butch's suggestion that the
posting be delayed till the following day very nearly started a Third
World War. So if the posting was all that was needed to make Bev
happy, pretty soon the letters were beyond recall.

What started him on the drinking session that evening none of us
ever knew. Possibly it was his wedding anniversary or the date of his
son's birthday as it was with so many others. The only other time I
was to see Bev touch alcohol was at our Christmas party in Holland
and his reaction was exactly the same. He was killed two days later
when the squadron tangled with a superior number of enemy fighters.

Our next airfield was to be Newchurch on the Romney Marshes,
where we joined Second TAF in April 1944 and we were billeted in
tents in preparation for following the invasion forces to France which
came in September 1944. However, before that happened we were
involved in the V1 campaign.

Again, the form was shipping strikes and low level attacks over
France with rail and road targets. It was a most exciting period in
history, we could feel the tension mounting. Then came D-Day. It
could turn out to be the Battle of Britain in reverse with the enemy
opposition at its peak. But what a let down for us. We flew once on
D-Day and not a German aircraft was to be seen.

From our grandstand view the water below seemed covered with
ships and it was possible to believe that one could walk from France
to Blighty by merely stepping from one ship to the next. Up above it
was so peaceful and hard to appreciate that down below war was being
conducted with all its barbarous side effects and that fellow human
beings, with all their hopes and plans, were dying in the most brutal
way.

For me D-Day, Minus Eleven was a day that I will long remember.
With a fellow pilot our briefing was to do a dusk patrol down the
French coast, observe and report. Off Le Havre the flak was heavy

and accurate. While weaving furiously to unsight the gunners, it seemed as though a baby hurricane had suddenly swept into the cockpit from below.

It was to be a night landing. No problem. We had practiced them often enough. The only difference being that at Tangmere the runways were long and sealed and the latest runway lighting was installed. Here, at Newchurch, night landings were to be on a grass field where the runway was covered by a type of wire matting, which was quick to lay and the flare path was lit by goose neck flares. On this evening, just 11 days preceeding D-Day, the field was packed with aircraft all set for the big show which was not long to come. A ground loop at night can cause problems, but at night on metal runways with the field littered with squadrons of parked aircraft, the pilot can do a helluva lot of damage.

No sooner had my aircraft touched down than it began to swing wildly in a vicious ground loop. There was nothing that I could do but hang on and hope as it carved it's way through a line of parked aircraft and tortured metal flew all over the place, some of it so hot that it could be seen in the darkness. After crawling out of the wreck and making my way to our dispersal, I found the place deserted, for while we had been aloft, the Wing had been called to the briefings.

None of my flying mates were interested in my little 'sideshow'; all they could think of was the mass of targets that would be round when the army stormed ashore in a few days time.

When the Engineering Officer sorted out the mess he discovered that not only had bursting flak punctured holes in the bottom of my cockpit but also it had punctured a tyre and that had been the cause of the baby hurricane that had so surprised me. With no air to cushion the impact the wheel rim had dug into the Somerfelt matting and from then on all hell broke lose as dirt and dust blew up from the cockpit floor. Later, on the eve of the Rhine crossing, I was to have a repetition of pre D-Day. On that occasion I was to lead 486 on a sweep deep into enemy territory and as it was possible that there could be strong enemy reaction, Bruce Cole, with 3 Squadron, flew as our high cover. At the briefing we had been warned that the thrust into Hitler's homeland was not unexpected and that squadrons of fighters had been withdrawn from the Russian Front to support the home based ones and that the indications were that we could expect a lively trip. As we taxied out, Bruce and his pilots were seated in their aircraft and it was expected that they would follow us out and form up in their allotted position. Aloft and in position, there was no sign of any movement from 3 Squadron. Committed to radio silence and with limited fuel it was then a case of setting course and trusting that we would be able to deal with any trouble that should arise. Upon our return Bruce was there to meet me.

'Sorry, Jim. Letting you down was none of my doing, it was all part of a big cover up by Group. As soon as you were airborne we were briefed for the Rhine crossing which is to take place at first light tomorrow'.

Bruce was a gentleman and to have to stay behind and desert friends who were expecting trouble and counting on his being around to help out, must have weighed heavily with him. I will wager that it was with anxious eyes that he counted our aircraft back as we swung into the Volkel circuit. We had been used as guinea pigs. Well, war is not for the feint hearted.[1]

As regards my ground loop on 26 May, I was an eye witness to a similar accident which happened to Rick Tanner[2] and it was on the same airfield. As his Tempest touched down, the wheels appeared to dig in and the aircraft did a forward somersault at over one hundred miles an hour. When we pulled Rick out of the heap of twisted metal there were buckets of blood around, or so it seemed to me. I found it hard to believe that a body could lose so much blood and survive. Rick was a lucky boy but as it turned out the physical injuries were the least of his troubles. His nerves had taken a battering and there was not a thing that we could do to help him. There never was a more obvious case where we could truthfully say, 'but for the Grace of God, there go I'.

To those of us who had watched Rick's plane do what appeared to be a normal approach and landing, it was not a comforting sight to see our comrade strapped into what was left of that cockpit and not even be able to suggest a reason for his plane's behaviour. During future landings one could not help thinking, will it be my turn this time and if so will I be as lucky as Rick.

This accident happened near the end of the flying bomb invasion and we were up there on patrol stooging up and down, and as nothing seemed to be happening, we were bored to distraction, which was a dangerous feeling. My worst experience, when bored, which could have been my last, after a heavy night sitting up there in that hot cockpit with the sun streaming down, was when I dropped off to sleep and awoke to find my aircraft in a gentle dive and not far from the

---

[1] Squadron Leader R B Cole DFC and bar. Desert Air Force 1941-43. CO 3 Squadron 1945-47

[2] Flight Lieutenant E W Tanner, injured in crash 25 Aug 1944

French coast! Rick, on that last patrol, must have been equally bored and probably started to play around with the brake lever and attempted to land with the brakes locked on. It was a great relief to us all when the Engineering Officer was able to pinpoint the cause of Rick's accident. Another lesson learned the hard way—leave the brakes alone until you need them.

As the days slipped past and our army stormed ashore, it was a case of sit on the ground and wait, and so limited was the enemy air activity that our services were not required. Stuck out on the Romney Marshes under canvas, we were under starters orders, which meant that we could not leave dispersal. Our only diversion was taking meals at the field kitchen which was situated only a few hundred yards from our parked aircraft. The best that could be said for the meals was that our health was unlikely to suffer through over-eating. So we kept on waiting . . . though we did not know what for.

CHAPTER XI

DOODLEBUGS

You could feel that something was going to happen. There was antici-pation in the air. We were also sure that our Commanding Officer, Johnny Iremonger, and our 'Spy' (the IO), knew more than they were telling us. In some mysterious way we seemed to know that whatever it was, it had nothing to do with the landings in France. It is in such a situation that the rumour-mongers and 'gen' men swing into action. There is no limit to what a fertile imagination can dream up. A German counter-invasion was expected; enemy paratroopers were planning to land on the home airfields and blow up all our aircraft; it was even suggested that several airfields had already been put out of action. Then one evening a strange aircraft, with a jet of flame shooting out the back and making a noise that we had never heard before, flew in from the Channel and headed in the direction of London. As we watched and tried to make up our minds as to what the strange aircraft could be, Kevin McCarthy said, 'It looks like a Doodle Bug'. This was the first time I was to hear a name which was soon to become a household word in Britain.

Next morning we were told to report to the Spy's tent for briefing. No member of the armed forces can be more mysterious, or frustrating for that matter, when what he knows is his exclusive property and his audience are bursting with curiosity. The Spy, his voice just above an audible whisper (he must have felt that a German ear was pressed against every keyhole within a hundred miles!), warned us that what we were about to hear was most secret and not a word was to be breathed outside that tent. In hindsight, it amazes me that he did not forbid us to talk about it in our sleep. If the Spy had his facts straight, the authorities were expecting an attack by pilotless aircraft that would make the Battle of Britain look like a dress rehearsal and such would be the destruction of British cities that there was a possibility of panic amongst our civilian population.

Our Spy was really enjoying his little role and to add to the drama, we had noticed Military Police stationed at various points around the field. Even for the pre D-Day briefing, security had not been so strict.

We had been a constant worry to the Spy; he just could not get us to take the war seriously. Now he was in the box seat and had us hanging on his every word.

One of the first things that had got our backs up was the bombing of the 'No Ball' targets which we had considered a wasteless loss of lives, bombs and aircraft. Why we were kept in the dark as to what these targets actually were will always be a mystery to me. Our intensive bombing must have alerted the Germans to the fact that the British Government knew what they had in the pipelines, so why not tell us. It was our necks that were on the chopping block and our mates that were being shot down day after day. It would have made things a lot easier for us who were up front, if we had been told why we were being sent into that inferno of flak, day after day. Finally we were told that what we had been bombing day after day were launching ramps for pilotless aircraft, or more precisely, a large bomb fitted with wings and a jet propulsion unit.

It was predicted that it was the German intention first to destroy London and then proceed to wipe out all our major cities by swamping England with hundreds of these projectiles. The bomb was fired off it's launching pad in the direction of it's target and the distance regulated by the amount of fuel carried. Once the engine stopped, the distance the bomb would glide before hitting the ground could be calculated to within a very narrow range. So seriously had the threat been taken that there was a plan to move the entire population out of London. Our bombing had delayed the initial attack but now it seemed that the Germans had developed a much smaller launching ramp, some of which were under ground and others so well camouflaged that it was impossible to see them from above. The plane we had seen the previous evening was the first bomb to reach England but soon we would see large numbers passing overhead once the Germans commenced around the clock launching. They would even launch them from bomber aircraft over the sea. All this, of course, was based on the assumption that the information reaching England from across the Channel was accurate.

Three lines of defence had been planned to deal with the expected flying-bomb attack. Firstly a constant fighter patrol along the south coast of England where the attack was expected to cross. Further inland a belt of anti-aircraft guns were positioned which in turn were to be backed up by a balloon barrage which it was hoped would deal with any bombs which slipped through the aircraft and gun defence. This little scheme seemed logical, the only snag being at that time that there were neither balloons nor guns so all that stood between London and the enemy were three squadrons of Tempests, the only aircraft with the speed and fire power to deal with the intruders. One of these was 486, so it seemed that we were in for a lively time. Later, of course, Spitfires and Mustangs were able to catch them as well as Mosquito night fighters.

As usual the choicest piece of news was kept for the last. It was estimated that because of it's speed, the only way an aircraft would be able to attack successfully would be from directly astern, with the result that when the bomb, which contained half a ton of explosives, was detonated it would more than likely blow up the attacking fighter! We were a sombre and silent bunch as we left that briefing tent. On my one and only patrol over the Beach Head I had looked down from my lofty perch and felt sorry for the invading troops. Had I known what was coming I might well have saved a little bit of sympathy for myself.

Just in case we believed that this was perhaps a little over dramatic, my chum Bruce had to force land north-east of Rye, when his target V1 blew up. This was the same day we lost Joe Wright—28 June, 1944 (see page 117).

Sightings were frequent, interceptions difficult for although our ground speed was over four hundred miles an hour our target was as fast, some of them faster and it was frustrating to have a flying bomb leave you floundering in its wake as it headed towards London. In warfare, tactics are never static. The bombs flew at two thousand feet or lower, so the intercepting fighter had to be positioned another two thousand feet above and directed onto its target by radar. In theory it seemed fool proof. In practice, in hurtling down at near the speed of sound, the bomb because of its dark colouring, was almost invisible against the ground and when seen, the attacker was almost on top of it and the closing speed was frightening.

On one occasion, concentrating on the interception and at the same time checking the angle of dive in order to level out directly behind my victim, the bomb did not become visible until less than a hundred yards ahead. It was a case of the hunter becoming the hunted as my plane seemed intent on doing a first-class ramming job. All thought of shooting had vanished. There was only one way to miss that half ton of high explosives and that was to push the control column forward. The motor, which was not fitted with an anti-gee carburettor, cut through being starved of fuel and at the same time my head hit the canopy top with a resounding bang. Another lesson learned the hard way, never fly with loose straps. It did not help to hear the plaintive voice of the controller complaining that I must have passed within a few feet of the bomb without seeing it. Somehow it did not appear to be my day!

Success when it came was something of an anticlimax. A short chase, then as the dot of the reflector sight settled on the target, a burst of cannon fire and ball of flame. The explosion seemed to blow everything outwards thus forming a tunnel through which the pursuing fighter could safely pass. Occasionally a bomb would react out of character, like the occasion when the burning fuel removed most of the paint from Jim McCaw's Tempest.

No sooner did we discover that we could deal successfully with the new menace without the Spy's gloomy predictions coming totally true, than boredom once more set in. There really is no fun in shooting at an enemy who cannot shoot back. True, we had our share of accidents, some caused by engine failure and others by bomb collisions and with them the resultant casualties. Once when I was on a night patrol with Dusty Miller (3 July) he came on the air to say that his motor had packed up. Looking down into the blackness below, with not even a light visible, there was no way that Dusty was going to survive a forced landing in those conditions, so my advice to my old mate was to bale out while there was still time. As there was no reply from Dusty it was obvious that he was in no need of my advice, so after making sure that Control was aware of the position it was a case of sweating out the remainder of the patrol, then landing and heading for the local pub. Surprise, surprise, who should be standing by the bar, a pint under his arm and his moustache quivering with excitement, but Dusty, surrounded by an admiring crowd as he told of his misadventure. It seemed as though he had landed in or near the pub. It had all the earmarks of a put up job, but that could not be; Dusty's navigation was not that perfect!

Dusty seemed to get into all sorts of flying scraps but the 'Miller luck' never deserted him. Once he was to make his way back across the Channel with a long flicker of flame trailing out behind which was caused by a punctured wing tank which had caught fire. On another occasion while returning from France, a sea bird somehow found its way into the cockpit or it might be more correct to say what was left of it did. Even worse, quite a large portion, including a quantity of it's feathers found their way into his oxygen mask! What a mess. With the quantity of feathers available, Dusty did not need an aeroplane, he could have become airborne without one. Just before the end of the war in Europe, Dusty was in trouble again and spent what was left of it hiding with a Dutch family. If Dusty was to be believed he spent most of the time hiding under the lady of the house's bed, and the only reason why he was *under* instead of *in* that bed was because she had a very large husband who took up all the available space and there just was no room for Dusty. I eventually helped him to get his DFC in the following manner.[1]

At the end of the war, 486 had spent a considerable time in the Army of Occupation and then in September 1945 we flew into Dunsfold where we left the Spitfire XVIs which we had flown back from Germany to disband. The major problem was to keep the pilots sober and out of trouble while their clearances were being attended to, then send them off to London. It was unbelievable the amount of paperwork involved in disbanding a squadron. Eventually it was all behind me, no aircraft, no pilots, and I was able to hand the ground crew, and their many problems, over to the Adj; it was like being released from bondage. Eventually the shackles were removed and I was able to make my way to London a free man without a worry in the world. Sitting in the New Zealand forces club, sipping a handle of beer I was at peace with my surroundings when who should I see making his way in my direction, but Jimmy Wilson.

Woe, as I had always known him, would be one of my oldest squadron friends. I had met him on my first night at Tangmere and we had been room mates until he had left me to take up residence in the Officer's Mess there. His arrival had made my day. I had not seen him since he left 486, tour expired and in the meantime he had been back to New Zealand, did not like what he saw, so prevailed on Scottie to organise his return to our side of the world. Woe had joined a Typhoon squadron for a second tour of duty and from reports that drifted around Fighter Command he had been shot down and badly knocked about. Now here he was about to join me and it was a chance of catching up on all that had passed since we had last seen each other.

Woe had a problem and it did not take me long to realise that somehow I was involved in it. As was his way Jimmy did not beat about the bush.

'I've just seen Old Dusty and he is upset about all the DFCs that have been dished out to the 486 pilots and he has been overlooked.'

---

[1] Flight Lieutenant W L Miller from Waimate, joined RNZAF in 1940

Well, it was something that I had not thought about. I had been a junior member of the squadron when Dusty had been shot down and as was the way with operational aircrew, out of sight, out of mind. Life had been lived at such a hectic pace that once a pilot disappeared he was wiped out of your mind as though he had never existed. It had to be like that if you were to survive. As Woe told it, Dusty was so upset that he was not even wearing his campaign ribbons and the final straw for Dusty was when he saw one of our latest recipients of the DFC walking around London wearing the ribbon on his tunic the wrong way round! While I readily agreed with Woe, Dusty had not been with us during my period of Commanding Officer, the war had been over for a considerable time and with no orderly room records, with the best will in the world there did not seem to be a thing that we could do about it.

That was the end of what should have been a great evening out. Woe was depressed and having known Dusty and his war effort since joining the New Zealand squadron, it was clear that there had been a miscarriage of natural justice. Instead of an enjoyable evening around the West End I was in bed early, sober and could not get Dusty off my mind. When eventually I dropped off I even dreamt about him. What topped it all was the next day, for there was Dusty with his tunic, apart from his flying badge, completely bare. Nothing ventured, nothing gained, so I made my way to New Zealand House and did my best to interest somebody in Dusty, but nobody seemed to care. The opinion seemed to be, it is your problem, if you think he has earned a decoration there is a room, a table and paper and pen, the ball is in your court, make out a recommendation and citation.

The first step had to be to obtain Dusty's log book without telling him the real reason as it would be criminal to build up his hopes and not produce the goods. The act was to dream up some story about NZ House wanting to do a story on several pilots and asking me to try and obtain their log books. As he was one of those selected, did he mind if I borrowed his book for twenty four hours? That part of the operation went far more smoothly than expected. Pilots are usually very reluctant to let their log books out of their sight. With the precious document in my possession, it was a case of obtaining the necessary information and getting it back into Dusty's hands before some misfortune could overtake it. It was while leafing through the book that I was to discover that he had earlier done a tour on Malta.[1] Every time

---

[1] With No. 126 Squadron 1942 flying Spitfires

that Dusty became airborne there were a gang of Messerschmitt 109s waiting to collect the Miller scalp and hang it on their belt. Dusty would have to be about the most shot at pilot who ever served on that Island base. They certainly wasted a lot of ammunition trying to shoot him down and that was quite a valuable war effort on it's own, without the damage he did to the enemy while he was out there. The next time I saw Dusty the campaign ribbons were back where they belonged plus the DFC ribbon. He had received an immediate award which said heaps for my literary achievement, and it was all my own work.

I am little ahead of events as they happened, so back to the flying bomb patrols. Two other incidents of note; Black Mac blew up a 'Diver' and the resultant explosion burnt the paint from his aircraft. Eagelson followed a Diver into cloud and on emerging into clear air could not see it. A glance in the mirror and there was his victim tootling along behind and so close that it could have been in line astern formation!

It had not taken long to set up the balloon barrage, once the flying bombs started to arrive; then the flak units seemed to appear almost overnight. With the guns so close to London a lot of bombs, although they had been partially immobilised by ground fire, were still able to reach a built up area so it was decided to move some of the guns down to the coast and to position the patrolling fighters to seaward. Again it was amazing how quickly the guns and their associated equipment and personnel were uprooted and transported out to the coast. It was at this time that the proximity fuses were brought on stream and watching from aloft it was fantastic. Any bomb that managed to allude the fighters rarely managed to make it past the guns. Had the enemy developed this fuse, there would have been no future in attacking ground targets.

As the attacks began to taper off and the gunners became used to the fuse our role reverted to patrols up and down the Channel. Occasionally a bomb would manage to make it past the guns and then it was our opportunity to pursue and attempt to destroy.

On 28 June, 1944 Joe Wright, while on a seaward patrol at night, had pursued a bomb inland and after destroying it was heading back to his offshore patrol line when some American gunners shot his air-craft down and Joe was killed. From the ground at night, it should have been a physical impossibility to mistake an aircraft for a flying bomb with that long sheet of flame trailing out astern but the American gunners managed to do it. Joe was a popular member of our team and it made us bitter to see him killed in this way.

We would have welcomed the opportunity of making a strafing

attack on the gunners responsible. It would have done them the world
of good to have been on the receiving end of war for a change. The
last message from Joe was that he was being fired on by our gunners
and that his Tempest had been hit and he was going to attempt a
forced landing. In the area he was over, a forced landing in daylight
would have been a dicey do, at night he had no show. At the time he
was over land and with enough height to have successfully baled out.
Why he did not was difficult to understand.

Kevin McCarthy was another Tempest Flying Bomb casualty and
although he survived the crash his flying days were over. When next
I saw Mac he was in McIndoe's special hospital at East Grinstead
having his face straightened out.

I had a reputation of being lucky but my time was running out.
When disaster struck—on 5 July—it was the result of the action of a
fellow pilot and of all people the individual was our Wing Commander
R P Beamont. Even if I had not recognised the letters on the aircraft
there was no mistaking the fellow in the cockpit. I had just scored
numerous hits on a Diver and was watching as it headed towards the
ground, when in front of me there appeared another Tempest and
the smoke drifting back from the wings indicated that the pilot was
shooting at my wounded bird. As the bomb increased it's angle of dive
I ranged up alongside and watched as the marksman continued to
fire, without any visible strikes. (I was later to discover that when he
returned to base he claimed a half share!)

Concerned with following the bomb down and watching it's final
destruction there were developments nearer to home that I was
unaware of. Bang. The engine ground to a stop and with it the propeller. At the speed at which a propeller turns it is invisible to a pilot
and it is something of a shock to see it hanging there useless on the
front end!

Flames were shooting out all over the aircraft and with the associated smoke it was almost like cloud flying. Much too low to attempt
to use my parachute, my only hope of survival was to try and find a
clear patch and attempt to do a wheels-up landing. The area of Sussex
that I was flying over, just inland from Hastings, was heavily wooded
and fields scarce and small. In the general panic the one I did pick was
just not big enough and by the time I reached its far end, my Tempest
was still airborne and travelling much too fast. There was no alternative but to pull up over a high hawthorn hedge and hope that on the
far side a suitable area for a crash landing would be available.

By this time fear and panic had departed and training took over. It
was simply a case of dealing with the rapidly changing situation as it

unfolded. I went over or through that hedge and on the far side, conditions could not have been worse. Directly in front of me was a large plantation of trees with no hope of going over or around them. My last memory was of trees crashing over as the Tempest started a forward somersault. Later, much later, I slowly drifted back to the world of the living to discover that I was completely paralysed and could move neither hand nor foot. By far the most distressing thing was the swarms of flies that had been attracted by the blood that covered my face on this warm July day.

I had heard of the dialect spoken by the Sussex country folk, now I was to learn why it was referred to as silly Sussex. The first to arrive was a local village boy but he might well have just arrived from outer space for all the sense his lingo made to me. I tried to tell him to get help and I wanted him to try and lift me up in order that I might breathe, but we were just not communicating. That boy just stood there and when he did attempt to speak it appeared to be in a foreign language.

Help came at last. I drifted off and when I did come to I was in a bed in the East Sussex hospital. It was idle then, and it is idle now, to speculate as to what took place; was I thrown through the hood or did the plane just break up and leave me behind as it charged into and through that plantation at over one hundred miles an hour? I just don't know. That seven-ton aircraft was so broken up and scattered over such an area that the Royal Air Force recovery team did not even bother to collect it. An inspection of what was left of the wreck revealed the cause of the engine failure. When the Wing Commander was assisting me to shoot down the bomb, one of his empty shells had lodged in the Tempest's radiator and it's contents had escaped through the hole.

As for me, in addition to the numerous bruises on the front half, there was a bruise on my back from which, later, a doctor was to remove fifty fluid ounces. My left rib cage had been flattened and the rib ends pushed out the front. In an accident of this nature, shock causes dehydration and to counter this, as much fluid as possible is given to the patient. For the first twenty four hours of my stay in that hospital a nurse was in continuous attendance. The first nurse was a young red-headed girl from Southern Ireland and if she felt any sympathy for her patient she certainly did not show it. Every ten minutes or so she would lift my head up and more or less force me to swallow a small amount of water but no sooner had my head regained the pillow than my stomach would repel and eject the fluid straight up into the air. Gravity would then take over and the liquid would shower down over the both of us. This performance went on for most of the night, and when I could gather enough strength I would curse my tormentor from the top of her red head to where I judged her big flat Irish feet to be. All that I asked was for her to get the hell out of there and let me die in peace.

I was glad when the night came to an end and also it could not have been a very pleasant experience for my modern day Florence Nightingale, but to give the young lady her due not by word or deed did she betray what she must have been thinking. Left alone at last I dropped off into an uneasy sleep and I can recall dreaming about my brother Alex who had been killed on air operations only a short time before.

My greatest fear was that I was paralysed and in my panic I imagined that I could move neither my feet nor legs. After a few days I just had to know, so after lights out, and alone, I dragged myself over the side of the bed and the relief was terrific when I found that not only could I stand but also was able to take a few shaky steps. From then on this procedure was to become part of my nightly routine, and soon I was able to move around the room without hanging onto things. Eventually my doctor considered it safe for me to sit in a chair for a short period daily and after two weeks on my back, two nurses were on hand to prevent me falling flat on my face when my feet hit the floor. What a laugh. After a couple of weeks of exercising every night I had almost reached the sprinting stage. Just restitution no doubt. But that hospital had the last laugh, for while there, I was to meet a nurse who later was to become my wife.

Joan was a nurse in the East Sussex hospital and her father was a West End business man. He and his partner had five shops which sold luxury goods, four shops in the Burlington Arcade and one in Jermyn Street. I believe that my old father-in-law was quite a pal of the Prince of Wales who used to buy a lot of gifts there for his lady friends. They traded under the name of Henry Derfields and all but one of the shops were knocked around during the bombing of London.

Our eventual wedding, when the war ended, was attended by the squadron and Joan's father wanted it featured in his favourite paper, which was the *Times*, but once in that paper there was no doubt the other National papers would have picked it up. I didn't need such publicity, so Bruce Lawless, who was my best man, and I worked a swifty and a reporter and photographer did not turn up as expected. Poor old Ted Bex, he was still moaning about it when I said goodbye before leaving for home.

CHAPTER XII

OUR LAST WEEKS IN ENGLAND

On my first night back at Newchurch with the squadron in August I went out to the local pub with the rest of the gang. After four weeks of inactivity the results were a disaster. After consuming less than half my usual nightly ration of beer I found myself out on the back lawn and so shaky that I had to sit before I fell down. At this time a flying bomb decided to get in on the act and as its distinctive noise signalled its approach the mob decided to troop out and watch its passing. It was a very dark night and rigid observance of the black out regulations ensured that I was invisible.

Apart from the few squadron members who were on night flying duties, most of our boys were gathered around me. It was a heaven sent opportunity for my mates to dispose of surplus fluid, from which they had removed most of the alcohol. To be piddled on by some of my mates was hardly the welcome home I had expected!

The following morning, as I was not rostered to fly till the afternoon, I was curled up in my camp bed, together with my hangover, when another flying bomb could be heard approaching and just when I poked my head out of the tent its motor cut out; its distance and angle of dive left me in no doubt that if it did not hit my tent at least it would land very close to it. We were just far enough from the coast that a lot of metal, thrown up by the gunners, was falling around the tent lines and to be hit by a lump of it, on its return to earth, would not have been a very pleasant experience. Just behind my tent a pilot had dug a shelter in the form of a shallow grave which he had partially covered with a sheet of scrap metal and he had his bed down there. With nowhere else to go and the bomb getting closer by the second I dived headlong into the trench landing on top of its occupier just as the Diver exploded only a short distance away. The arrival of a body plus a lot of dirt and other rubbish could hardly be described as one of the more pleasant ways of being awakened for this poor unfortunate.

After my crash, my next flights were on 20 August—two in one day. It was back to anti-Diver work again. I destroyed my last on the 23rd, and it exploded on the ground at precisely 8.41 pm. Patrols were still flown on the 24th, 25th and 26th, then three on the 27th, then once on each of the 28th, 29th and 31st. My Number Two on the 29th, Stafford, got a V1 that day.

One might have imagined I would be a bit nervous of flying against the V1s following my untimely exit from the scene back on 5 July. After any crash, and I had my share, there were moments of nervousness but as always, once the action started there just was not time to think about anything apart from the job in hand. Although all my friends and relations tell me that I am highly strung and living on my nerves, it never did apply to operational flying.

I can remember when I was a young lad of about 12, going into hospital for a minor operation and having an injection with a blunt needle. It was such a terrifying experience that I used to break into a cold sweat whenever I saw a nurse with a needle, even if it wasn't for me.

On entering the Services though, there was such a battery of injections that I had to beat my fears before they beat me. My answer was to put the approaching ordeal completely out of my mind until it was about to happen. I later applied this to flying and the only time that it did not work was while awaiting start-up. We often had to be in our aircraft three minutes before start-up and it was so quiet that just sitting there, tightly secured by the straps, your mind would begin to work. I can recall looking at the airmen, awaiting my signal to pull the chocks away, and thinking, they will still be alive in half an hour, will I be?

Another time which was hard to live with was when control reported large numbers of enemy aircraft heading in our direction. But once a sighting was made and smoke and tracer began to appear, everything changed—there was just not time to feel nervous. As bad luck would have it, I had no sooner got back into my stride when it all happened again, on the last day of August. I was to take a Tempest aloft on what was to be a refresher flight. Following a period of level flight, a few gentle aerobatics, then bang, it was a repetition of my previous flight; a motor which had ceased to function. Once again a vertical propeller blade stuck up there in front of me and smoke and flames all over the place. It was just too soon after the last flight and for the one and only time in my five years of flying I panicked and experienced a moment of sheer terror. I literally had to put my head down, close my eyes and force myself to come to terms with the situation. That few moments of indecision made the difference between being able to bale out or having to go down with the machine, but luckily there was reasonably clear ground ahead and the big motor knocked over any obstructions that were in our path till eventually it broke clear and left myself and the rest of the fuselage behind. Strange as it may seem I was able to step out of what had once been part of an aeroplane without a scratch. The poor old Tempest was, of course, a complete write-off.

Once we discovered that the actual danger of being blown up by an exploding flying bomb was only wishful thinking on the part of our Spy, we had returned to our old free and easy ways; the Spy was much older than any of us and very proud of his boys, as he referred to us. Some of our antics, however, must have just about broken his heart.

One evening, for instance, after we all had drunk more than we should have, Jack Stafford, who nobody in their right mind would ever be guilty of referring to as a religious type, started to tell me about his past life and how as a boy he had enjoyed attending church on a Sunday morning. He almost seemed to resent the fact that he was now having to associate with such ungodly people as his fellow pilots. To put it bluntly poor old Jack was almost crying drunk and had picked my shoulder to weep on.[1]

Awaiting a suitable opportunity, I approached one of our Padres, disclosing that one of his 'sinners' had confided in me that he wished to return to the fold. After briefing him on Jack's problem, I advised diplomacy as any undue haste could result in his victim escaping, as Jack was a very gentle soul and easily upset. Jack happened to be alone in his tent at that moment and the good man did not need much urging to strike while the iron was hot. To me it seemed unbelievable that anybody could be as gullible as that young padre. In the past he had listened to some of my stories with such wide-eyed innocence that I had almost begun to believe them myself.

After my efforts on Jack's behalf this was one show I had no intention of missing, but to see and hear all that was taking place in a tent was quite a problem. The Padre was holding his victim gently by his arm and while peering earnestly into Jack's eyes was saying something like, 'Is there anything you would like to talk to me about my son?' Jack was hanging back, the whites of his eyes showing! He

---

[1] Flight Lieutenant J H Stafford DFC, from New Lynn, joined RNZAF 1942

reminded me of a young horse put into a trailer for the first time; ears
forward and eyes staring.

Some movement or other on my part must have drawn Jack's
attention and in a flash all had been revealed. It was no place for me
as Jack could become violent if provoked. As I hastened away I heard
him say, 'So you have been listening to some more of Sheddan's
bullshit.' That Padre was quite a friend of mine and I used to spend
many an idle hour entertaining him but now I'd blown it. Whenever
he saw me approaching after that, he seemed to remember that he
had an urgent appointment in the opposite direction. If at any time I
had, like Jack, been in the need of spiritual comforting, I was certainly
not going to receive it from that quarter!

At Newchurch the Officers had a tent, complete with bar, while the
NCOs had to go off station when in search of an evening supping.
On one occasion that I can recall, our Commanding Officer, Johnny
Iremonger, was the Senior Officer on the field and invited his NCO
pilots to a party in the Officer's Mess.

Eagelson turned on a real western act but instead of arriving on a
horse and demanding service while still in the saddle he turned up on
a big motor bike. Eagle had problems controlling the machine when
surrounded by nothing more lethal than open country. So, in the
Officer's Mess, amongst the furniture and confronted by a bar, he had
no show. Iremonger must have had his problems explaining away the
wrecked bar and furniture but somehow he managed to do so as we
heard no more of the incident.

Next to the tent that Bruce Lawless and I occupied was that of Joe
Wright and Butch Steedman, both North Island farmer's sons.[1] How
Butch was so named was, and is, still something of a mystery but in
some way, Joe Wright was responsible. On one occasion, when entering their tent, I found Joe was sound asleep on his camp bed with a
baby fire blazing away merrily on his chest, while on the adjacent
camp bed his tent mate was calmly observing developments and
making no attempt to alert Joe as to the dangerous situation that was
developing. My first reaction was to awaken Joe, and extinguish the
blaze, by the simple process of throwing a bucket of water over him;
then the abuse started. Joe was abusing Butch for letting the situation
develop and me because of the mess he and his bed were now in.
Butch was upset because Joe's favourite act was to go to sleep

---

[1] Flying Officer J Steedman, from Whangarei, joined RNZAF 1942

while smoking and Butch on these occasions had waited hopefully for the lighted fag to start just such a blaze. Many times it had almost happened but at the critical stage Joe always awoke. Now when Butch's hopes had been realised and he was keenly waiting for Joe's reaction, I had to arrive and spoil the act.

On another occasion, when I arrived, both Joe and his mate were out so I stretched out on Butch's bed while awaiting their return. As I lay there, the outline or shadow of a bird was plainly visible directly above. When fully clothed and ready for duty we usually had a thirty eight revolver, fully primed, slung around our waist. In hindsight, why we were issued with them was a mystery as without practice any attempt to use one was most likely to end up in our becoming the victim. Anyhow, the bird presented an irresistible target. That bird, if he had suicide in mind, had picked on a poor assistant in me, but whatever his intentions were it flew off after each attempt on it's life, then immediately returned to it's former position.

'Up to some more of your tricks, Sheddan?' said Butch, for he had heard the racket and come to investigate and was now standing in the tent opening and did not look pleased.

'Butch', I said, 'you have no idea how hard it is to hit a target when it is on the outside of a tent and you have to judge its position by its shadow.'

'That might well be,' retorted Butch, 'but I have a fair idea just how difficult it is going to be to keep my head out of the wet, the next time it rains!'

I must admit I saw his point of view.

Towards the end of the bomb patrols, Group decided that pilots would be on duty for twenty four hours, then be off duty for the next twenty four. The result of this was that we had time to visit London on our days off—but often arrived back in no condition to face a further spell of duty, some of which would involve night patrols.

One day I reported at midday and was immediately sent off on a patrol which involved flying up and down on the seaward side of the English coast. It was one of those days, so typical of the South of England, when the sun beat down out of a cloudless sky. No bombs were coming across and it was hot sitting there under the plastic hood. It was a case of fly in one direction for about ten minutes, turn one hundred and eighty degrees and fly back over the same course. I was quickly tired, then bored and the clock seemed to have come to a dead stop. The obvious happened. I dropped off to sleep to awaken with a start to find myself nearer to France than England and the Tempest in a gentle dive! During my little snooze, which had started at five thousand feet, my Tempest had now descended to just a few hundred feet above the sea. A near thing which does not bear thinking about.

We were all relieved when the squadron was ordered to fly North to Matlaske from where we were to cross to Belgium and join the invasion forces.

While at Matlaske, awaiting orders to cross to Brussels, I had another of those close calls which seemed to be occurring with monotonous regularity. Four of us were detailed to fly across the North Sea and shoot up an electric train which, if information received in London could be relied upon, made a trip at the same time each day between Rotterdam and a station further north. We were in position at the appointed time but our train did not appear and as it was a lovely day with no cloud above, or movement below, we went down almost to ground level for a closer look.

Much as we were enjoying ourselves, flying around the countryside and being waved to by the local population, all too soon it was time to start the long journey home. As we closed up into formation and started to increase speed it sounded as if a whistle was being blown in the cockpit and the faster we went the louder this shrill noise became. My first thought was that the radio telephone was playing up but switching this off did not help; if anything the noise seemed to increase. As usual, when something like this occurred, when we returned we described the symptoms to our ground crew and left it to them to sort the problem out.

In this case it did not take long to discover the cause. As we had been flying around Holland at low level, Germans had been firing at us with service rifles and so on, and one of their bullets had passed through my cockpit and lodged in the wing which had been uppermost during a turn. When lining up its line of flight, from where it had entered and left, it was difficult to believe that it could have passed through without collecting me on the way! Closer inspection disclosed two holes in the front of my battledress tunic at a level with my chest and I hadn't been aware of a thing. I was getting to the stage when I was beginning to ask myself just how much longer I could expect my luck to hold out.

We usually spent the evening at the Mess bar or went out to one of the local pubs and if not flying the following morning invariably had a hangover. Depending on the degree of pain, we either suffered it out or went to our own doctor who would mix up some sort of potent concoction. Sometimes it helped, more often it only made the condition worse.

One particular day in September, while the old Witch Doctor was brewing up his hangover medicine, I was trying my eyesight out on the wall eye chart. The right one was not too bad considering the punishment it had received the previous night, then it was the left one's turn. Believe it or not the moment the right eye was closed I could not see the letter or anything else for that matter; that eye was just a passenger. To find that you are blind in one eye, especially when your life depends on having perfect sight in both, would be the perfect cure for a hangover. When the doctor turned around his patient had left.

I'd been formation flying both during the day and at night, in preparation for D-Day, shooting up trains and road transport, shooting down flying bombs and had recently spent a month in hospitals yet at no time had there been an indication that my sight was less than perfect. To give up operational flying was unthinkable so my first act was to take a Tempest up and see if I could cope. This was no problem because our 'Chiefy' always seemed to have a machine which had just come out of maintenance and which he wanted air tested. All went well until attempting to land, when my problem was in levelling off too high, then forestalling the approaching stall with a burst of motor and going around again and making another attempt. It took three attempts before I was safely back on the ground and in no way could it be described as a landing. It would have been much more accurate to have termed it an arrival. Altogether it was a disgraceful exhibition of flying by a pilot of my experience and worse still, the entire field had realised that something was wrong and were watching the performance. I was in trouble.

My problem was to be compounded by the rule that all pilots must wear goggles at all times while flying and the hood must be open whenever possible while taking off or landing. The reason was that should a shell fragment or any other foreign body start flying around the cockpit, your eyes at least had some protection against dust or splinters. Also, in the case of fire, they would protect your eyes while escaping or being dragged out. The same applied with the hood. With a trapped pilot trying to fight his way through a jammed hood or a rescuer facing the same situation, vital seconds could be lost which would mean the difference between getting clear or being burnt to death.

Most, if not all, pilots, land an aircraft, like a Spitfire or Tempest, by looking along the left side of their big motors because it is impossible to see through the motor and over the cowling. Also, because this is the side on which the throttle is situated. The procedure was that when a pilot messed up a landing or whatever, he would push the throttle open and go around for another attempt, which gave him time to sort his problems out. This, by the way, was the reason why a lot of Royal Air Force pilots came to grief when attempting to fly German aircraft. It was second nature to push the throttle forward when more power was required. German aircraft had reversed throttles and if not thinking too clearly, the unfortunate pilot closed the motor down when he needed to increase power.

Now, back to my problem. Being neither used to using goggles or putting my head out into the slipstream, and now with the left eye out of action, it was now a case of trying to look sideways and judge height and direction. Worse was to follow. I had not noticed any problems the previous day, nor during the previous three months, so it seemed that the eye had packed up overnight and if that could happen to one eye there was no reason why the other should not follow suit. The thought of being taken off operational flying was bad enough but the realisation that total blindness could be just around the corner was devastating.. There was no other course than confessing my problem to our CO, who arranged for me to see an eye specialist, and thankfully the problem was a lot minor than I had feared. A cyst had developed under the eyelid and was pressing on a nerve. After diagnosing the cause, it was then a simple matter to remove it, in hospital, under local anaesthetic. The amazing thing was that the eye specialist was of the opinion that the cyst had taken at least six months to develop to its present size and that I must have been blind in that eye for three months or more. I had obviously been flying on my instincts alone throughout this time.

It was at Matlaske that another incident occurred which could have involved me in a spot of trouble. Flying late in the day, when I landed there was only time to fire up the old Austin and head out for the local pub in order to arrive before last orders were called. Two sergeants came along with me, one being Jimmy Brash who was one of our Squadron armourers. When we arrived at the local, the public bar was crowded with soldiers so we moved into the private one. Dressed in battle dress with sweat marks on my face, it would seem I was not the type to associate with the flashily suited gentlemen and their even flashier ladies. The war was over, as far as those people were concerned and now we were only an embarrassment. The private bar was not a large room, the windows were still decked out with their blackout shutters, which would have required a massive undertaking to remove, and apart from a small sliding panel connecting the bar, the only other entrance was by opening a massive oak door.

When I fronted up to the slide and politely asked for three glasses of beer, the frosty-faced landlady informed me that if I required service, the public bar was the place for me. What angered me even more, as we made our way out of that room, was the smart look on a lot of faces. Obviously, by the look of them, they had remained in civvy street and made money while we had done their fighting for them. As I closed the door behind me I noticed that the key was still in the lock. It was at least nine inches long and massive so it was a simple matter to turn the key and drop it into the front of my battle dress before moving into the public bar. We stood surveying the situation but it was obvious that we had no show of getting near the bar let alone obtaining service. But noticeable to me, at any rate, was that a fair amount of panic was beginning to develop in the 'Toffs' bar. Worried faces were beginning to cluster around the slide and the hatchet-faced landlady was obviously getting in on the act. The final straw was when the old girl dragged a stool out and used it as a stepping stone to make her way up onto the bar, from where she announced that not another drink would be served in the hotel until the key was replaced and the door unlocked. A drunken soldier threw a jug which missed the landlady's head by a matter of inches, whence she decided that a place under the bar was far safer than on top of it. Fists and jugs began to fly; it was quite an enjoyable performance providing that you were not on the receiving end. It was no place for we 'gentlemen' of the air force so we took off and left them to it!

Time was running out for me, I'd had a long tour, several bad accidents, a spell in hospital then to cap it all the loss of sight which could have finished me off. However, instead of a posting to a training unit where there was no escape from being an instructor and where I would have to fill in the required six months 'rest', it was decided to send me to a rehabilitation centre where the score was gentle exercise and early to bed. As can be imagined I was not exactly thrilled to death with that sort of treatment.

After about a fortnight I suggested to the Officer in charge that it was time that I reported back to my squadron and as he did not raise any objections I was off before my records turned up. Since leaving Operational Training Unit, nearly two and a half years before, I had never been out of 11 Group, Fighter Command, so I knew all the dodges. It was a simple matter to turn up at Northolt and climb aboard a Dakota which was flying out supplies and personnel to the squadrons based in Holland. 486 Squadron had moved to the Continent on 30 September, as part of 2nd TAF. Now it was November 1944 and the

Squadron was at Volkel. The Adjutant of 486 nearly threw a fit when I walked in. It would appear that the intention had been for me to spend a six-month rest period then be posted to a pool of fighter pilots and from there be sent out to a squadron which had requested a replacement pilot. Johnny Iremonger was pleased to see me, though, and with him on my side there was not a thing that the Adj could do. Looking back, my rest period would have to be considered as one of the shortest on record.

CHAPTER XIII

2ND TACTICAL AIR FORCE

I NOW found myself involved in a rapidly changing war. For one thing, based on the Continent of Europe, there was no longer any need to sit on that hard rubber boat and survival gear in the cockpit, which had been so necessary for survival when having to cross a stretch of water with the possibility of finishing up in it. Even in the event of having to make a landing or parachute descent in enemy-held territory, it greatly helped to avoid capture to have the survival kit available.

Of all the Allied fighters in action during the last twelve months of the war the Hawker Tempest, powered by a Napier Sabre sleeve valve engine, was in a class of its own. In the hands of an experienced pilot it was more than a match for any aircraft flying on either side of the lines. That is, up to fifteen thousand feet when it's performance began to fall off. In addition to being a superb air-to-air combat machine it was the perfect gun platform when used for ground strafing. A Merlin, by comparison, was a slow revving motor, cruising revs being in the vicinity of eighteen hundred per minute while maximum revs were in the twenty eight hundred range. Thus there was a flat spot between when the pilot asked for maximum effort from his Spitfire and when he received it. This time lag could be crucial when bounced by the enemy. The Napier Sabre, by comparison, cruised at thirty five hundred and had a maximum of thirty seven fifty. There was so little difference between cruising and flat out that it could be claimed that a Tempest was almost operating at its maximum performance at all times. This had an advantage in that it was difficult for enemy fighters to position themselves to bounce it but a disadvantage was that should a pilot get left behind, say in a turn, it was very difficult to make up the lost ground. Just like the old Typhoon really.

For ground attack, trains being our number one target, the procedure was to cruise at about eight thousand feet. At that height it was possible to see without being seen, dive almost vertically when a speed of about six hundred miles an hour would be reached, then after the attack, zoom back to our original patrol height. The main advantages of a Tempest for this form of attack was its ability to pick up speed when diving, its steadiness and ease of handling at high speeds and its initial zoom climb. Pull the nose straight up and it fairly rocketed to the five thousand foot mark, the height where the ground tracer fire was beginning to curl over. Above this height and the light flak could not touch it.

When I mention light flak, I am referring to the point five to forty millimetre range. Towards the end of the war trains often had flak carriages spaced through their entire length, and it does nothing for your nerves when your aircraft seems to be surrounded by tracer and you know that for every one you can see there is at least four that are invisible! The Germans also used heavily armed trains as flak traps. One of my worst moments was when 'Smokey' Schrader drew my attention to a train which I was trying hard not to see, as I knew in my heart that it was a plant—too much smoke, too little movement. It was all very well for him sitting up there and reporting and I was not the least bit impressed by his offer to cover me and see that no German fighters interfered! I was between the Devil and the deep blue sea. I had been at this game for longer than I cared to remember and knew that this was one train that I should keep away from but with Smokey, who commanded 486 shortly before I did and who'd been a flight commander on the squadron, watching and waiting for my decision, I just had to take the risk and attack.[1]

No sooner had I committed myself, than all hell broke loose as the flak came showering up in waves. Crunch! About a foot of the end of my port wing folded over. Now I was in real trouble! Any sudden change of direction and that wing would stall, causing a spin. Down below was what looked like a train full of guns and all firing at a single aircraft. It seemed that my luck was finally running out, and that this was the end of the road. As usual I had organised the dive to undershoot so I had to pull out slowly, so as not to over-tax that damaged wing, then line up the flak wagons. It still looked as if my run was

---

[1] Later Wing Commander W E Schrader DFC and bar, from Wellington. Joined BNZAF in 1941 and saw action in the Middle East and Europe

about to come to an end, but thought if I survived there would be a few German gunners on the receiving end.

There was no way that my plane should have passed through the wall of lead without receiving further damage. However I survived—just! Back at base, it was necessary to land at a much higher speed that normal to avoid stalling that damaged wing while on the approach. It was while attacking a similar train in this area that Gus Hooper was shot down and spent what was left of the war as a prisoner.[1]

While stationed in the South of England we had become very much part of the local scene and mixed freely with the civilian population when off station. In Holland not only was there a language problem but also a fear that the Germans might return and the Dutch had no intention of becoming overly involved in any activity that might antagonise the dreaded Boche should they once again sweep across their land.

Evenings were spent mostly in the Mess bar, the Officers being billetted in a Monastery, the top floor of which was still occupied by the Friars. After one of our wild parties, the good Friars departed somewhat hastily and did not return; well, at least while we were still ensconced there.

The cause of their departure was Colin McDonald, a tall, fair lad, who was one of the pilots who always seemed to be around when you needed him and the only way that I can describe him was that he was just Colin. If you wanted his opinion or advice all you had to do was to ask for it. When it arrived you could be sure that he had thought about what he was saying and even if you did not agree, well it was well worth listening to and thinking about. Later, when CO of 486, I leaned heavily on Colin and he never let me down. Colin, when he cast aside his normal serious air and let his hair down, was a completely different person and knowing them 'both' it would be hard for me to state a preference. If a gang of us were at a Lord Mayor's party and decided to debag our Host, Colin would be the one to put in charge of the operation. Always the perfect gentleman he would have it done in such a way that not even the victim could take offence.

On one particular night at Volkel we had all drunk more than we should have and Colin, though still in high spirits and the life of the party, discovered that his legs would no longer function or it might be more correct to say that they had developed a will of their own and

---

[1] Flying Officer G J Hooper DFC, RNZAF POW 2 Feb 1945

would no longer respond to their owner's commands. Never let it be said that 486 ever deserted a comrade in his hour of need. We dragged the body up a flight of stairs to an ex-Monks cubicle and emptied it onto the little wooden bunk. Flat on his back and still in high spirits, Colin dragged his six gun out of it's holster and demanded a target. The only one readily available was Colin's officer dress hat and held in the right position, he fired the bullets through it in the direction where the window glass would have been if it had not been hastily opened. So it was one shot for the hat and then one for the Monks roosting above. Next morning the only visible signs of the previous night's binge was three holes in the crown of Colin's hat and three holes in the ceiling directly above his bunk. Later that day I felt a twinge of remorse as I watched a procession of Monks file down the back stairs and head out over the frozen courtyard with it's coating of snow, their few worldly possessions dangling from their shoulders. I was reminded of a couple of lines from a ballad by Gordon, a poet who roamed the Australian outback at the turn of the century, when referring to himself and his dog:—

'Across the trackless wastes
We go no matter when or where
Few our future home shall know
and fewer still will care'

Various daytime activities were thought up by the pilots to while away the idle hours when they were not involved in flying or when conditions were such that the squadron was grounded. Two of the most hair raising were Pip Powell exclusives.[1] Both required a steady nerve and a complete disregard for one's personal safety.

Pip had found, or built, a sledge which he attached to the squadron jeep by means of a five-metre tow line. His next problem was to find a pilot who was nearly as crazy as he was and who was prepared to drive the jeep down the frozen run until it reached the cross-runway, by which time the jeep had achieved its maximum velocity of about sixty kilometres an hour. While this was taking place Pip would be stretched out on the sledge when the jeep arrived at the cross-runway, its driver would wind on maximum lock and at the same time apply full break. This had the effect of causing the jeep to spin around like a top with the sledge airborne on the outside of the circle. If Pip had lost his hold he would have been half way to Berlin before returning to the ground!

---

[1] Flight Lieutenant N J Powell, from Dargaville, joined RNZAF in 1941

Pip's second performance, which also involved the squadron jeep, was even more spectacular but it was rather significant that for the driver, it was a single performance and he was always a new boy who had recently joined the squadron.

Before the squadron had moved to Volkel, the airfield had been bombed by the RAF and was heavily pockmarked with bomb craters which were at least three to four metres across, and most of them over a metre in depth. The only section of the field that did not have bomb craters was the runways because they had been filled in. A blanket of snow now covered the holes and to the unsuspecting there was no indication as to what lay beneath. The field was a favoured habitat for hares and while the driver and his jeep chased after these, Pip would stand on the seat alongside with his gun at the ready while hoping to get close enough to get in a telling shot. To the audience, who were always on hand to watch the performance, it was obvious what was about to happen. As sure as night follows day that jeep would disappear into a crater, head first. There would be a period of inactivity before a very disillusioned driver would clamber out and head for home. Sometimes he would make it but more often he would flounder into another crater and without the jeep to help, we would have to lay on a recovery operation. Pip would get the aircraft recovery boys to haul the jeep out and shooting would be suspended until the next sucker arrived.

Pip had another little trick which he practised at night in the bar and which was all part of making a new boy feel at home. On his first night in the Mess bar, a new boy would be no doubt watching and trying to take it all in, when Pip would get a mouth full of paraffin and after waiting a few moments for it to warm up he would sneak up behind the new arrival and holding a lighted match just behind his ear, blow the paraffin over the top of it. There would be a loud 'whoosh' and a ball of liquid fire would shoot past. If the new boy's nerves could stand that sort of treatment there was no chance of the war frightening him to death. How Pip survived the war was a mystery to most of us but he did, only to return to his home land and be killed in a boating accident.

Lord Trenchard called on us at Volkel and while he was in the process of telling us that when he first joined the air force all the pilots knew each other by their christian names, the air raid siren sounded. He assured us that we had nothing to worry about as no airfield had ever been bombed while he was present. No sooner had he made that claim than a 262 loomed up overhead and dropped a bomb in the middle of the field. The next time I was to see the Old Gentleman was at Kastrup. The Wing was gathered around him as we listened to one of his many stories and a new Sergeant Pilot was peering over his Lordship's shoulder. I expect he had never seen so many ribbons at one look. Suddenly Trenchard stopped what it was he was trying to tell us, turned around about one hundred degrees and asked, 'What do you think about it, Sergeant?' That poor Sergeant, his mouth fell open and he was incapable of thinking anything.

Jerry, with these kind of unpredictable tricks, disposed of any feeling of boredom that I may have had. Let me explain. The Tempest Wing at Volkel was mostly engaged in ground strafing. Our task was to roam over Northern Germany and shoot up any road transport or trains that were foolhardy enough to attempt to move during daylight. But suddenly, from time to time, large gaggles of Fw190s and Me109s would appear on the Western Front and then just as suddenly disappear. Had we flown together, all five squadrons in the Wing[1] at the same time, we would have been able to cope with the enemy fighters when they did appear. The Germans had their Y-Service too which monitored our air-to-air and air-to-ground conversation, also radar by which they could work out approximate numbers, speed and direction of any aircraft we had in the air no matter at what height they were flying. Having worked out the speed, their Controller could be reasonably sure that it was a wing of hostile fighters that had appeared on his screen and more than likely be able to say they must be Tempests as no other fighters had such a high cruising speed. (Nobody was sure where the Germans obtained their information but, wherever, it was up to date and quite a gimmick when interrogating a captured RAF pilot.

If the victim was being difficult, the interrogating officer would say there is little that you can tell us which we do not know already. Just turn around and look at the wall. There he would see a complete layout of the Wing, the various squadrons attached, the names of the flying personnel involved and his own squadron, possibly with the names of all its pilots listed—even his own.)

With all this information available the German Control could work out how long the Tempest Wing could remain on patrol, the time that it would take to return to base and re-arm and refuel, then return to its patrol area. Once the area was clear the German transport knew exactly how much time they had to be about their normal duties before

---

[1] 122 Wing consisted of 3, 56, 80, 274 and 486 Squadrons

having to park up again. For our side it was just as effective to stop the flow of transport as to destroy it because the number of trains or road transport that could be destroyed was limited and while our fighters were in the area the whole transport system was under threat.

Our Control, in their wisdom, or lack of it, decided that in order to maintain a continuous patrol over the area, they would fly single squadrons of Tempests which meant that apart from the squadron that was patrolling, there would be one possibly on its way back to base, a relief squadron ready to take off, another refuelling and rearming and the fifth on standby ready to be called on if needed. This was all very well in theory but, because of our losses through ground fire, we were short of pilots and reduced to flying with a squadron of eight aircraft instead of twelve. Although eight was a more manageable number, when set upon by a hundred or more German fighters and usually when you were at least a hundred miles into enemy territory, it was not so much a case of trying to destroy the enemy, but to try to keep yourself and your aircraft in one piece until you made your escape.

Had we known that the fighters were there and waiting we could have come to terms with the situation but it was the uncertainty of not knowing, the ever present thought that it could be our turn this time, that was so wearing on the nerves. Then it would be on.

'Kenway to Music Leader, are you receiving me, over?'

'Music Leader to Kenway, loud and clear, over.'

'Kenway to Music Leader, caution advised. We have a plot of seventy plus at six o'clock above, range twenty miles, over.'

'Music Leader, thank you. Kenway listening out.'

Then again, 'Kenway to Music Leader, fifty plus at three o'clock. We do not have a height at present.'

'Music Leader to Kenway, message understood, out.'

As we listened to all this unusual activity, it could mean only one thing. Hitler's hatchet men were gathering for the kill. Yet as we flew through the boundless sky at over four hundred miles an hour our Tempests seemed to hang almost motionless as though suspended in space. All seemed so serene and peaceful that it was hard to believe that somewhere out there, hostile eyes were watching and for some of us death could be only moments away.

Next thing would be the calm voice of one of the Music pilots reporting the first sighting and Music Leader calling the break as the German fighters attacked. Outnumbered twenty to one, the sky would be full of turning, twisting aircraft as friend and foe intermingled. It was on such a mix up that Bev Hall was lost. On the last sighting of Bev he was behind an Me109, smoke drifting back as his cannon were firing and bits falling off the enemy fighter.

An occasion which will live long in my memory was on 23 January 1945 when eight of us were over Rhine airfield, at about ten thousand feet, and a large number of aircraft were reported in the circuit below, some landing, some preparing to do so, and the rest flying around awaiting their turn. It looked like the perfect bounce; for once the wily Hun had been caught with his pants down. A shout from Spike Umbers, 'Break port Music, their high cover is almost on top of us!' The biter bit.

Great ugly brutes sliding past in all directions and smoke drifting back from their wings which indicated that their cannons were firing. I appeared to be surrounded by aircraft and each one seemed to have a cross on it. There just did not appear to be a friendly face around. After a lot of twisting and turning I managed to fasten onto the tail of a 109 whose pilot pulled directly up into the sun. The bright light prevented me from seeing if any damage was being done but it helped me just to fire the guns.

As was the way of air battles one moment there are aircraft all over the place, the next you are alone. On this occasion there were seven aircraft heading in the direction of where our base should have been and they had to be Tempests. At my forlorn cry of, 'Wait for me, Spike!' the aircraft started to orbit. Never have I felt so miserable and alone than during the few minutes it took me to catch up. When our combat films were shown on the screen, the aiming point showed up and it was possible to tell whether the target had been hit. In my film the 109 showed quite plainly, in spite of shooting into the sun, and it appeared that my shooting had been right on target.

I ignored Staff's suggestion that I claim a possible. If that Jerry had survived the wall of lead which appeared to be headed in his direction the best of British luck to him. I was more than pleased to have come through the encounter without getting my hide creased.

This was not the only time on which I had failed to make a claim although on that occasion I saw my cannon shells tearing the enemy aircraft apart and watched it dive into the ground where it burst into flames, the pilot still in the cockpit. One other was in March 1945. 'Whackie' Kalka and I were shooting up German transport just behind their front line when two light German aircraft appeared and on seeing us flew low over the trenches, no doubt in the hope that the light flak would scare us off. Only an idiot would have attacked under those conditions but the thought of personal danger never crossed our minds. All that seemed to matter was that there was aircraft to shoot at. Two of the RAF's top fighters each capable of over four hundred miles an hour and both armed with four twenty millimetre cannon against two slow, unarmed aircraft. It should have been a one horse race but it did not turn out quite like that.

They kept low where ground features offered the maximum protection and when we did get into a position to attack, they would pull incredibly tight turns, that it was impossible to hold them in the sights long enough to get in a telling shot. Eventually we lost sight of one of them, who must have landed in a convenient field or taken advantage of a ground feature to make off unobserved.

The obvious solution to our problem was for Whackie to keep our remaining victim turning while I did a wide turn and so position my aircraft so that he would have to fly through my cone of lead. It was a high-winged monoplane, and when my shells hit the top of its wing, a combination of lead and slipstream caused the fabric covering of the wings to roll back and for a fraction of time it looked as though its pilot was sitting in the centre of a bunch of sticks. Then Whackie called up to say that his aircraft had been hit by ground fire and that he was going to try and make it back to our side of the lines and bale out. Whackie had baled out a few days previously and had so enjoyed the experience that he had expressed the intention of baling out again if the opportunity should present itself.

Together we climbed up about three thousand feet and my mate's aircraft appeared to be flying and handling normally but Whackie was in charge and in no way was I going to try and advise him to attempt a landing. To see one of our pilots use a parachute was a new experience for me so I flew alongside in order not to miss any part of the performance. Whackie appeared to carry out the correct procedure. Firstly, he jettisoned the hood and when it had detached itself and disappeared astern there was the pilot sitting there in an open cockpit. It was a step backward into my Tiger flying days. From where I was watching, Whackie appeared to be enjoying himself, with that roguish grin of his and a wave of his gloved hand he went over the side much in the manner of a swimmer leaving the high board. Unfortunately I was on his starboard side and as he went out the port, I became unsighted until he reappeared astern. He tumbled, then the parachute blossomed and he began to swing gently from side to side.

For me it was a case of throttling back to a speed just above the point of stall and ranging up alongside for a closer look but now there was no grin or hand waving. He just seemed to hang there and to be completely unaware of my presence. From the height and position that Whackie left his aircraft the River Maas looked like a silver string stretching across the horizon but as the wind carried the parachute and its passenger rapidly eastward, it became obvious that Whackie was going to land in the river or beyond it, yet he made no attempt to change the direction by pulling on the shrouds and spilling air out of one side of the 'chute. The final descent was exactly in the middle of the Maas but I was not unduly worried. When in London on leave, most of us spent the time trying to see who could collect the biggest hangover while Whackie, a teetotaller, spent his time looking at places with a historical interest or swimming, his passion.

There was little that I could do other than report his approximate position and then head back to base. It would not be difficult to imagine my feelings when shortly afterwards news arrived that a Dutch girl, who had been on hand to witness the descent, had swum out and retrieved the parachute but there had been no sign of the pilot. One moment Whackie was his bright and breezy self, the next he did not seem to be aware of what was going on. He must have been swept backwards by the slipstream and collided with the tailplane. It had been my intention that we each claim a half share of that aircraft, now with Whackie gone there was no way that I was going to claim any part of our victim. We had lost an operational pilot and a valuable aircraft and what did we have to show for it? One small aircraft which would have had no influence on the war one way or the other.[1]

Towards the end of 1944, there seemed to be a lack of German fighter aircraft about. We knew the Luftwaffe were taking a beating, but there was a definite lull just before and just after Christmas. In hindsight, we now know the Germans were planning a mass fighter attack on the American bomber formations but this in turn, became the force which, on New Year's morning, was used to strike at the British and American airfields in Belgium and Holland.

The Ardennes offensive had started, and we were stuck on the ground in the initial stages because of the severe weather. The weather improved on 1 January, and the Luftwaffe took this opportunity to strike soon after first light. Luckily for us at Volkel, with the break in the weather, we had been ordered off shortly after 9 am to fly an Armed Recce sortie to Hannover, led by Spike Umbers. 56 Squadron,

---

[1] Flying Officer W A Kalka, from Auckland. Killed in action 25 March 1945
  The Dutch girl was Miss Rit Hannsen and whilst she was in the water, someone stole her bicycle. Later when RNZAF HQ heard of her gallant attempt, and her loss, the New Zealand War Services Association presented her with a new 'cycle. An article and photograph appeared in the NZ Forces paper *Southern Cross*, but unfortunately nobody thought to inform 486 Squadron of the ceremony and it was not represented.

which was with us at Volkel, took off just ahead of us to go to Pader-born, so we missed the attack on the airfield.

Whilst on patrol, our Kenway control called Spike, telling him that enemy aircraft were attacking the field and that there were eight Fw190s in the Deurne area, on the deck, heading for Volkel. Spike gave the drop-tank signal, but I knew nothing of the panic. We were keeping strict radio silence, of course, and when Spike turned the squadron around and headed back to base, I had no idea that my radio was out of action, so I was totally unaware of all the information that the boys were getting.

I had never seen German aircraft over our side of the lines so when I arrived back at Volkel and saw Me109s and Fw190s flying around as though they owned the place, I had to make up my mind as to whether I was dreaming or not. I fastened onto the tail of a 190 which was flying just north of the airfield, in company with another 190 and a 109, opened fire and saw strikes along its wing. The pilot then com-menced a steep turn but hit the ground and exploded into small pieces. The rest of the boys got into action and in total we shot down four Focke Wulfs and a Messerschmitt, with another 190 and two 109s damaged.

One month and one day after this spectacular day, I was flying Green 4 with Bremner and Jack Stafford, south of Paderborn shortly after midday. Suddenly, Bremner reported a twin-engined aircraft approaching an airfield directly in front and obviously about to land. He attacked, followed by myself. Jack, as leader, then turned and followed us in. I had seen my fire score strikes on the Dornier 217—which we had now identified as such—and when Jack attacked, the bomber was just touching down and starting to burn. There was suddenly a lot of flak about, but as we weaved away and looked back, we could see the Dornier well alight and then it exploded.

On 6 April 1945, I was flying an evening patrol to Stolzenau with Tubby Ross as my wingman. Flying near Dummer Lake, our forward contact car, call-sign 'Scallywag', called to say that some Ju87s were dive-bombing the bridge over the River Weser. We then saw some AA fire and whilst orbiting saw one Ju87 attempting to drop his bombs. It then started a vertical climb towards cloud. I followed closely, fired, and saw strikes as it disappeared into the cloud. I went in after it, but then Tubby saw two parachutes emerge from below the cloud. Meantime, my Tempest stalled and I spun down out of it. On regaining control and straightening out, I saw another Stuka about a mile away. So great was my overtaking speed that I had only time to fire a few shots before breaking off the attack. After about three or four of these seemingly abortive attempts, the crew baled out and the aircraft hit the ground and blew up.

In mid-April the Squadron was quite busy with lots of air and ground targets. We were out every day, shooting and strafing anything and everything that moved. On the 12th, for instance, my log-book shows me that I damaged one Fw190 on the ground, claimed seven MT as flamers with eight more damaged. The next day I led an Armed Recce in the early evening and south east of Parchim spotted a small grass airfield. We could see aircraft on it, parked beside trees on the south east and south west sides.

They were a mixed bunch of Ju88s and He111s, and with Warrant Officer Maddaford on my wing, we headed down for a group of three Junkers parked in line astern on the south-west corner. We shot them up from tail to fuselage, raking all three, while Kendall and McDonald blasted five Heinkels and another 88.

That there were plenty of targets is proved by the fact that the very next afternoon, flying on the deck near Ludwigslust on a weather recce, we found a train and went for it. Pulling up from that I spotted a silver-coloured aircraft, flying very low, heading north. We had now climbed to 2000 feet and gave chase by diving towards it. At 700 yards I could see it was a 190, so closing to 100 yards let him have it from dead line astern. Pieces came away from its wings and fuselage and as I broke away to the right, I watched as the 190 dropped a wing, rolled over onto its back and hit the ground where it exploded.

As I have mentioned before, the thing that was feared most by all pilots when ground strafing, was the so-called flak trap. This consisted of about an acre of flak guns draped around an attractive target which made it appear that it was trying to hide what was still visible, to attract the attention of patrolling Allied aircraft. The form, when attacking ground targets, was to see before being seen and then all together; to attack individually was fatal as far as the last attacking aircraft were concerned. First in would wake up the flak gunners and the last to attack would be on the receiving end. This form of attack was made to order for the flak trap. The German whose task it was to push the button, had only to wait until the attacking aircraft were in or near the centre of the pattern and down would go the finger. For the airmen there was no turning back; the only solution was to keep your head down and hope there was not a shell around with your name on it.

Rarely was a Commander shot down by opposing fighters, as by the time they had reached the rank of Squadron Leader, they were wily birds; but with flak it was a different matter. Some of our most experienced pilots were to lose their lives when attacking heavily defended ground targets, and we lost two successive COs in this way.

While at Volkel, Johnny Iremonger left us, tour expired, and Spike Umbers replaced him. What a 'press-on' character Spike was, with his motto of 'never shoot till you could see the whites of their eyes'. While attacking shipping in a Dutch harbour, Spike boasted that he had been so low that they had to open the dock gates to let him out. During his early days with 486, Spike acquired the name by which he was to become known throughout Fighter Command. Not being present at the time I cannot vouch for the accuracy of the story but Harvey Sweetman declares that this is how it happened. While at a party, Spike clapped his eyes on an attractive young lady and I expect that she was not averse to a spot of flirting with a handsome fighter pilot. Just when it seemed that the future seemed to be developing all sorts of attractive possibilities, a giant of a man turned up who the girl introduced as her husband. As the big fellow peered down at the little airman he said, 'That spiked your guns, old boy'. From that moment it had to be Spike.

On the completion of his first tour, Spike had spent his rest period as a test pilot for Hawkers and during that time had married Pam Worthington, a handsome lass. Now they were expecting their first baby. 14 February was one of those days at Volkel. The squadron was out on a sweep and those of us who were not flying were hanging around the flight office with nothing to do or nowhere to go. Spike was there with us awaiting the arrival of the duty Anson which was to take him to Brussels from where he was to fly over to London in a Dakota. When I answered the telephone in the flight office it was Control to say that the Anson had been held up and could not be expected at Volkel for at least another couple of hours; it was already an hour late.

Spike was fed up and I readily agreed to his suggestion that we make a short flight into Germany, so away we went taking a couple of new pilots with us. We flew due east above cloud for about three quarters of an hour when Spike spotted a hole in the overcast and down we went to ground level and headed for home. Hazy, with cloud base at less than a thousand feet, these were precisely the conditions in which to find a German aircraft being air tested. As we crossed the Dortmund–Ems canal there were a couple of barges moored against its east bank and at Spike's shout of 'Barges', my heart sank. Those two had 'flak trap' written all over them.

I was becoming an expert at recognising this sort of warfare, having been caught several times during the last month and only shortly before this had been the occasion when I had the end of my wing blown off. Spike did a climbing turn to cloud base and down we went, Spike attacking one barge as I lined up the other, then all hell seemed to break loose. Just far enough back to watch Spike I had to admire his shooting—it was spot on. As he passed over the barge, his Tempest appeared to stand on its tail in a vertical climb and at the same time my plane sounded as though it was being attacked with a big stick, as flak seemed to be tearing through it in all directions and then there was a bang as rocket flak tore through a wing leaving a hole that I could see the ground through. Next thing I knew, the motor cut.

Like my Channel landing, it all appeared to be happening in slow motion. I just seemed to hang there. While this was taking place, I saw Spike's plane continue what appeared to be a tight loop. The nose dropped and it dived into the mud at the side of the canal. I could see Spike quite plainly and he just seemed to be sitting there. All that saved me from a similar fate was my turning down the canal, not because I realised that here I would be safe from the vertical flak but my plane was banging and clattering and losing height so rapidly that over the water was the only area that was clear of obstructions. Back at base I found our two mates. They had not collected a single piece of flak between them. They must have seen what was happening and wisely headed for home as no way could they have attacked those barges without receiving the same treatment that had been dished out to Spike and myself.

Our next CO was Taylor-Cannon, known to us all as Hyphen.[1] Like Spike he was also on his second tour and also like Spike he had completed his first tour with 486 while we were at Tangmere.

On this particular morning in April 1945 I had taken out the early morning show and found a road on the west bank of the Elbe packed with transport travelling nose to bumper. By the time we had run out of ammunition and left for base, the road was full of burning vehicles, deep ditches on both sides preventing any chance of escape. Burning fuel from accompanying tankers had spread along the hard surface like a river of fire, completing the picture of desolation and destruction.

Hyphen was leading the next sweep, due to take off as soon as the planes had been refuelled and rearmed and they planned to return to the same area as we had covered that morning, I advised caution as there was a lot of flak about and no point in risking anyone's neck

---

[1] Squadron Leader K G Taylor-Cannon DFC and bar, killed in action 13 April 1945

shooting up a lot of transport that was unlikely to take any further part in the war. I can still see that slow grin of his as he said, 'Don't worry, James, I will not take any risk'.

Sadly, the flak gunners were ready and waiting, and Hyphen's plane received a direct hit and as he baled out his parachute caught fire and to those watching he seemed to make a heavy landing. Hyphen's fate, after landing near those flak gunners, will never be known. His name is listed at Runnymede as one of those who have no known grave. Spike, now Hyphen—how much longer would it be before the flak struck me down. Why did it have to happen to them when the end was so near?

Three days after Hyphen went in, we lost our Wing Leader, Pete Brooker. On the day he failed to return I was leading 486. The Wing Commander and his three pilots, who were from one of the other squadrons, took off just in front of us. On reaching the Elbe they were to turn south and on reaching the river I was to turn north towards Hamburg. It was agreed at briefing that as we would be in radio contact, if they were to meet up with enemy aircraft he was to give me a call and we would turn about and do what we could do to help. Now if they had attacked a ground target we would have heard them arranging their method of attack, and again if they had been engaging or been attacked by enemy aircraft, one of them would have reported a sighting. We carried out our patrol and returned to base without seeing or hearing anything. When we landed there was the Wing Commander's station waggon parked where he had left it and he and his wingmen just seemed to have disappeared. The only logical explanation is that they were bounced and shot down before any one of them had a chance to use their radio.[1]

Again we were without a CO. One day I was acting in that capacity, the next, Smokey Schrader. It was a return to the period when Iremonger departed and Umbers took over and it was doing nothing for the morale of 486. Spike then Hyphen had moulded us into a top fighter squadron, now that was being endangered by lack of direction from the top. It upset me greatly.

I went to Group Captain Jameson and expressed my concern, adding that in my opinion Flight Lieutenant Schrader would make a first class Commanding Officer and one that I would be happy to serve under. Jamie took my advice and Smokey put up his third ring but it

---

[1] Brooker and Sergeant W F Turner of 80 Squadron, were shot down by Fw190s near Wittenberge

was not long before Smokey was to be promoted to Wing Commander and given command of the Meteor Squadron.[1]

Once again 486 was without a Commanding Officer and I received an order to report to the Group Captain's office. Jamie did not beat about the bush. 'Sheddan, last time you had your way, now it's my turn. Put up your third ring and take over 486'.

It was with mixed feelings that I settled into that chair in which Scottie had been sitting when I had first walked into the 486 flight office so long ago at Tangmere. Jacko, Spike, then Hyphen had all been cut down by flak while commanding fighter squadrons, the last two within a short time of each other and now I was in the hot seat. We had all been at Tangmere together. Spike had been killed shortly after starting his second tour, Hyphen had followed an almost identical path and now, after that abortive rest of mine would I be the third member to return to 486 for a second tour and chopped by flak? At this stage of the war, just staying alive was an achievement. How much longer could I continue to dodge the flak? It would be an understatement to say that I'd been on borrowed time for a considerable period and now I had the fate of a squadron on my plate.

This is a ditty composed by Jack Stafford, a great songster. It was his and the Squadron's favourite when we were spending an evening in the bar at Volkel.

ON AN AIRFIELD UP IN HOLLAND,
WHERE THE BROWN JOBS LOOK FOR MINES,
SAT A WINCO AND HIS PILOTS,
DRINKING BEER AND SHOOTING LINES.

NAME WAS KENWAY* ALWAYS KENWAY,
NEVER PRESSED THE TIT ON TIME;
USED TO LINGER, WITH ITS FINGER,
FULLY IN AND FULLY FINE.

ONE-OH-NINE'S AT TWENTY THOUSAND,
TWO-SIX-TWO'S AT FORTY NINE,
NO CORRECTION FOR DEFLECTION,
FULLY IN AND FULLY FINE.

* 486 Squadron's call-sign.

---

[1] 616 Squadron—Schrader commanded this from May to August 1945

CHAPTER XIV

SQUADRON COMMANDER

Paperwork was a side of commanding a squadron that many Commanding Officers found irksome and most of them did no more than was necessary. Since Iremonger's departure this was the side of 486 that had been neglected. Spike was a pilot's CO, Hyphen ditto; the less they saw of paperwork the happier they were. Smokey had stayed only long enough to get his name in the record book before passing on to greater things and now it was my turn. My task was to clear up the mountain of correspondence plus flying once, and sometimes twice a day, as well as attending to the other administrative duties that went with running a front-line fighter squadron.

For example, when a pilot was killed or posted missing, it was expected that the next of kin receive a personal message from his Commanding Officer and this was not the sort of task that could be left to the orderly room. After all, it was a husband or son that you were talking about and one that they had lost or might never see again. Were I to suffer the same fate as Spike and Hyphen, before the task was completed, it was possible that a Commanding Officer would be posted in from another squadron and be faced with the task that now confronted me. If that were to happen, it would be a stranger writing to strangers about a stranger. At least I had lived, played and flown with most of these boys for two years or more and though it was not a pleasant task, the relations and I had some kind of mutual interest. Accordingly, it was pilots who were relative newcomers that I found the most difficult to write about.

Not only did we have our operational problems but also personal ones as well, and one of the pilots responsible for causing his mates a lot of worry, was Brian O'Connor.[1] 'Oc', as he was always known, was one of the old hands who had joined us at Tangmere and was always the life and soul of any party. Most evenings he could be found at his usual place at the bar, surrounded by a mob of pilots whom he would be entertaining with his stories which he told with an Irish wit. No matter how sad or depressed you might feel, you could always get a laugh out of Oc.

Then we became aware that something was amiss. Oc just did not seem to be around as much as he used to be. He had seen more than his fair share of the war and in any other pilot his strange behaviour would have indicated that it was time he was sent on rest, but this was obviously not the case with Brian. He seemed to spend a lot of time writing letters and when we did manage to persuade him to join us at the bar he was his usual cheerful self but he was just not drinking his normal quantity of beer; it was all very upsetting. There had to be a reason and there was. The boy was in love.

An English girl had caught Oc's eye and during his last leave they had become unofficially engaged, and it was in order to save up enough to buy a ring that he had eased up on the beer. The situation was even worse than we thought. He was due to go on leave again in a few days and by the time he returned to us he could be married! We were his friends and we just couldn't let such a thing happen to a brave comrade.

Sid Short was due to go on leave at about the same time and he was a very dear friend of Oc's.[2] It would not be too difficult to arrange that they go together and for Sid to keep O'Connor in a twilight world for most of his stay in London. If Sid did the job of which he was able, girls would be the last thing his friend would be capable of thinking about. Sid readily agreed to undertaking his part of our little scheme but displayed a mercenary side of his nature which none of us had suspected. Happy as he was to undertake the proposed mission, he could see no valid reason why he should finance it and suggested that we all should divvy up. It looked as if we had some thirsty days coming along too!

Oc, meantime, had written to his lady friend and made arrangements to meet her in London but when, after two days of searching, she found the pair in a West End bar, Oc was in such a state that the only thing he was capable of was peering at the girl through red

[1] Flying Officer B J O'Connor DFC, from Napier. Joined RNZAF in 1940
[2] Flying Officer S J Short from Cardiff, Wales. Joined RNZAF in 1942

rimmed eyes, muttering, 'Should I know you?' The young lady was so upset by the experience that she met a Yank and on the rebound, married him.

When I met O'Connor shortly after returning from overseas, he was still complaining bitterly about that disastrous leave. As Sid had not disclosed our part in the plot I was able to help him abuse Sid. As a matter of fact I was finding it hard to believe myself that Sid was capable of such a treacherous act!

I shared my last German fighter on 16 April with Warrant Officer W J Shaw, who was flying wingman to O'Connor. It was an early Armed Recce to the Pritzwalk-Parchim-Luneberg areas and we found and strafed some MT. Then we spotted activity around the airfield at Neustadt and went down. We were at 4,000 feet when Oc reported an Fw190 in the air. As leader, I initially sent their section down to deal with it but as their attack did not appear to be effective, although Shaw had scored some hits, I also went down. O'Connor lost sight of the low-flying Focke Wulf as he dropped his wing tanks, so Shaw attacked it but overshot. The 190 was beginning to pull away. He attacked again, forcing the 190 away from the airfield but he then had to break too, to avoid crossing the airfield himself.

The 190 was now heading north as I intervened behind it and as my cannon shells hit the Focke Wulf it flicked onto its back and went into the ground.

My last operation was on 2 May when Dave Thompson[1] and I attacked a multi-engined flying boat which had just taken off from a seaplane base just north of Lubeck. Thompson thought it was a Blohm und Voss 138. The plane must have had some fairly important personnel aboard for not only were the flak gunners, surrounding the base, fully on alert, but also circling around it were a ring of German fighters. As we dived to the attack the flak guns opened up and created so much cloud that we were able to hide amongst it while we demolished that plane, one engine at a time with an occasional squirt at the cabin to make sure the Jerrys kept their heads down. Our problem was that the flying boat or seaplane, I am not sure which, was so huge that it would have been easy to misjudge distances and fly into it. Also compared with our speed it was so slow that it was a case of flying across behind shooting as you went, then stall-turning in order to be in position for a second attack. Strangely enough the German fighters

---

[1] Flying Officer D J Thompson, flying Tempest EJ659

did not attempt to interfere. I suspect that they reneged at searching
for us amidst all that flak. The outcome was that the German plane
caught fire and spiralled down to blow itself to bits on the edge of the
base. Back at our base Tommy was not sure whether he had fired or
not but an inspection of his aeroplane disclosed that the patches were
no longer over the cannon muzzles so we claimed half each.

Looking back now, I would like to list a few more of the incidents
that I was involved in over the years. Strangely enough, I cannot recall
other pilots being there but they must have because we never flew
alone, well, not at the start of an operation, though it was not unusual
to find yourself alone during or after a mix up. When we first started
flying Typhoons with a five-hundred bomb under each wing it was
thought possible that the aeroplane's undercarriage was not strong
enough to withstand the added weight when landing, and as such
a collapse on top of the bombs could be disastrous for both plane
and pilot, we were told not to attempt to land without first unloading
our bombs. It was the rule, therefore, that if a suitable target could
not be found, the bombs should be dropped in the Channel on the
way home.

On one occasion, after cruising over France and unable to locate
our, or an alternative, target we were heading for home when I rashly
decided to unload my bombs over land instead of the sea, as normal.
The villages near the French coast had been cleared of locals and were
mostly occupied by Germans. To drop slightly behind was no problem,
as I was flying at the rear of the squadron. The difficult part was to
judge the correct place to press the bomb release. My effort must have
been about the best bombing of the war for as I peered over my
shoulder while hurrying to catch up, I was to see twin explosions in
the middle of the target. The next problem was to have a convincing
excuse ready in case my act had been seen but it appeared that it had
not for, on landing, nobody mentioned it. That night in the bar I was
to receive something of a shock, however, when Woe Wilson told the
assembly, 'The poor old Frenchmen were lined up at their local post
office to collect their old age pensions when along comes nasty old
Sheddan and drops a couple of bombs on the building. Shame on you,
Sheddan'.

When the Germans were retreating during the final weeks of war a
lot of horse-drawn wagons were being used. These were loaded with
hay and made to resemble farm carts but if our information was to be
relied upon there were German soldiers hiding under the hay. I was
a Section Leader at the time and our trick was to strafe the wagon
from the side to avoid hitting the horse, but the shooting naturally

used to panic the animal which would take off at full gallop through gates and fences, over ditches with harness flapping and bits flying off the cart while the hay and what remained of the transport blazed merrily. There was no need to hit the Jerrys hiding under the hay, as the entire performance would quite possibly have frightened them to death.

Another enjoyable prank was to spot a German despatch rider riding his motorcycle and then to attack him. More often than not, the rider would 'bale out' while his machine was still at speed and we would see a motor cycle heading in one direction while the German, on his big flat feet, would be heading in another. If the victim lay on his stomach he was reasonably safe, but turn on his back in order to watch and he would be scared half to death by our aircraft, with the attacking pilot witnessing a white face getting whiter by the second.

As with the Goon hiding under the hay there would be no need to hit the despatch rider, the fact that he had an aeroplane and four cannon all to himself plus a few high explosive shells bursting around would have such a shattering effect on his nerves that he would be of no further use to the German war effort. It would be fair comment to say that in future, even if safe in an air raid shelter, every time he heard an aeroplane he would have to change his underpants!

A lot of the secondary roads had, typically, trees evenly spaced on both sides and as most of these trees were oak, their foliage completely covered the highway. On occasion, an attacking pilot would know that there was a staff car down there, but the only way of locating it would be to fly parallel to the road at ground level. Once the target had been pinpointed you had never to lose sight of the covering tree whilst at the same time gaining enough height to point the aircraft in the attacking position and undershoot the target in order to peep under the tree from the opposite direction. The problem then being that with the closing speed, the time between when the attacking aircraft was near enough to open fire and when the pilot had to pull up, in order to avoid hitting the trees, was so limited that the exercise was a risky operation. The driver of the staff car could, of course, by picking the right time to move, spoil the attack.

In the case I have in mind the driver must have been an old hand but he made the mistake of leaving the safety of the trees and taking cover behind a house. This move would have been okay providing that he had been able to make the change undetected, but he was unlucky in that I just caught sight of the vehicle disappearing behind the building. It was a simple matter to estimate the approximate position of the staff car and aim through the house. The stream of cannon shells did not do much for the house but they had the desired effect as was indicated by the quantity of flames and black smoke that shot skyward as the car and its petrol tank blew up.

On another occasion while a vehicle was racing along a country road which had been carved out of the side of a hill, the car disappeared into what seemed to be a tunnel but what must have been a garage carved into the hill because no sooner had the vehicle disappeared than a camouflaged door was pulled across the opening. Luckily or unluckily, depending on which side you were on, I was able to keep that door in view while getting into position and attacking. After a short burst the door blew out followed by a cloud of smoke and flames.

On another occasion still, while attacking a tanker in a small village, I was so impressed by the white cloud that I called up to say, 'I knocked that joker off, look at the smoke'. One of my mates with a doubtful sense of humour replied, 'You're terrible, Sheddan. All those little Hiennies lined up waiting for their milk ration and you blow up their tanker'.

Once, while the squadron was shooting up an airfield, a fuel tanker pulled out from behind a hangar just when one of the attacking aircraft was in position to take advantage of the opportunity. Why that tanker driver made such a boob was hard to understand. With aircraft shooting at ground targets, and airfield flak shooting at the attacking aircraft, he must have been totally confused by it all. I happened to be in a position to watch the performance and at the time thought it amusing, but if some of the flak that was streaming up had been a little more accurate it would have been a different story. Anyway, the attacking aircraft fired a short burst, the tanker exploded at the same time as its driver baled out, only to be drenched by burning fuel. That poor German looked like a flaming torch as he raced for the safety of a slit trench which must have been full to capacity because his mates displayed even greater haste in leaving than he did in getting there.

At the same airfield, at a later date, the Squadron were chasing an Me109 down the runway, eight against one. There could be no doubt as to what the final outcome would be so I decided to climb up and watch the performance. Suddenly the German pilot pulled his plane into a vertical climb. He obviously caught the Tempests by surprise as they made no attempt to follow him, but instead of continuing to climb he completed what could be best described as a giant loop, which totally encircled my plane as he started on his way down. I had to admire the control of that pilot. In order to recover from the dive he had to pull back on the control column as the vapour tails began to creep in from the wing tips, indicating that the wing loading had increased to a point where a high speed stall was imminent. He then eased the pressure off. From where I was watching it was a matter of continually keeping the wing loading just below crisis point and hoping. Another fifty feet and he would have made it, but as it turned out he ran out of height and went slap into the middle of his own runway.

Five years living with death and violence was something that could not be forgotten just because somebody said, 'The show is over, go home and take up where you left off'. Shortly after returning from England I pulled an act which today seems unthinkable. My people were farmers and Mother's kitchen had a walk-in pantry attached. A mouse had taken up residence there and Mother was upset because on the odd occasion that she had seen the mouse, it was increasing in size and it was obvious that it would not be long before there would be some additions to the mouse population. Traps had been ignored and the family cat, though it had a reputation as a mouser had failed to produce. As a last resort a neighbour's Tom was called in but a strange cat in a strange house is not a very successful combination. That cat panicked and in its attempt to escape knocked over and destroyed some of Mother's favourite ornaments. The amount of destruction one small mouse was capable of had to be seen to be believed.

After all the frustration, Mother readily agreed when I suggested that I take over the problem. After defying the might of the German Air Force I had to be capable of dealing with the new enemy. What I did was to place some bait on the pantry floor and with the door just wide enough to see without being seen, sat outside on a stool with a gun fully charged and ready. Presently an eye and a whisker appeared as the animal surveyed the surroundings from behind a biscuit barrel. Next, it bounded across the floor with the obvious intention of collecting the decoy on the wing and disappearing into one of its many hide-outs. I was well ahead of that mouse in my thinking and had fastened the hunk of cheese to the floor with a big nail.

Mother was a gentle person and very religious. No doubt her first act was to thank God that I had decided to use a gun instead of burning her house down in my campaign to destroy the little rodent.

On 6 May we left Jamie's Wing which was then at Fasburg and joined Group Captain Johnnie Johnson's Wing[1] flying from Celle which was a pre-war German airfield.

---

[1] Group Captain J E Johnson DSO and 2 bars, DFC and bar, the highest scoring pilot in the European Theatre and in 1945 CO of No. 125 Wing

After Tangmere, we were stationed at numerous, hastily con-
structed, wartime airfields, but even the splendour of Tangmere
was nothing when compared with the German pre-war fighter
stations. Swimming pools attached to the Officer's Mess, married
quarters, even the single pilots had luxurious flats where they could
entertain their lady friends. At Celle, in a room attached to the bar,
was a row of chrome-plated bowls which had big openings where
normally a bung would be placed. These bowls were attached to the
drainage system and had concealed flushing with a foot control.
Each bowl had a handle on either side, obviously meant for hanging
on to. Puzzled by these strange looking gadgets I asked an English
speaking waiter to explain. He did better than that and gave me
a demonstration. Grasping the handles and with his foot on the
flushing control he lowered his head into the bowl and from the
strange noises it was obvious what he was attempting to do.

On the first night at Celle at my usual place, the bar, I was listening
to a Nursing Sister talking about Belsen Concentration Camp which
had just been discovered by our troops. The tales of horror were
a little over done I thought. Frankly I did not believe her and said
so. 'Okay Squadron Leader, it will do some of you the world of good
to see the conditions inside that camp. Tomorrow you are coming
with me'.

Man's inhumanity to man, the stench of filth and human flesh could
be smelled for at least ten miles down wind. As for some of the
inmates who stood listlessly in their barbed wire enclosures, starv-
ation and torture had reduced them to a stage where their survival
rate would not be more than one in fifty. I finally believed—the
unbelievable.

My first mission on our new Wing was when Johnnie asked me to
fly up to Denmark and report on an airfield situated on the outskirts
of Copenhagen, and return the same day. Johnnie's Wing moved
up there a few days later. I took Joe Kendall and Colin McDonald
with me and we had a happy three day binge in Copenhagen, having
met 'Digger' Cotes-Preedy[1] who had spent the final period of the
war in a forward control car directing the RAF fighters onto selected
targets. When about to return to Germany Joe and Colin's aircraft
refused to start so I flew back alone. At this late date I suspect that
it was reluctant pilots and not aircraft that were refusing to leave that
northern city. Arriving back at Celle, the Wing was in the process of

---

[1] Squadron Leader D V C Cotes-Preedy GC, DFC

leaving for the north and I do not think that our absence had been noticed! So we settled in Johnnie's Wing at Rastrup while on the other side of Copenhagen a fully operational German fighter wing occupied another airfield.

CHAPTER XV

COPENHAGEN

ONCE settled at Kastrup the Group Captain suggested that I move into the Senior Officer's Mess. This invitation I politely declined on the grounds that if those wild colonial pilots of mine started to let their hair down and I was not around to tone down their high spirits they were capable of demolishing Copenhagen. This remark Johnnie never let me forget on the numerous occasions I was called into his office and asked to explain some of their horse play and tried to defend them by explaining that my boys were just not capable of committing the felonies suggested.

'No, Sir, not my pilots. There must be some mistake'.

The Group Captain and I were as one in our thinking. Our pilots had survived a torrid trek across Europe and providing they kept their antics within the Wing, we were prepared to look the other way.

On numerous occasions Johnnie and his Wing Commander, Mike Ingle-Finch[1] were off the field so, being the senior Squadron Leader, it was my lot to handle the day-to-day problems involved in running a Fighter Wing.

When summoned to the Groupy's office I could form a fairly accurate assessment as to the reason, by the reception I received.

'Good morning, Shed'. Johnnie was about to ask a favour or suggest a day's shooting.

'Good morning, Sheddan'. Wait for it, what nonsense had my gang been up to.

Copenhagen was the city everybody seemed to want to visit. Senior Officers, politicians, big noises from New Zealand, all seemed to

---

[1] Wing Commander M R Ingle-Finch DFC and bar

discover a reason for paying a visit to 486. Never had we been so popular. When a Wing Commander or above arrived it was expected that I be on hand, clad in my best blue, to greet the visitor. It was a bit of a bind but a small price to pay for the privilege of living in Copenhagen.

It helped no end by having a jewel of a batman. Paddy hailed from Dublin and his cheerful manner and smiling face were a tonic, no matter what the condition that I had arrived home in or how bad the hangover might be. While officially my exclusive property, the rest of the Officers imposed on his good nature and as he seemed happy to run around after them I did not interfere. Unfortunately Paddy's reign was speedily coming to an end and when it did he was irreplaceable.

Johnny Wood and Ginger Eagelson decided to do a midnight jaunt into Copenhagen by car and took Paddy with them. On their return they drove into the Guard's box at the airfield entrance and not only wrecked the sentry box and their automobile but the three finished up in the Station Sick Quarters. The next morning when I went along to view the damage it was to find the two villains sitting up in bed and as chirpy as a couple of sparrows but poor old Paddy was in a bad way. I gladly would have traded the two pilots, dead or alive, for my batman but it was not to be and when he was well enough to leave hospital we sent him off on 'survival leave' and I was not to see him again. Paddy would, in the long history of Fighter Command, be the only batman to have been awarded this dubious honour.

Incidentally during the night some enterprising Dane had pinched what had been left of the vehicle and the guard, who had been in the box when it was attacked, was in no condition to give a reliable report so the case against the two conspirators lapsed for want of evidence.

There were at least two incidents I can recall that tested my powers of diplomacy. On one occasion a telegram arrived which contained the news that a New Zealand Wing Commander was arriving in a Dakota which was due in about seven thirty the following morning. Senior officers were a constant trial, as they always expected red carpet treatment. Why could they not act like ordinary mortals? Anyhow, I was on hand to meet the Dakota with every intention of collecting my visitor and unloading him into the Senior Officer's Mess where no doubt someone would keep an eye on him for me.

The transport duly arrived, about forty minutes late, as usual, which did nothing for my state of mind but apart from a load of freight the only spare body was a Flight Sergeant air gunner who had New Zealand shoulder flashes. It soon became obvious that I'd been conned or sold a pup, in other words. I had to admire the airman's cheek but he had outsmarted himself. If he had climbed aboard the Dakota at Northolt and just arrived, he could have bedded down with the 486 NCOs and no-one would have been any the wiser but he had drawn attention to himself by having that telegram sent.

Always one for a lark, I decided to play along. Luckily I was wearing a Mac, so apart from my hat disclosing that I was an Officer there was no way that bogus Wing Commander could tell that he was face to face with the Commanding Officer of 486.

'Flight Sergeant', I said, 'I was asked by the CO of 486 to meet this Dakota and collect a New Zealand Wing Commander who is to visit the squadron but there does not seem to be one around. They were not referring to you by any chance?'

'There must have been a mistake in the wording of the tele-gram, Sir'.

That air gunner looked the type who would become involved in just such a 'mistake'. If I'd had my wits about me I would have told him to return to Blighty on that same Dakota, as he had trouble written all over him.

'OK, Flight, throw your kit in that jeep over there and I'll drop you off at the 486 Orderly Room and introduce you to the Old Man. A word of warning, the CO is a livery old bird even when he is at his best. With a hangover, he's a terror and I know he had a fairly rough night and most of his squadron will be keeping out of his road'.

By the look of my passenger he could see rough water ahead. Obviously this visit to Copenhagen was beginning to turn more than a little sour.

'Good morning, Sir'. Always very conscious of rank the Adjutant bounded to his feet as I entered the office, followed by my passenger.

'Adj you did not mention that we had an air gunner posted to us'.

'I did not know myself, Sir'. The Adj stood there, his eyes blinking behind his glasses and his mouth opening and closing like a stranded whale. Poor old Adj, he never seemed to be able to work out when I was serious or when I was pulling his leg.

The joke had gone on long enough and my stomach was beginning to remind me that I had better hasten over to the Mess or I would miss out on breakfast.

'Right, get hold of Jim Duncan or if he is not available, another of our NCOs and tell them to take over this character. They are to find him a bed. Keep an eye on him and he is to stay a week, then back to England and I am holding you responsible to see that my orders are carried out'. As I departed I noticed the look on the Adj's face.

If looks could have killed that Flight Sergeant would have been on his way to the undertaker.

Next morning it was 'Squadron Leader Sheddan report to the Group Captain's office immediately'. Johnnie Johnson did not beat about the bush.

'Sheddan, one of your NCO pilots created a disturbance in Copenhagen last night but according to the Service Police it was a New Zealand air gunner. There must be a mistake; we don't have air gunners on a fighter squadron'.

That bloody air gunner! 'Leave it to me, Sir, I'll find out what they are talking about and deal with it.'

Johnnie was a wise old bird and it was obvious that I knew more about the air gunner than I was letting on. If we had been accused of being the owner of an air gunner in error, my loud protest would have been heard half way to England.

The Wing Adjutant had wasted no time in moving the ball back into my corner, for by the time I had returned to the Flight office there was a Service Policeman there with all the gruesome details. The gang had gone into the city and had spotted a Danish milkman delivering milk to the shops. While he was away from his horse and cart our air gunner had mounted the animal and set off at a gallop along the street.

One air gunner to report to my office immediately. The previous day I had been amused by the situation but there was no way that I could raise a laugh over that act of vandalism.

'Yesterday I was prepared to turn a blind eye to your antics and you repaid my generosity by creating a disturbance in the city last night. There is a transport leaving for England in a couple of hours and you are going to be on it. In the meantime, clean up those dirty buttons and polish your shoes which look as though they haven't seen a brush since you've owned them. Also get that uniform pressed and report back here in one hour when the Adjutant will inspect you and if he does not like what he sees, you're for the high jump. I will have an Officer down at the plane to see you safely aboard and any more of your tricks and you will be escorted aboard and when you arrive in England you will be facing a court martial for impersonating a senior officer and for destroying Danish equipment. Now get out of my sight.

The orderly room corporal had been a silent observer and it would not be long before the rest of the ground staff would hear the details. Well, it would do no harm for the squadron to find out just how tough the Old Man could get if his toes were trodden on.

The next case was much more serious as it involved an international incident and could have resulted in the squadron being sent back to

England in disgrace. A German warship was tied up in the harbour with a skeleton crew aboard which included its Captain and a couple of officers plus enough German crew to keep the ship in running order while awaiting a decision from the Allies as to what its fate was going to be. A New Zealand officer, with a civilian companion, had forced their way aboard at gun point, ransacked the boat and the officer had signed a chit which listed the items taken. The incident had been reported to London and by this time our German opponents were beginning to be looked on as heroes, so we were asked to investigate, and if the officer responsible could be identified he was to face a court martial.

Luckily, instead of sending over a trained investigator they instructed Group Captain Johnson to sort out the details and report. Summoned to Johnnie's office in order to help try and sort out the mess, I was in no doubt as to the identity of the pilot involved as the only member of our team who was always in the company of a civilian was Warrant Officer Maddaford. Fortunately the German officer did not know the difference between an officer who held the King's commission and a Warrant Officer who did not. At the time this act of piracy had taken place, I could account for every one of my officers so the obvious conclusion was that some villain had somehow obtained a New Zealand officer's uniform and had used it to mislead the Germans.

Whilst in Denmark, I lost another of my old mates. Rupert 'Bluey' Dall was a red-haired Australian who had joined the NZ Air Force and was with 486 at Tangmere when I arrived. Shortly after he left us and joined 198 Typhoon Squadron as a flight commander. On completion of their tours both he and Woe Wilson returned to New Zealand where Bluey had a wife, and then, not liking what they saw, had Scott pull some strings and both returned to the UK and wangled their way back onto operational squadrons in Europe. Wilson was shot down by flak and ended up in hospital while Bluey, as usual, managed to dodge all the Germans thrown in his direction. While we were in Denmark Bluey flew up and spent about ten days as my guest before returning to Wunstorf where his squadron was stationed.

Shortly afterwards I flew down to spend a few days with Bluey, and it was arranged that he would lay on a spot of pig and deer shooting. As I taxied in I was surprised at the absence of pilots. Normally when a Tempest visited a Typhoon Wing there was a welcoming committee. When I enquired after my friend from the airman who was there to receive me and my plane, I learnt that he was dead and all the Wing were at his funeral. It seemed that Bluey had wangled a posting to

SEAC and had gone aloft for a last flight. This was to be literally so because he had pulled a 'Cobber Kain' act, too many slow rolls too close to the ground. As his plane hit the ground, moving sideways, Bluey had been thrown out and had bowled along the ground. When they picked the body up, all that was holding it in one piece was the skin and the battle dress. As soon as my plane had been refuelled I taxied out, took off and returned to Kastrup.

When based in England, squadrons had less than a hundred ground personnel to service their aircraft and relied on the base for such amenities as major overhauls on aircraft, stores, pay accounts, sick bay attendants, the lot. Once kitted up for Second TAF, squadrons became complete units, and ground personnel was increased to over five hundred; the thinking was that once it had followed the Allied Armies across the Channel all Second TAF needed was space enough to operate its aircraft and then it could function as a separate unit, without any outside assistance, no matter in what situation it was to find itself.

A Squadron Leader, therefore, was virtually the captain of his ship and this included holding court from time to time and handing out what punishment he considered the crime deserved. Of course, the accused had the option of requesting trial by court martial, but there was a war to fight and the authorities were tough on any airman who was prepared to involve the service in a time-wasting trial in order to avoid his just desserts. The result of this was that the accused had be fairly sure of his facts before he refused to accept the CO's ruling.

It was quite a performance. The Decip. Flight Sergeant would march the criminal in and he would have to stand rigidly to attention whilst his crime was disclosed for my benefit. Then it was his turn to offer what defence he thought would make the most impression on me. Sometimes I could tell by the expression on the Flight's face that I was being handed a load of bull but I only had two options, accept the tale that I was being handed or adjourn the case until the following day, and as soon as our victim had departed ask the Chiefy what it was that was being put across me. This I refused to do, if the airman was able to tell a convincing story which had a ring of truth; in these cases I gave him the benefit of the doubt.

When one of our 'bush lawyers' put one across me I knew that he just could not resist telling his mates and in a very short time I would have the complete story fed back to me. It would not be very long before my turn would come and this time I'd take no notice of excuses, no matter how valid. I would throw the book at him and add on a little extra for the previous occasion. It gave me great pleasure on occasions to enquire if he would like to appear before a Court Martial. A little bit of rough justice and it was surprising how soon the persistent malingerers found other less expensive forms of entertainment.

There seemed to be a constant parade of Wing Padres into my office seeking assistance to iron out some of their flock's problems. In my opinion they were doing a good job and I never refused to see them and listen to their tales of woe. On one particular morning I was intercepted by the Roman Catholic Priest who indicated that he would like to talk to me. I had seen quite a lot of the little Irishman and could almost predict what his problem would be. What a surprise I had in store for me. It appeared that it was my performance that was troubling the holy man. It seemed that he had received a complaint from one of my pilots that I was not holding enough church parades!

It was quite a shock to be abused by the Padre and even a bigger shock to discover that one of my mob had a religious streak. Up to then I thought that I was in charge of the biggest pack of heathens in Second TAF. When I expressed that opinion to my visitor he said, 'Flight Lieutenant . . . is very devout.'

Well, if he had said all that he intended to, I had lots of work to do. I made it very plain that as far as I was concerned the interview was over. This Flight Lieutenant had arrived on the squadron during the closing stages of the war, and had had a brother who had also been a fighter pilot but who had been killed a couple of years earlier.

My first move was to get Johnny Iremonger on the scrambler. Johnny was now a Wing Commander stationed in Brussels and his duty was to organise postings. I wasted no time in coming to the point.

'Sir, I have a Flight Lieutenant on the squadron who I would like to post. Can you organise it?'

'Jim, the only one available would be more suitable for a new Pilot Officer who has had a rush of blood to the head'.

'That would be most suitable, Sir. There is an Anson leaving here during the afternoon. I will tell him to report to you when he arrives in Brussels'.

I liked Johnny. I had been on the squadron during the twelve months that he had been its Commanding Officer. After a bit of chit chat as to how I was coping and our doings in Denmark, he hung up.

The next job was to impart the good news to one devout pilot!

'Flight Lieutenant, you have been posted, so get a clearance and catch the Anson this afternoon. When you arrive in Brussels report to Wing Commander Iremonger who is expecting you. Time is somewhat limited so get cracking and if it was within my power I would have that holy man of yours on the plane with you. Close the door behind you on your way out'.

That Catholic Padre had as many problems, more or less, as any of the other clergy attached to the Wing but after this little incident I heard no more from him.

Only on two other occasions did I have to wave the big stick. The first was when a Flying Officer pilot offended and the other occasion was when a Wing Commander doctor upset me and strangely enough both occasions occurred while we were in Copenhagen.

On the first occasion two of the pilots who were rostered to fly during an Air Display at Kastrup, failed to turn up. Next morning the first of the culprits had no excuse to offer apart from the fact that he had been at a party the previous night, had drunk too much and did not recover until about noon the following day. Well, it was a valid enough reason so I handed him the usual bull about what a bad show it was and not the sort of performance that I expected from my officers. It was not too difficult for me to remember similar situations when I had also offended. The next officer adopted a different approach. He thought there were plenty of pilots who were equally capable of doing the job, and he seemed to think that what he had done was excusable and was surprised that I was taking exception to what he had done. Well I had news for him; he wasn't going to bullshit me!

We had left most of our transport in Germany and a Senior NCO and a small number of airmen behind to look after them. I had told the Adj to rotate the personnel on a weekly basis in order that all would have a chance to sample the pleasures of Denmark. This was just the place to send an officer who had offended and he stayed there until the squadron flew back to Germany three weeks later.

Our Chief Medical Officer, a Wing Commander, was an entirely different kettle of fish. So rapid had been the expansion of the Royal Air Force and its medical requirements that a lot of doctors had been drafted into the service straight from medical school. Most of these young doctors could handle the rapid promotion but at Kastrup we had a Flying Officer acting Flight Lieutenant acting Squadron Leader acting Wing Commander; he was so high up in the clouds that he had lost touch with us ordinary mortals.

No sooner had we arrived in Denmark than Ralph Evans was admitted to sick quarters with suspected 'flu.[1] On my first visit I was

---

[1] Flight Lieutenant A R Evans DFC, from Coromandel, joined RNZAF in 1942

not happy with what I saw or the doctor's diagnosis. While I was a temporary patient in hospital, prewar, there had been a number of patients, mostly girls in their late teens, who were infected with TB and having reached the stage where nothing more could be done for them they were more or less just waiting to die. Sallow complexions, graveyard hollow coughs and bright roses appeared in their cheeks from time to time. When I looked at Evans it was as though I had moved back in time fifteen years. When I suggested to our Wing Commander that Ralph might have TB, his immediate reaction was to enquire as to what school I had done my medical training. As you can imagine I was not very impressed by that response.

Bill Jordon was the New Zealand government's representative in London (High Commissioner) and anything that concerned his boys, as he called us, also concerned him. Following a personal call expressing my dissatisfaction with the treatment Evans was receiving, Ralph was on his way to base hospital within twenty-four hours. Shortly afterwards I received a report that not only confirmed that Evans had TB but also that his condition was much worse than even I had suspected. I was up those stairs, two steps at a time. I had no intention of mincing words as far as that puffed up medical student was concerned, but I was too late.

With Bill Jordon on our side we were on solid ground and he was capable of cabling the New Zealand Prime Minister and asking him to take the matter up with Churchill if he considered that we were getting less than justice. In this case he did and the upshot of the Wing Co's faux pas was that he had now caused trouble between the British top brass and the New Zealand government and as a consequence he was demoted to his substantive rank of Flying Officer and posted to South-East Asia. It would be fair comment to say that the ex-Wing Co would have no future as far as the Royal Air Force was concerned. I wonder if I was right?

When we moved to Kastrup the airfield was littered with German transport but as the days passed it became noticeable that those with tyres still attached were becoming fewer, so I thought I'd better ask for an explanation from Warrant Officer Maddaford. If Rocky was to be believed there was a big demand for tyres and tubes, so what some enterprising airmen were doing was removing them and unloading them to the Danes. Right, my instructions were for Rocky to organise a team of airmen to remove all existing tyres from any remaining vehicles so clad and when anyone completed the recovery exercise, Rocky was to find a suitable buyer and then the two of us were to split the proceeds down the middle. By the look on Rocky's face I could not have found a more willing or suitable assistant. I have no doubt that Rocky, being Rocky, received more than his fair share of the proceeds but the wad of notes that I received was a lot more than the annual salary of a Squadron Leader and enabled me to finance the gang's parties, and especially the dinners that Eagelson was so fond of dishing up. Unfortunately the Danes changed their currency shortly before we left so I was unable to dispose of my temporary wealth.

As far as 486 was concerned Rocky was not our only racketeer; Eagle was at least his equal. At that time there was a brewery in Copenhagen which had a problem in that it had traded exclusively with the Germans, and now the Danes were refusing to drink any of its beer. This was a situation made to order for Eagle who purchased the entire contents on the understanding that the RAF would do the paying. When the Group Captain discovered what was going on he lost no time in informing me that if I had any ideas of the Air Force supplying free beer for my gang of pirates I could forget it. So that ended Eagle's game. In addition to his other achievements, Eagle was a first rate cook and delighted in preparing and serving a first rate meal. Supplies were never a problem, I had no intention of hoarding my nest egg.

A squadron that was with us in Denmark had a couple of large Harley Davidson motor cycles which it had 'acquired' during its trek across Europe. As they were not on squadron strength, their Squadron Commander asked me if I would like to take them over as his outfit were due to return to Blighty to disband. Transport was hard to find and they were just what my two flight commanders, McDonald and Eagelson, wanted. Colin's friend was a very attractive Danish girl, an only child of wealthy parents and she was frequently to be seen perched on the rear of the big Harley, her long blond hair streaming back in the airflow as they whizzed around the city. While we were up there the girl turned twenty one and her parents threw a suitable party to celebrate the event. Colin was the star guest and being his friend I was invited to take part in the celebrations.

In the normal course of events drinks would have been served at seven and after a happy hour, feasting would have commenced about eight. Colin, accompanied by the glamorous daughter and myself, did not arrive till after ten, by which time we had already drunk more than we should. Her parents did a first rate job in covering up the disappointment that they undoubtedly felt. Our hostess must have spent a considerable part of the afternoon in the kitchen instructing the cook in the construction of tit-bits which she imagined would appeal to her

New Zealand guests but as things turned out it was a waste of time and effort.

Colin had just chewed the head off a chocolate Kiwi and was making short work of the body when our hostess put an end to the orgy by asking him if he recognised what it was that he was eating. By this time the only visible portion was a hind leg and Colin was past the stage when he was able to judge the species of animal that it belonged to—and said so!

On another occasion, a gang of us had been invited to a late party at the Zoo restaurant by its owner, Stan Muller, and during the course of the evening a discussion developed as to who was the best revolver shot. Stan Muller invited us to settle the argument by having a shoot out. Upstairs there was a number of guest bedrooms sighted on both sides of a long passageway. Stan hung a target on the wall at one end of the passage and assembled the contestants at the other end. By this time most of us were incapable of hitting the wall let alone the target attached to it. Every so often, during the battle, a bedroom door would open and a guest's head would appear. A casual glance was enough to convince the owner that there were safer places.

Colin and I were invited to spend what was left of the night in the guest's room. Next morning, long after the sun had appeared, Colin made his way to a bedroom window and I gathered from his mutterings that he thought that he could see an elephant. If we are to believe the stories, these sightings only begin when the person involved is well on the way to becoming an alcoholic. However, there was no call for alarm; where else in Europe could one expect to see an elephant, other than in a zoo, At that time of the morning and in Colin's condition, it would have been difficult to be sure whether it was pink or grey.

On another occasion after an all-night party I arrived back at my billet, just as daylight was appearing, to see a body sound asleep under a hedge. A casual glance left me no doubt as to who it was but as it was a warm night there was no point in disturbing the sleeper. On entering the billet, I found the downstairs rooms awash and a steady flow of water down the stairs was adding to the mess. Following the water to its source I was to find Bert Collins sound asleep in the bath with the cold tap turned on and when the bath had reached capacity the water was finding its way onto a lower level. A vigorous shake and, 'What the hell is going on, Bert?' resulted in the sleeper opening one bloodshot eye and with an expression which seemed to say that only an idiot would ask such a question. The answer to the question was obvious, 'I'm having a bath, Sir'.

I'd been around Fighter Command for a considerable time and believed that I'd seen and heard everything but when the boys started to take cold baths in the middle of the night while still dressed in their best blue, complete with shoes and flat hat, I had to admit that there were still a few surprises left.

Later that morning, while taking a pre-lunch drink, Colin told me about the previous evening. He had been at one of the many parties which seemed to go on continually and, at this late stage, I cannot remember whether his vehicle had refused to start or his taxi had failed to appear but he had decided to walk home and in the process became lost. After wandering around for what seemed hours he decided to relax under an inviting hedge and await the arrival of daylight. On the road again he eventually began to recognise familiar objects and was able to direct his steps towards home. Why spoil a good story by telling him what I'd seen?

Junior officers were not the only ones with problems. Group Captains Jameson and Johnson once left a late night, or maybe it was an early morning, party, in their run about, as they called it. That car was so long that a back seat passenger would have needed closed-circuit television to have been able to see what its driver was up to. There seemed some doubt as to who was in the driver's seat but none as to the outcome. Instead of going around a traffic island the driver took the short route, straight across the top, with the result that the car and its two occupants started on a gigantic swing. All might have been well if a corner shop had not somehow managed to get itself in the road. The spinning car removed the shop without disturbing the owners who were asleep in an upstairs apartment which jutted out over the shop. Johnnie was the only casualty, a small cut above his left eye which is visible in the picture of the Group Captain talking to the Queen of Denmark and reproduced in his book, *Wing Leader*.

During my five years in the air force, I put up some fair-sized 'blacks' but my Copenhagen effort, described below, was by far my best, if I do say so myself! All the Senior Officers from Kastrup were invited aboard a British Navy Cruiser which was paying a courtesy call. The object of the exercise was to meet Field Marshal Montgomery who was visiting Copenhagen.

We arrived early and Monty, as usual, kept us waiting. This, coupled with the hospitality of the Senior Services Ward Room was to prove a disaster. My whisky glass was never allowed to become empty, and my big mistake was in remaining seated. When Monty swept into the Ward Room, although my head was clear and appeared to be operating normally, the same could not be said for my legs. The

Navy was well aware of their guest's aversion to alcohol and all bottles and glasses had mysteriously disappeared. Thinking back, I have no doubt that I was the victim of a pre-arranged plan; realising that they had been more successful than expected, my naval friends proceeded to cope with the situation in true naval fashion. Standing close together in line, it was not too difficult for the officer on each side to push in my direction and by the sheer weight of their bodies, keep me in an upright position until the crisis had passed.

On my comings and goings from the Officer's Mess, I used to use a short cut down a side alley and in the process struck up an acquaintance with a Danish business man. Friendships develop quickly in times of war and after, and it was not long before I was a frequent visitor to his home. There was only one snag, my new friend lived alone except for an only child which was a very attractive girl in her middle teens though she looked much older. Girls seemed to mature early in that part of the world.

Like most local girls her ambition was to attend one of our Mess parties, and I was the obvious choice to secure an invitation and act as escort. With true feminine wiles she started in on Dad and then with him on her side she turned her big blue eyes on me. Her father put me in a position from which there was no retreat by saying that I was the only person who he would trust to take his little girl to such a party. Not only was I being pressurised into taking the lovely damsel along as my guest but also I was being made responsible for her welfare!

I could imagine what would happen when those young officers of mine clapped eyes on my lovely companion. I would more than likely be trampled in the rush. The only solution was to forestall trouble and my way of doing it was to tell Colin to line the gang up and inform them that if the CO saw any of them even so much as looking at the girl who he was bringing to the party, they could expect an immediate posting and there would be no reprieve. Colin seemed to think that it was a little rough but those were my instructions and that was the way it was going to be. Poor girl, she must have thought that she had lost her sex appeal. No sooner had she given an officer the glad eye than he seemed to find a reason to hurriedly leave the area. It was obvious that the young lady was not enjoying herself, in fact, she was very near to tears, so to make amends I bundled her into my Jeep and we did a tour of the City's night clubs, arriving back just before daylight to find an anxious Dad up and waiting. It would not have been difficult to imagine what had been going through his mind during the previous few hours.

By this time, as far as my 'ward' was concerned, my gang were only a bunch of immature boys, and she was all for more mature men, with me number one in her sights. This was too much for me and I never visited that household again; besides I had more interesting ways of filling in my time without acting as nurse maid to a school girl.

Two nights before the Wing was to return to Germany, it put on a party at the Belview Hotel and invited all the Danes whose hospitality we had enjoyed. The show commenced at nine, when normal trading ceased and went on till five in the morning, when breakfast was served. We provided the whisky which cost us about five hundred pounds, at tuppence ha'penny a nip. That is a lot of booze! The Danes supplied the beer and champagne. Our Danish friends had not seen so much whisky since before the war and by midnight anyone who was sober enough to know where he lived was bundled into a transport and taken home with as many other drunken bodies as were available. In the morning it was their problem to sort out who was where.

I cannot say that I enjoyed the party as I was one of the unfortunates who Johnnie had charged with the responsibility of taking care of any problems that should arise. At one stage I found a Rhodesian Wing Commander unconscious in a toilet. It seemed that he had been bludgeoned over the head and then robbed. Even Denmark was not immune to that sort of carry on. I did a recovery job on the victim and straightened out his financial problem. When Colin McDonald emigrated to Rhodesia after the war, he was to meet this character who remembered what I had done for him and Colin was treated as one of his friends.

On our last night it was simply a matter of preparing for the morrow's departure, then cleaning up the last of Eagle's supply of bottled beer. There were so many empty beer bottles that some artistic type was able to write '486 NZ Squadron' across the floor in large letters. Jim Duncan tried to record it on film but only managed to capture a portion of it. The outside wall of the room had a quantity of small windows which covered most of the area. There would have been at least a dozen of them. Sitting there and surrounded by empties I thought that it would be a reasonable idea of knock a window out and heave our empties through the opening thus available. For the CO to heave a bottle was an open invitation for the rest of the gang to do likewise. A passer-by would have witnessed an explosion as empty bottles hurtled through windows from one end of the wall to the other.

Next morning I had the party goers out of bed shortly after daylight and we removed any of the jagged edges of glass that had survived the attack. About three windows had escaped but they only served to draw attention to what had happened to the rest so we brought them into line by knocking the glass out and tidying up any bits of glass that would draw attention. When the Squadron Leader (Admin) did a final inspection we hurried him through that building and he actually congratulated us on the condition in which we had left our billets. It was possible that the next lot of pilots to move into that room could have been opening and shutting those windows for a fortnight before discovering that they were permanently 'open'.

Back in Germany, at Lubeck, a non-fraternisation order was in force so we were more or less confined to the airfield. We paid occasional visits to the officer's club in Lubeck but it did not take long for us to wear out our welcome. One evening we were having a bit of a sing-song when an old World War One General objected to the noise. He was one of the many who had been mothballed for the duration of the war but who now seemed to be popping up all over the place like spring flowers. The old fellow happened to be the most senior officer present at the time and by virtue of his rank what he said, went. He issued us an ultimatum. Either we ceased our merry-making or he would close down the bar. That old boy was obviously a stranger to the ways of fighter pilots.

Being the CO I could not aid and abet, but there was nothing to prevent my looking the other way while the junior members turned on a performance that the old stuffed shirt was likely to remember for a considerable time. They debagged the old fellow and hung his trousers up to a chandelier by the braces. He looked a real Charley as he stood there complete with suspenders and monocle, his walrus moustache quivering with indignation. As expected, Johnnie received a report on the night's performance but as I had endeavoured to make myself as invisible as possible, I could honestly say that I had been with the squadron all evening and had not seen the incident complained of. Johnnie did not seem unduly concerned, so maybe he'd also had problems with that old billy goat. The result of our little brush with authority was that the Lubeck officer's club was now out of bounds to New Zealand officers but this did not cause us any pain.

On another occasion we decided to visit the officer's club in Hamburg and take our NCO pilots with us. In those early days of occupation, officers were allowed to enter the club wearing battle dress so we had no difficulty in finding officer dress. Our problem was that Pony Atkison was so small that there just was not a uniform around that even started to fit. The legs were too long and the sleeves ditto, while the tunic gave you the impression that it would have been possible to fit another body inside without removing Pony. We solved the problem by tucking the surplus leg material up inside and doing likewise with the sleeves. We attracted some strange looks but nobody interfered with us.

When we arrived at Lubeck 487 (NZ) Mosquito Squadron was already there but it was due to return to England to disband. Its Commanding Officer made 486 a present of their squadron band but as there was none of my gang interested in this kind of equipment all it was doing was cluttering up my room. The Squadron Leader Admin found out about the band and had ideas of unloading it at a handsome profit providing that I could be persuaded to part with it. Also interested in the band was an army captain who had ideas of forming an army band, so instead of letting the Admin Officer flog it off for gold, I struck a deal with the Captain, exchanging guns and rifles for instruments. I had no idea where he was getting his supplies from but before long there were so many firearms in my bedroom that there was hardly any room for me. The upshot was that the Captain had his band and all of 486, myself included, had a fairly impressive supply of field guns and sporting rifles.

It was obvious that it would not be long before the squadron was disbanding, but when and where was not yet known, so I decided to take my muskets over to England now and park them in a safe place, the plan being to land at Tangmere where there was no customs control, and then go on to Northolt. All went according to plan until taking off from Tangmere, when the motor started to clatter and bang and obviously was about to pack up. The correct procedure was to attempt to get the wheels up and force land straight ahead but all that I could think of was the three guns and a rifle stored in the fuselage behind the armour plating. If that motor had quit during the turn I was history, but it kept thumping away while I completed a one hundred and eighty degree turn and landed back down the runway from which I had taken off. No sooner had the wheels touched the ground than the motor stopped. After travelling to London for a couple of nights and days celebrating my escape, I made my way to Northolt where I boarded a Dakota which was leaving for Lubeck. There were several new boys aboard, who were going out to the Wing and crouched in that old plane, feeling like death warmed up, I dearly wanted to be sick, but no way was I going to have those young pilots arrive at Lubeck and report that the CO of 486 had been air sick on the way over. However by the time we reached Brussels the weather had packed in and we spent the night there and by morning I had staged a partial recovery.

For the occupying forces, especially pilots whose flying was restricted to a few hours a month, life became tedious except for those of us who were interested in wild fowling, and deer and pig hunting. It was a sportman's paradise. There had been little game shooting in Germany during the war and after it, all firearms, including sporting rifles and smooth bores, had been collected by the Army of Occupation. But we had guns.

Though birds were plentiful there were just not enough hunters around the various lakes to keep them moving. We solved this by having a Tempest patrolling and when the pilot saw a collection of water fowl congregating in a safe area a few cannon shells had them on the move again. The keenest shooters were Johnson, Eagelson and myself. Unfortunately, before leaving Denmark I had invested in an expensive gun and although pre-war I had been a first-rate game and trap shooter, from the moment I started to use that gun my shooting was deplorable. For some reason I never suspected the firearm and it was not until many years after returning to New Zealand that I was to discover that my problem was in trying to shoot with a gun with a short stock. The solution was to get a gunsmith to add a couple of inches to the stock which was all that was required to make the difference between me being a poor shot and a good one.

I spent many happy hours out with Johnnie's dog Sally, tramping through the fields in pursuit of pheasant and ironically, on one of these trips I had my closest call of the war. In order to avoid the foxes, pheasant used to roost in 'nigger heads' which abounded on the wet lands and on this occasion I had shot a pheasant which had fallen out amongst the rushes. Unable to direct Sally, I left the dog and gun on solid ground and made my way in the direction of the kill by stepping from one nigger head to the next. Eventually I slid off a rush but was not unduly worried as I expected to find solid footing not far below the surface. It was not until I was almost down to my waist that I realised that I had blundered into a bottomless swamp. I managed to drag a nigger head under me and just at the critical point Sally floundered out and tried to join me, but the rush proved unable to support our combined weight and I sank further down. All that saved me was that another bunch of rushes happened to be close enough for me to grab, otherwise I would have been a gonner. When I eventually reached solid ground I just lay there and shook like a jelly; the thought of sinking into that oozing black mess had terrified me.

There were large flocks of Canadian geese on the lakes in Northern

Germany but getting close enough for a shot was a real problem. No matter how carefully camouflaged, they always seemed to know that you were there and stayed just out of gun range. Then Johnson dreamed up the idea of taking them on in their own element. After all we were 'airmen'! We would use a light aircraft to get within range and while the pilot maintained position the passengers would do the shooting. It was the original version of what the army now call 'gun ships'.

On 28 September, the aircraft the Group Captain chose was a captured German Fieseler Storch and he was to do the flying while Wing Commander Mike Ingle-Finch and myself were to be the marksmen. Although space was at a premium we took Sally along; she was always an essential part of any performance and it did not enter our heads to leave her behind. There were so many geese around that finding a mob of them was not a problem, but lining up a bird was a horse of a different colour. The plane was faster than the birds and when they found that they were being overtaken the mob split up, so we had to chase after individual birds. No German could dodge and turn like some of those old ganders. This, and the fact that our field of fire was limited to a right angle, meant there was no way that we could shoot straight ahead and this did not make hitting the target any easier. I had the misfortune to have a sixteen gauge shell amongst the twelves and, of course, it *had* to be the first one that I picked up and dropped into the twelve bore. After this my shooting was restricted to a single barrel.

As for the recovery of game, it was only those shot down over the lake that it was possible to retrieve. Unfortuately quite a few had only been winged and, apart from their inability to fly were fully mobile. The wounded birds were easy to identify and our pilot brought the Storch down almost to water level in the hope that we might get in a killing shot but it was a waste of time and effort. Long before we were within lethal range, the geese dived and stayed down till danger had passed. After landing as close as was reasonably safe to the shore we commandeered a boat and set off to collect the bodies. Why we all went along, and that included Sally, I will never know. The extra weight had the effect of causing the boat to sink deeper into the water and slow up the operation. Had our boat been powered by a motor extra weight would not have mattered but as it was we had a large boat and only one set of oars.

By the time we had arrived back at the aircraft it was dark and we found that its wheels had sunk into the soft ground so we had to heave and push until we managed to manhandle the Storch up onto firmer ground. It would have made much more sense if one of us had stayed behind and, after sorting out a take off run, taxied the plane into position while it was still daylight. Now we were floundering around in the dark trying to make sure that there were no fences, trees, soft patches or ditches which could impede the take off run and possibly cause a fatal crash. Being the Junior member, my two mates tried to pull rank and suggested, as the plane was grossly overloaded, that I stay behind and one of them would fly up and collect me in the morning. With visions of a long cold night ahead I did not approve of that suggestion. No way was I going to stay there on my own. If they were so concerned about the overweight why not leave Sally and the geese behind I thought, but these were already aboard and there was no suggestion that they be off-loaded.

Couched down in the rear of the fuselage with a wet dog, which ponged, and about a dozen birds which were producing an even more disgusting odour, that trip back to base would have to rate as the most uncomfortable of my five years of flying. As we took off I could feel the wheels bouncing over obstructions and in and out of holes. It seemed an eternity before we were airborne, and even then, all danger had not passed as we were well below the height of the numerous trees that were around and because of the excess weight, our plane was gaining height only slowly. Clear at last our troubles were still not over. That little plane was not equipped for night flying and in order that Johnnie could see the compass, Mike had to lean over his shoulder and strike a match. As soon as the match burnt itself out it seemed darker than ever and Johnnie had to guess in which direction base lay.

Finding Lubeck was only one of the immediate problems; because there was no flare-path operating it was going to have to be a chancy landing in the dark. So there we were, three 'aces', who between us had shot down a considerable number of German aircraft, and now it seemed that a small enemy aircraft was about to do in one evening, what the German air force had been unable to accomplish in five years of war. Against the odds, we made it down safely.

This was not to be my last shaky night landing in a light plane. As recorded earlier, on 20 December 1943, my brother Alex had been shot down and killed while on a night bombing raid, and I know knew that he had been buried on an island off the Dutch coast. I decided to fly from Lubeck to the island on 10 October in a small two-seater Army Auster and our engineering officer, Flying Officer Stuart Cooper, decided to go along for the ride.

On the way out it was a piece of cake as we flew from the Baltic to the North Sea with a couple of refuelling stops but even then we had to divert quite a distance south to find airfields which were occupied by RAF personnel. It was our intention to call at the same fields on the return journey but it did not work out quite like that.

We finally landed in a small field bordering the cemetery but it was when we attempted to take off again that things started to go haywire. After visiting Alex's grave, we returned to the field which had no take-off path to find the entire population of the village had come out to welcome us and they crowded around the plane in a circle. None of the sightseers appeared to speak our language, or at least a language which we could understand, so my passenger alighted and persuaded those directly in front to clear a gap, but by the time he had made his way back to the cockpit the take off area that he had so laboriously cleared, had closed again. The result of all this was that we had been delayed for over an hour, so when we eventually got away we decided to take the short way home and refuel at an airfield which was marked on our map as working; when we arrived, however we discovered that it had been abandoned. Further on, with petrol getting low I had no option other than to side-slip into the only small field available.

With a main highway close by which was carrying a lot of military traffic at the time, there was no problem in cadging enough petrol to supply our need but getting airborne again was the difficulty. I had been able to side-slip the little aeroplane in, but there was no way that I could reverse the procedure to get out. The solution was to have a number of soldiers anchor the tail while I pushed the throttle wide open, and at a wave of Cooper's arm our helpers released their hold and the Auster shot forward like a runner off the starting blocks, just managing to become airborne and high enough to scrape over a fence directly in our path.

As we flew along the autobahn the light now started to fade and the easiest solution would have been to land on the wide highway below and spend the night there. Unfortunately even Squadron Leaders are capable of making wrong decisions and in this case I made directly for Lubeck which involved crossing over Hamburg. The city had been bombed flat and was just a heap of rubble so there was no way that an aircraft could be landed there and as there was no cockpit lighting, I was only guessing as to the quantity of petrol we had left. Just when I was beginning to believe that we were going to make Lubeck the motor gave a couple of coughs and quit. I had no idea what lay below and there was only one light visible which fortunately was within gliding distance so, as we could not stay up there, we had to make for that light and hope for the best.

A small landing strip had been bulldozed on the edge of Hamburg and a Canadian squadron was flying Spitfire XVIs from it. Believe it or not it was this strip that I found in the dark; interestingly, when we returned to Dunsfold to disband it was in the aircraft of this very same squadron that we made our last flight.

CHAPTER XVI

FINALE

In the early days of the no-fraternisation rule which said that in occupied territory there was to be no contact between ourselves and the German civilians, there was a curfew which meant nobody was to be off the airfield from midnight till eight in the morning. Also we had been advised not to go out alone or after dark because the self-styled 'werewolves' favourite act had been to cut a telephone line and when the repair crew went to investigate they were ambushed and found hanging from a cross arm.

On one occasion, when I was hurrying home late and alone, the lights of the jeep illuminated a German in the middle of the road making frantic gestures which indicated that he wanted me to stop. Although my safest course would have been to head straight for him, he obviously had no intention of moving out the way, so somehow it seemed too much like cold-blooded murder and I could not bring myself to do it. The German kept pointing towards the house and shouting, 'Komrade, Komrade', the indications being that he wanted me to follow him. At the same time I became aware of a crashed jeep that had wrapped itself completely around a tree. Whoever had been in that vehicle would have to be history. Whatever the outcome, I was committed, so I followed my German guide indoors to find more Germans grouped around a bed on which a South African Flight Lieutenant lay and although in a bad way he was still conscious. One of our Squadron Commanders had recently been repatriated and this chap was now in temporary command of one of the Wing Squadrons.[1]

---

[1] It was not unusual to have a Flight Lieutenant as an acting CO while awaiting the appointment of a new Squadron Commander

That South African implored me to get him back to the airfield as quickly and discretely as possible. We transferred the patient to the rear of the jeep and covered him with a blanket, after which I set off hoping that the guards would not be too difficult at that late hour.

Before joining Johnnie's Wing, junior officers had always been lumbered with the tiresome job of Duty Officer but Johnnie, for some reason best known to himself, decided that Senior Officers perform this task, so as my turn came along every nine or ten days I was personally known to the guards and they happily waved me through with, 'Good night, Sir'.

Arriving at the billet I did not want to draw attention to ourselves so I managed to drag the body out and struggle inside with it on my own. By this time the pilot was deeply unconscious and it was obvious, even to me, that without professional attention that chap was not going to last the night. What to do? I had two options, one was to walk away and when the body was discovered deny that I had been involved. It would not take the authorities long to find the wrecked jeep and then it would be the German's word against mine. The guards would have to support me as they should have reported my late arrival... The other was to contact the sick quarters and get medical assistance at which point all chances of a cover-up would have vanished. It boiled down to my future against the South African's life and really I did not have an option. A doctor was called in and worked on his patient all night with blood transfusions and what have you and even then it was a very close thing.

This was a case where honesty was the only course so I called on the Group Captain first thing in the morning and told the story, omitting nothing. While I was wading through the sordid details, Johnnie's eyes never left my face and when I finished, all he said was, 'Jim, I'll do my best to cover it up'. His best was good enough because I never heard any more about the incident.

Three of the finest Englishmen I was to meet during my service with the Royal Air Force, were Johnny Iremonger, Jacko Holmes and Johnnie Johnson. Strangely enough they were all at home with New Zealanders though we must have tried them sorely at times. While at Lubeck, Hawkeye Wells paid us a visit and spent the night in a spare bed in Johnnie's room.[1] The 'Hawk' left early and with him went his

---

[1] Group Captain E P Wells DSO, DFC and bar, RAF. Joined RNZAF in 1939. CO 485 (NZ) Squadron 1942, Wing Leader Kenley 1942-43 and Tangmere Wing 1944

host's pair of new shoes. When Johnnie surfaced later the only foot-wear available was an old pair of shoes which were badly in need of repair. Later in the day, Johnson was to greet me with, 'Bloody Kiwis, they would steal worms from a blind hen'.

We were lucky to have Johnson as our Group Captain during our period in the Army of Occupation. He realised that, for pilots, the switch from war to peace was going to be a long, painful business and no matter what happened or what we did, he was always on our side.

At the end of the war, a couple of incidents occured which were very difficult to explain. They involved two of our pilots, Ross Mellies and Shaw, who were late-comers to the squadron and were a couple who did not seem to get into the sort of scrapes the others indulged in from time to time. Whatever skull-duggery was afoot, I could eliminate those pair in my search for the culprit, which was to make their later performances that much harder to understand. Mellies by the way was shot down by flak in the closing stages of the war and before he managed to walk back through the lines, we had already sent off a telegram to his Mother reporting that he was missing on air operations.[1]

Shaw, who had never been known to put a foot out of place, unex-plicably went unauthorised low flying, crashed and was still in hospital long after the Squadron had disbanded. Mellies, with an equally blameless record, on 17 October helped himself to the engineer's motor cycle and presumably went off to say goodbye to a German girlfriend, as this was to be our last day at Lubeck. This possibly was the first time Mellies had ever ridden a motor bicycle and while stag-gering along the highway, with his machine more or less out of control, he pulled out to pass a truck that he was overtaking, and had a head-on collision with a Canadian despatch rider who must have been doing a ton. Such was the mess that apart from the New Zealand shoulder tabs and a piece of a shirt collar with Ross on it there was no way that we could identify the victim. We had Tubby Ross and Ross Mellies unaccounted for at the time but it was not till we located Tubby that we were sure which pilot had been involved. The accident took place at three in the afternoon. We attended Ross' funeral the following morning and flew out of Lubeck after midday. It was a good thing we were leaving.

With typical service efficiency we were ordered to fly our Tempests

---

[1] Shot down 27 April, 1945

to Flensberg and then after a couple of days fly them back to Lubeck, from where we were taken by road transport to Utersen in order to fly Spitfire XVIs back to England. I was not entirely happy with this set up. Having landed the Auster at this base some weeks earlier, I knew the strip had been bulldozed through rubble on the outskirts of Hamburg and there was a minimum take-off distance; in addition, if we were to strike a crosswind during take-off, it could be disastrous, as very few of the pilots had flown Spitfires. Take-off we did, though, and after a refuelling stop at Gilze Reijen in Holland, thence across the North Sea, we eventually arrived at Dunsfold. As I slid back the hood and watched the last Spitfire taxi to its dispersal pen, I felt as though a great weight had been lifted from my shoulders. For three years I had been continually flying fighters and then for seven months had been responsible for over five hundred ground crew, twenty six aircraft and nearly as many pilots. The ground crews were normal human beings and their antics were predictable. Alas the traits that we had encouraged in fighter pilots, during wartime, were the very qualities that were now proving such an embarrassment in peacetime.

I had seen these young pilots arrive at the squadron unsure and apprehensive and watched their reaction when they realised that it was kill or be killed. They'd had their bad and good days and at the end of each had been able to return to some degree of sanity, sometimes with the aid of alcohol. Now they faced the long road back to what they had been and a lot of them were not going to make it intact.

Most of us had lived in an unreal world for too long and I had no wish to see any of the boys falling foul of authority at this late stage. It had therefore been my resolve that no pilot would leave 486 with a blot on his record and during the last few months I had acted in all three roles of Judge, Prosecution Officer, Defence Council; and although it had not been easy I had managed to get my pilots out of the various scrapes into which they seemed to become involved just as naturally as night follows day.

Now the last evening in which we were to be together as a squadron had arrived and a pub crawl with a thrash to beat all thrashes was to be expected. For me it was the end of the road, with no more wilful pilots or ground crew with matrimonial problems to nurse maid, but on what should have been the happiest day in nearly five years, I felt more washed out and weary than at any stage of my service career. To use a crude expression I felt buggered and I did not want to think about the past, the present, or even what the future might have in store for me.

We sallied forth into the local village accompanied by various members of the ground crew, but if any of my gang had visions of finding an innocent young thing who would fall for their line of patter, they were in for a shock. Dunsfold was the station where numerous fighter squadrons had disbanded already and young though the local girls may have been in years, they were old in the ways of the world—and the ways of fighter pilots.

Well, we had our night out and as usual managed to bring home a quantity of beer and this, plus the various quantities that had been brought over from Europe, ensured that the party went on unabated until the early hours. Lucky me, the rest of the squadron could stay in bed with their hangovers, but I had a full day of supervising and signing official papers if the disbanding of 486 was to be completed on schedule.

Trying to follow an Adjutant's explanation as to what can and cannot be done under the umbrella of King's Regulations can be difficult and just when I began to see a clear path ahead, a message arrived to inform me to report to some senior officer immediately. At that stage of the proceedings, I was past jumping to attention every time authority blew a whistle, and in addition, I had met that particular chap the previous night, and was not impressed. He was what my branch of the service termed a 'Wingless Wonder'. He'd had an armchair ride during the war and now that the bullets had stopped flying, he was of the opinion that the aircrew had greatly exaggerated the part they had played in the war. To me, that individual looked sound in wind and limb and I could see no obvious reason why he could not have earned himself a set of wings and taken part in the battle, instead of hiding behind a desk.

I would not have won any medals for diplomacy and I caused a temporary deflation by telling him exactly what I was thinking. It was one of our doubtful pleasures in the air force that you could abuse an officer of equal rank and there was not a hell of a lot that he could do about it. Our Adj was panicking and the Station Adj was equally concerned as telephone messages flowed back and forth but I was not in the least worried. If the little 'pip squeak' wanted me that badly there was no problem. I had not gone into hiding—he would have to come to me. Eventually the Station Adjutant arrived, all hot and bothered and almost begged me to put an end to the performance by returning with him to see the man.

He had some story about one of our 486 officers physically assaulting a Corporal and while I found this difficult to believe there was no point in making things more difficult, so I agreed to go along. By the time we had made our way to the man's office, my mood had improved

and I was looking forward to bearding the little horror in his den. If
the tale I was listening to was to be believed the Corporal was cycling
past our billets and Flight Lieutenant Collins had knocked him off his
cycle. If true it was a very serious matter and Collins would have to
face a Court Martial. But I would deal with it in my own way.

'Right, let's have the Corporal in, I want to hear his story'. I was
not too interested in hearing his story actually. The first thing to do
was to kill the complaint at source and afterwards Collins could make
his own explanations to me and if it was as bad as it sounded I had
my own way of dealing with it.

Strategically placed behind the Corporal's Commanding Officer's
chair, I tore into that Corporal for not standing to attention while
addressing Senior Officers, then, spotting a tunic button that had
escaped when its mates were being polished, I drew attention to it and
handed out a stern lecture about how poor an example it was to the
airmen under him. A few more interruptions as he tried to gather his
wits and get on with his story put him off his tack, and if it had not
been so serious I could have found it in my heart to feel sorry for that
airman. As the stop, start, tale unfolded, it was becoming hard to
decide who had attacked who.

'Right, Corporal, I've heard all I want to hear. Wait outside and we
will call you in if we need you. By what I've heard you could be facing
a charge for wrongly accusing an Officer'.

That poor airman. No doubt he'd worked hard for those two stripes
and now it looked as if he could loose them.

Now that I had managed to confuse the Corporal and had him safely
parked outside it was the little Squadron Leader's turn.

The first thing to cover was Collins' war record. If even half of what
I said was true he would have been a national hero in his own country.
I was tempted to claim that he was the New Zealand Prime Minister's
son but that might be overdoing it a little, so I had to settle for the
Deputy PM!

With Collins' war record and the people involved, it was more than
likely the higher-ups would try to sweep the whole unsavoury episode
under the carpet even if it meant requesting my little friend to resign
his commission. Not surprisingly the Squadron Leader readily agreed
to my suggestion that the matter be dropped. He had thought that he
was attacking a white mouse but somehow he had managed to get into
the wrong cage and found he had a tiger by the tail.

Now for the true story and I was disgusted when I heard it. After
the previous night's binge the pilots were still half under the weather
and instead of breakfast they had started drinking Schnapps. Bert and

one of his drunken mates had then produced a length of string and taking up stations on each side of the roadway they held the length of twine between them and as each WAAF came along they refused to drop the string and let the girls pass, until they had said good morning. The Corporal had attempted to barge past, the string had become entangled in the front wheel of his bicycle and he had finished up on his back in the middle of the roadway.

This was the last straw for me. Bert had two hours to have the mob sobered up, cleaned up, dressed up and report to the flight office with their clothing cards. If any of them wished to retain their flying gear that was all right as far as I was concerned. My signature signified that all gear had been returned to stores and they were on their way to London. Frankly, I was now absolutely fed up with being help mate to a lot of pilots who were refusing to accept the fact that the war was over, and that the time was past when their stupid games could be excused as just high spirits. It was time for me to move on.

I had been with 486 so long that I thought that I should have felt a twinge of sadness to see it pass into history. But on the contrary, when I saw that bunch of pilots, all spruced up and in a condition any Commanding Officer would have been proud of, boarding a transport en route to London and realised that I was no longer responsible for their antics, it would have to be one of the most satisfactory moments of my service.

APPENDIX I

Record of Service

Squadron Leader C J Sheddan DFC

Born Waimate, New Zealand, 3 March 1918.
Joined RNZAF 13 April 1941
No. 1 Elementary Flying Training School, Taieri, New Zealand.
No. 2 Elementary Flying Training School, Woodbourne, New Zealand.
No. 2 Service Training School, Woodbourne.
No. 9 Flying Training School, Hullavington, England.
No. 57 Operational Training Unit, Hawarden, England.
No. 485 (RNZAF) Squadron, Kingscliff, England, Oct 1942, Sergeant Pilot.
No. 1 Air Delivery Flight, Croydon, January 1943.
No. 486 (RNZAF) Squadron, Tangmere, May 1943.
No. 486 (RNZAF) Squadron, Beaulieu, Castle Camps, Ayr, Newchurch, 1944.
No. 486 (RNZAF) Squadron, Volkel (B. 80), Holland, November 1944.
No. 486 (RNZAF) Squadron, Hopsten (B. 112), Germany, April 1945
No. 486 (RNZAF) Squadron, Fassberg (B. 152), Germany, April 1945.
No. 486 (RNZAF) Squadron, Celle, (B. 118), Germany, May 1945.
No. 486 (RNZAF) Squadron, Kastrup, (B. 160), Germany, May 1945
No. 486 (RNZAF) Squadron, Lubeck, (B. 158), Denmark, July 1945.

Promoted to Warrant Officer, May 1944.   Promoted to Flight Lieutenant, April 1945.
Promoted to Pilot Officer, December 1944.   Promoted to Acting Squadron Leader, 2 May 1945.
Promoted to Flying Officer, January 1945.   Left RNZAF 13 April 1946.

Awarded Distinguished Flying Cross—*London Gazette* 12 June 1945.

'This Officer has displayed the highest standard of devotion to duty. He has participated in a very large number of varied sorties during which much damage has been inflicted on such enemy targets as locomotives, barges, industrial buildings and mechanical transport. On one occasion Flying Officer Sheddan was forced to bring his damaged aircraft down in the sea. He was subsequently adrift in the dinghy for 19 hours before being rescued. On resuming flying Ops, Flying Officer Sheddan quickly showed that this experience had in no way diminished his zest for battle and he set a fine example of courage and resolution in pressing home his attacks. Among his successes is the destruction of three enemy aircraft.'

(Jimmy Sheddan was presented with his DFC by General Sir Bernard 'Tiny' Freyberg VC, DSO, a soldier in the First War, and who had commanded the New Zealand Forces in Crete in 1941. Jimmy wrote in his log-book—'Tiny Freyberg hangs a gong on my jacket. Tiny's big moment'.)

APPENDIX II

C J Sheddan's Combat Reports

1 January 1945   **1 FW 190 Destroyed**

'I was flying Green 3 and whilst in the circuit over Base I saw Ack-Ack bursting at low altitude in the direction of Nijmegen. I flew on the deck towards Nijmegen and saw two FW190s and one Me109 in line abreast heading North East at zero feet. One of the 190s was behind and weaving and I fired a short burst at this one from about 300 yards range 10 degrees off. I observed no strikes. By this time I was a good 10 miles North East of Nijmegen. I closed on the FW190 to about 100 yards, 5 degrees off and fired a two-second burst allowing quarter of a ring deflection. I saw strikes around the cockpit and on the starboard wing. The FW190 immediately went into a steep turn, and after one complete turn, straightened out as if attempting to crash land but hit the ground, violently exploded and blew up into small pieces. My petrol was getting low and I had to return to base.'

2 February 1945   **1 Dornier 217 Destroyed (shared)**

'I was flying Green 4, when in the Paderborn area, Green 3 called up and said there was an aircraft underneath, flying on the deck. As I straightened up from my dive I saw an aircraft just touching down. I saw Green 3 shoot at it and observed numerous strikes. I went in fairly flat and fired a good three second burst from 300 yards range and saw several strikes. As I pulled up I looked back and saw the Do217 burning on the ground.

6 April 1945   **2 Ju87s Destroyed**

'I was flying Pink 3 on a patrol of the Dummer and Steinhuder Lakes when, near Stolzenau, we were advised by Forward Contact Car SCALWAG that Ju87s were attacking the bridge over the Weser at Stolzenau. We were orbiting at about 2500 ft and guided by Ack-Ack, which was reported firing at the Ju87s, I broke up into wispy cloud. At about 4000 ft I spotted a Ju87B flying due east. I opened fire from about 200 yards range in dead line astern and saw some strikes on the fuselage. I maintained fire until within approx 10 yards and broke violently to port to avoid ramming the Ju87. This took me into the cloud and the last I saw of the Ju87 was it pulling up into cloud and almost stalling. Pink 4 (F/O Ross) who was flying on my starboard during the whole of the attack, reports seeing two parachutes going down just east after the Ju87 went into cloud. After breaking into cloud I flew due east for approx two minutes—broke cloud and saw another Ju87B on my port and about a mile in front of me. I manoeuvred into line astern and opened fire from about 200 yards and gave three short bursts down to 10 yards but observed no strikes. I pulled out to port and made a further attack following this with another from starboard. Whilst positioning for a fourth attack I saw a parachute open and saw the Ju87 commence a gliding turn. I spiralled slowly towards the ground—at 500 feet I saw the second parachute open and the Ju87 hit the ground and blew up just north of Steinhuder Lake. During the attack on the second Ju87B, the gunner of the EA was firing the whole time but I was not hit.'

14 April 1945   **1 FW190 Destroyed**

'I was flying Pink 1 on a weather recce of the Berleberg-Ludwigslust area, when just west of Ludwigslust, whilst pulling-up after attacking a train I saw a silver-coloured aircraft at deck level, flying due North. My own height was 200 ft and I dived down behind it and gave chase, followed by the other three aircraft of my section. When about 700 yards from it I recognised it as a FW190. The 190 did not take any evasive action and I closed to 100 yards and opened fire with one second burst in deal line astern. I saw large pieces come away from the wings and fuselage and I pulled out to port of the 190 and slightly above. Looking back I saw the starboard wing of the 190 drop and it rolled onto its back, hit the ground and exploded.'

16 April 1945   **1 FW190 Destroyed (shared)**

'I was flying Pink 1 and leading the Squadron on an Armed Recce of the Pritzwalk-Parchim area when, in the vicinity of Neustadt A/D, Pink 3—F/O O'Connor—reported a FW190 to be taking off from the A/D. Pink 3 and 4 were instructed to go down to the attack and whilst I was orbiting the A/D at 4000 ft I saw the 190 being attacked by Pink 3 and 4 as it was orbiting. The enemy aircraft pulled away and headed north on the deck. I dived down behind it and when within 200 yards, the 190 made a slight turn to port. Allowing 1 ring deflection, I fired a short burst and the 190 went under my nose. I pulled out to starboard to avoid the enemy aircraft which flicked onto its back and as I pulled away, saw it hit the ground and explode.'

2 May 1945   **1 Multi-engined Flying Boat Destroyed (shared)**

'I was leading the Squadron on an Armed Recce of the Eutin area, when about one mile south of Grossenbrode I saw a Flying Boat orbiting. I recognised it as a multi-engined German Flying Boat and attacked it from line astern. I saw numerous strikes on the fuselage and the two starboard engines. Both engines began to stream smoke and the enemy aircraft lost height and landed on the water and swung onto the beach. By this time it had caught fire and when last seen it was a blazing mass with small explosions throwing debris up in the air. Flying Officer Thompson flying Pink 3, followed me into attack and I saw him fire and secure strikes just as the enemy aircraft hit the water.'

APPENDIX III

Some of the aircraft flown by C J Sheddan during WW2, whilst serving with 486 RNZAF Squadron.

Hawker Typhoon EK272 SA-J	3 September 1943, ASR sortie off Le Havre
JP676 SA-J	2 October 1943, shot down by flak—ditched
JP495 SA-A	25 October 1943, Ramrod, Maupertus, 2 January 1944, No 2 to Scotty, on his last show
JP845 SA-H	10 November 1943, dive-bombing Mimoyecques
Hawker Tempest JN801 SA-L	23 June 1944, shot down a V1 25 June 1944, shot down a V1
JN805 SA-E	3 July 1944, shot down a V1
JN808 SA-N	29 June 1944, shot down a V1
JN809 SA-M	22 June 1944, shot down a V1
JN854 SA-G	5 July 1944, shot down 1½ V1s—crash landed
JN873 SA-H	1 July 1944, shot down a V1
EJ748 SA-I	1 January 1945, shot down an FW190, 21 February 1945, strafed a train 22 February 1945, strafed three trains
EJ577 SA-F	23 August 1944, shot down a V1
EJ711 SA-Q	6 April 1945, shot down two Ju87s
EJ717 SA-P	3 April 1945, two MT damaged, 13 April 1945, 3 Ju88s damaged on the ground
SN129 SA-M	14 April 1945, shot down an FW190 16 April 1945, shot down an FW190 and two MT flamers 17 April 1945, seven MT flamers, one train damaged 19 April 1945, one MT flamer, 4 damaged 24 April 1945, five MT damaged 25 April 1945, six MT flamers 26 April 1945, one train destroyed, one train damaged; six MT flamers, 10 damaged, one Me109 destroyed on a transporter 30 April 1945, road convoy strafed, (Sqdn claimed 15 MT flamers, 20 MT damaged 2 May 1945, road convoys strafed, 8 MT flamers, 20 damaged 2nd sortie: 18 MT flamers, 25 damaged, 3rd sortie: 10 MT flamers, 21 damaged, shot down a Bv138 flying boat
SN176 SA-N	25 March 1945, two bowsers flamed; two truck flamers; 4 EA damaged on the ground 26 March 1945, three staff cars destroyed and road convoy strafed 28 March 1945, three MT and two trailers damaged 30 March 1945, 11 MT and two trains strafed, a/c hit by flak and badly shot up 12 April 1945, damaged an FW190 on the ground
NV719 SA-E	2 February 1945, two trains damaged, am; Shot-up 2 MT, 2 trains, 3 barges, pm
NV652 SA-K	2 February 1945, shared a Do217 shot down
NV969 SA-A	18 April 1945, 8 MT flamers, 1 petrol dump

APPENDIX IV

Combat Victories of 486 Squadron 1942-45

Typhoons

Date	Pilot	Destroyed	Prob	Remarks
1942				
17 Oct	PO G G Thomas / Sgt A N Sames	FW190		Fw Klaus Niesel 10/JG26
17 Dec	FS F Murphy	Me109		Ltn H Raucheisen 4(F)/123
17 Dec	Sgt K G Taylor-Cannon	Me109		Oblt H Ruck 4(F)/123
18 Dec	FO G G Thomas	Do217		II/KG40
19 Dec	Sgt A N Sames	FW190		Fw P Gellert 3(F)/122
22 Dec	FO A E Umbers / FS C N Gall	Do217		Either 2/KG2 or 4/KG40
24 Dec	FO G G Thomas	Me109		Fw A Ripplinger &
	FS F Murphy	Me109		Ltn B Frank 4(F)/123
1943				
17 Jan	Sgt K G Taylor-Cannon	Me109		Uffz E Lank 4(F)/123
16 Feb	FS F Murphy	Ju88		1(F)/123
1 Mar	FS W B Tyerman	FW190		Uffz E Laepple 10/JG2
14 Mar	FS R H Fitzgibbon	FW190		Fw D Sahre 5(F)/123
9 Apr	SL D J Scott / FL H N Sweetman / FL A E Umbers / FO I D Waddy		FW190	
14 Apr	SL D J Scott / FS R H Fitzgibbon	Me109		Uffz Detlef Walter
16 Apr	8 pilots	Me109		
29 Apr	FO A H Smith	Me109		Ltn E Senzbach 4(F)/123
29 Apr	PO F Murphy	Me109		Fw W Quante 4(F)/123
25 May	SL D J Scott	FW190		SKG/10
24 Jun	SL D J Scott	FW190		
24 Jun	FL A E Umbers	FW190		
15 Jul	SL D J Scott / PO R H Fitzgibbon	FW190 / FW190		
15 Jul	PO A N Sames			
15 Jul	FL A E Umbers		FW190	
15 Jul	PO F Murphy		FW190	
Tempests				
1944				
30 Sep	FL S S Williams	Me109		
19 Nov	FL K G Taylor-Cannon / PO O D Eagleson		Me262	
26 Nov	FL K G Taylor-Cannon / FL S S Williams	Ju88		
	PO J Steedman		Ju88	
25 Dec	FO J H Stafford / PO R D Bremner	Me262		
27 Dec	FL E W Tanner	FW190	FW190	10/JG54
27 Dec	FL K G Taylor-Cannon	FW190		10/JG54
27 Dec	FO K A Smith	FW190		10/JG54
27 Dec	PO S J Short	FW190		10/JG54
1945				
1 Jan	SL A E Umbers	FW190		JG6
1 Jan	SL A E Umbers	FW190		JG6
1 Jan	FO W A L Trott	FW190		JG6
1 Jan	PO J G Hooper	FW190		JG6
1 Jan	PO C J Sheddan	FW190		JG6
14 Jan	FO C J MacDonald	Me109		
14 Jan	WO J E Wood	Me109		
23 Jan	SL A E Umbers	Me109		
23 Jan	FO J H Stafford / WO A H Bailey	Me109		
23 Jan	FO R J Danzey		FW190	

Date	Pilot	Destroyed	Prob	Remarks
2 Feb	FO R D Bremner			
	FO J H Stafford	} Do217		
	PO C J Sheddan			
22 Feb	FL J H Stafford	Me109		
22 Feb	FO A R Evans	Me109		
24 Feb	SL K G Taylor-Cannon	Me109		
24 Feb	FL N J Powell	Me109		
6 Apr	FO C J Sheddan	Ju87		
6 Apr	FO C J Sheddan	Ju87		
10 Apr	FL W E Schrader	FW190		
12 Apr	FL J H Stafford	FW190		
14 Apr	FL C J Sheddan	FW190		
15 Apr	FL A I Ross	FW190		
15 Apr	FL W E Schrader	FW190		
15 Apr	FL W E Schrader	FW190		
15 Apr	FO A R Evans	FW190		
15 Apr	FO B J O'Connor	FW190		
15 Apr	WO R J Atkinson	FW190		
15 Apr	WO G Maddaford	FW190		
15 Apr	FS A R Mellies	FW190		
16 Apr	FO C J Sheddan	} FW190		
	WO W J Shaw			
16 Apr	FL W E Schrader	FW190		
16 Apr	FO J W Reid	FW190		
21 Apr	SL W E Schrader	Me109		
21 Apr	FO A R Evans	FW190		
25 Apr	FO K A Smith	Me262		
28 Apr	FL J W Reid	} Ju352		
	FO O D Eagleson			
29 Apr	SL W G Schrader	Me109		
29 Apr	SL W E Schrader	Me109		
29 Apr	SL W E Schrader	FW190		
29 Apr	SL W E Schrader	} Me109		
	WO N D Howard			12/SG 151 lost 7 a/c
29 Apr	FO J W Reid	FW190		II/JG 26 lost 3 a/c
29 Apr	FO O D Eagleson	FW190		
29 Apr	FO C J MacDonald	FW190		
29 Apr	WO J R Duncan	FW190		
29 Apr	FO A R Evans	FW190	FW190	
29 Apr	FO C S Kennedy	FW190		
1 May	SL W E Schrader	Me109		
2 May	SL C J Sheddan	} Bv138		
	FO D J Thompson			
2 May	FO O D Eagleson	FW44		
2 May	FO O D Eagleson	Fil56		
2 May	PO J W Shaw	} FW190		
	WO N D Howard	} Fil56		
3 May	FL C J MacDonald	Ju88		
3 May	WO J R Duncan	Ju88		

APPENDIX V

Victories of German V1 Rocket Bombs by 486 Squadron RNZAF

Date 1944	Pilot	Tempest	V1s	Time	Remarks
16 June	FL H M Sweetman	JN754	1	am	Hythe/Dungeness
16 June	PO K McCarthy	JN801	1	pm	N of Rye – in sea
17 June	FO T M Fenton	JN808	1	am	Sevenoaks
17 June	PO R J Danzey	JN809	1	eve	Faversham
18 June	FL H M Sweetman	JN754	1	am	French coast
18 June	FL N J Powell	JN804	1	am	Dungeness
18 June	FS O D Eagleson	JN811	1	am	Tonbridge
18 June	PO R J Danzey	JN797	1	am	N of Tonbridge
18 June	FO J R Cullen	JN770	1	am	
18 June	FO J G Wilson	JN809	1	am	Dartford
18 June	FL V StC Cooke	JN801	1	am	during air test
18 June	FS O D Eagleson	JN804	2	pm	Nth Newchurch/Rye

Date	Pilot	Tempest	VIs	Time	Remarks
18 June	FS B M Hall	JN801	1	eve	SE of Sevenoaks
18 June	FS R J Wright	JN770	1	eve	
18 June	FO J R Cullen	JN758	1	eve	Nth Foreland
18 June	FO S S Williams	JN820	1	eve	Nth Foreland
19 June	PO R J Danzey	JN805	1	am	damaged, hit balloon
19 June	FO W L Miller	JN811	1	am	
19 June	FO R J Cammock	JN820	1	am	
19 June	FS J H Stafford	JN805	1	eve	
19 June	FL H M Sweetman	JN754	1	eve	
19 June	FL J H McCaw	JN805	1	eve	
20 June	PO R J Danzey	JN820	1	am	
20 June	FS J H Stafford	JN811	1	eve	
20 June	FL J H McCaw	JN758	1	eve	during air test
22 June	FL J H McCaw	JN758	1	am	Bexhill
22 June	FL J H McCaw	JN797	1	am	second sortie
22 June	FO K McCarthy	JN821	2	am	Crowborough/Hastings
22 June	FO W L Miller	JN794	1	am	N of Hastings
22 June	WO G J Hooper	JN809	⅓	am	shared with Spitfires
22 June	FL J H McCaw	JN821	1	am	N of Newchurch
22 June	WO C J Sheddan	JN809	1	am	sea off Hastings
22 June	SL J H Iremonger	JN808	1	am	Crowborough
22 June	FS J H Stafford	JN803	1	eve	NE of Battle
23 June	PO R J Danzey	JN797	1½	am	½ with 3 Sqdn
23 June	PO F B Lawless	JN859	1	am	N of Hastings
23 June	FS B M Hall	JN809	1	am	NW of Battle
23 June	PO K McCarthy	JN854	2	pm	Willington/Newchurch
23 June	FS O D Eagleson	JN794	1	pm	East Hoatly
23 June	FO W L Miller	JN766	2	pm	Hastings/Pevensey
23 June	FO R J Cammock	JN820	1	pm	Pevensey Bay
23 June	WO C J Sheddan	JN801	1	eve	
23 June	FO R J Cammock	JN810	1	eve	Edenbridge
23 June	FO J R Cullen	JN770	½	eve	with 3 Sqdn
24 June	FO R J Cammock	JN808	2	am	
24 June	PO K McCarthy	JN803	1	am	
25 June	FO S S Williams	JN758	1	pm	N of Newchurch
25 June	FS S J Short	JN810	1	eve	NE Battle
25 June	FO R J Cammock	JN804	1	eve	S of Maidstone
25 June	PO J R Cullen	JN770	2	eve	Redhill/Hasdoorn
25 June	WO C J Sheddan	JN854	1	eve	N of Newchurch
25 June	FO R J Cammock	JN804	1	eve	N of Hastings
25 June	FO W A Hart	JN809	1	eve	N of Newchurch
26 June	FL J H McCaw	JN758	1	pm	Tonbridge
27 June	FL N J Powell	JN866	1	am	
27 June	WO J R Powell	JN866	1	am	
27 June	FL H M Sweetman	JN754	1	am	N of Rye
27 June	WO G J Hooper	JN803	2	pm	Hastings
27 June	FO W L Miller	JN811	1	pm	
27 June	WO O D Eagleson	JN794	1	pm	
27 June	FO W L Miller	JN811	1	eve	
27 June	FO W A Hart	JN803	1	eve	
27 June	FO R J Cammock	JN794	1	eve	
28 June	FO J G Wilson	JN866	1	am	
28 June	WO O D Eagleson	JN859	1	am	S of Sevenoaks
28 June	WO O D Eagleson	JN854	1	am	N of Rye (2nd op)
28 June	FO R J Cammock	JN810	1	am	
29 June	PO R J Danzey	JN797	1½	am	½ with Mosquito
29 June	PO R D Bremner	JN821	1	am	
29 June	FL H M Sweetman	JN821	1	am	
29 June	FL H M Sweetman	JN810	1	pm	
29 June	WO C J Sheddan	JN808	1	pm	
29 June	WO S J Short	JN806	2	pm	
29 June	FO J R Cullen	JN810	1	eve	
30 June	WO S J Short	JN810	1	am	a/c dam by debris
30 June	PO B M Hall	JN821	1	pm	
30 June	PO F B Lawless	JN811	1	pm	
30 June	FL E W Tanner	JN770	3	pm	
30 June	WO J H Stafford	JN801	1	eve	
30 June	PO B M Hall	JN854	1	eve	
1 July	FO F B Lawless	JN770	1	am	
1 July	FO R J Cammock	JN866	1	eve	Nr Horsham
1 July	WO C J Sheddan	JN873	½	eve	½ with Spitfires
1 July	FL L J Appleton	JN821	1	eve	NE Pevensey
3 July	PO R D Bremner	JN801	1	am	
3 July	FO J R Cullen	JN863	1	eve	N of Hastings
3 July	WO O D Eagleson	JN873	1	eve	
3 July	PO K A Smith	JN801	2	eve	
3 July	WO C J Sheddan	JN805	1	eve	

Date	Pilot	Tempest	VIs	Time	Remarks
4 July	FO H M Mason	JN805	1	am	S of Brooklands
4 July	FL J R Cullen	JN770	1	am	N of Hastings
4 July	WO O D Eagleson	EJ537	1	am	Sevenoaks
4 July	WO W A Kalka	JN809	2	pm	Polegate/Leatherhead
4 July	FO F B Lawless	EJ537	1	pm	NE of Eastbourne
4 July	FL H M Sweetman	JN809	1	pm	NE of Eastbourne
4 July	PO R D Bremner	JN854	1	pm	N of Hailsham
4 July	FL N J Powell	EJ527	1	pm	Tunbridge Wells
4 July	WO J H Stafford	JN854	2	eve	Hailsham/Tonbridge
4 July	FO H M Mason	JN809	½	eve	
4 July	PO R J Danzey	JN805	1	eve	N of Eastbourne
5 July	WO C J Sheddan	JN854	1½	pm	Tempest crashed
5 July	WO B J O'Connor	JN803	1	pm	S of Beachy Head
6 July	WO B J O'Connor	JN803	1½	am	½ with Tempest
6 July	WO O D Eagleson	JN873	1	am	N of Hastings
6 July	WO G J Hooper	JN803	2½	pm	Friston/Beachy Head
7 July	FL H M Sweetman	} JN801	½	am	N of Beachy Head
7 July	PO R J Danzey	} JN809	½	am	N of Beachy Head
7 July	FL H M Sweetman	JN803	1	pm	N of Ashford
7 July	FO R J Cammock	JN873	1	pm	N of Pevensey
7 July	WO O D Eagleson	JN873	1	pm	on air test over base
7 July	FO J R Cullen	EJ527	1	pm	S of Beachy Head
7 July	WO O D Eagleson	JN873	1	pm	W of Dungeness
8 July	FO J R Cullen	JN770	1	am	off Dungeness
8 July	FL J H McCaw	JN758	4	eve	
8 July	PO F B Lawless	JN770	2	eve	
9 July	FO J R Cullen	JN873	1½	eve	Lydd/off Bexhill
9 July	WO G J Hooper	JN821	2	eve	Beachy Head/Hastings
12 July	PO B M Hall	JN805	½	pm	N of Tonbridge
12 July	FO S S Williams	EJ523	1	pm	
12 July	PO B M Hall	JN822	1	pm	E of Bexhill
12 July	WO W A Kalka	JN803	4	pm	Hastings & Bexhill
12 July	FS J S Ferguson	JN767	1½	pm	
13 July	FO H M Mason	JN732	2	am	Rye/Bexhill
13 July	PO W A L Trott	JN866	1	pm	Tunbridge Wells
13 July	WO B J O'Connor	JN866	1	pm	SW of Malling
14 July	FL J H McCaw	JN758	2	am	Bexhill
14 July	WO O D Eagleson	EJ523	1	am	N of Eastbourne
14 July	FO S S Williams	JN860	1	pm	Sevenoaks
14 July	FO H M Mason	JN732	½	pm	Bexhill
14 July	FO J R Cullen	JN770	1	pm	N of Hastings
15 July	FL J H McCaw	JN860	1	pm	Ashford
15 July	WO G J Hooper	JN803	1	pm	
16 July	PO B M Hall	JN821	½	pm	Hastings
16 July	FO R J Danzey	JN803	1	pm	N of Hastings
18 July	SL J H Iremonger	} JN763	½	pm	W of Tenterden
18 July	FO J R Cullen	} JN802	½	pm	W of Tenterden
18 July	FL H M Sweetman	JN754	1	eve	Hastings
18 July	FO J R Cullen	JN802	½	eve	N of Rye
19 July	FO S S Williams	EJ523	1	am	Rye
20 July	WO G J Hooper	} JN797	½	am	N of Hastings
20 July	PO R D Bremner	} JN802	½	am	N of Hastings
21 July	FL J H McCaw DFC	JN758	1	pm	
22 July	FO R J Cammock	JN863	1	pm	N of Ashford
22 July	FO J R Cullen	EJ537	1	pm	Sevenoaks
22 July	PO R J Danzey	JN801	1	pm	West Malling
22 July	FO J R Cullen	EJ523	1	eve	N of Rye
23 July	PO W A L Trott	JN758	2	pm	–/Etchingham
24 July	FL L J Appleton	JN863	1	am	SW Canterbury
24 July	FL E W Tanner	JN732	1	pm	E of Ninfield
26 July	PO R D Bremner	JN803	1	am	NW Rye
26 July	FO W A Hart	JN732	1	am	E of Tonbridge
26 July	FL J H McCaw DFC	JN770	1	am	N of Bexhill
26 July	FO R J Cammock	EJ523	1	am	N of Bexhill
26 July	FL V StC Cooke	JN763	½	am	W of Battle
26 July	PO K A Smith	JN803	1	am	N of Pevensey
26 July	FO R J Cammock	JN770	1	pm	SW Ashford
26 July	FO J R Cullen	JN770	1	eve	N of Pevensey
26 July	PO J H Stafford	JN803	1	eve	N of Hastings
27 July	PO R D Bremner	} JN803	½	pm	NW Tenterden
27 July	FO W A Hart	} JN754	½	pm	NW Tenterden
27 July	PO W A L Trott	JN763	1	pm	West Malling
27 July	FL J H McCaw DFC	JN770	1	pm	
27 July	FO R J Cammock	EJ523	2	pm	Tunbridge Wells
27 July	WO B J O'Connor	JN801	1	eve	
27 July	WO O D Eagleson	EJ523	1	eve	N of Ashford
27 July	FL J H McCaw DFC	EJ528	1	eve	Ashford

Date	Pilot	Tempest	VIs	Time	Remarks
28 July	PO F B Lawless	JN770	2	pm	
30 July	FL J H McCaw DFC	EJ528	1	pm	NW Mayfield
3 Aug	WO O D Eagleson	JN808	2	am	N of Bexhill
3 Aug	FO S S Williams	JN758	2	am	N of Tonbridge
3 Aug	PO R D Bremner	JN767	1	am	E of Battle
3 Aug	FO W A Hart	JN732	1	am	Pevensey
3 Aug	FL N J Powell	JN808	1	eve	
4 Aug	WO O D Eagleson	EJ528	1	pm	N of Hastings
4 Aug	WO B J O'Connor	JN801	1	pm	NW Rye
4 Aug	PO K A Smith	JN821	3	pm	Tun Wells 2/Maidstone
5 Aug	FO H M Mason	JN801	1	pm	SW Newchurch
6 Aug	FO J G Wilson	JN809	1	am	SW West Malling
6 Aug	PO W A L Trott	EJ528	1	pm	
6 Aug	FO R J Cammock	EJ523	1	pm	
7 Aug	FO R J Cammock	JN863	1	am	
9 Aug	FL H M Sweetman DFC	EJ577	1	am	
9 Aug	FL L J Appleton	JN808	1	am	
15 Aug	WO O D Eagleson	JN794	1	am	NW Newchurch
15 Aug	FO R J Cammock	EJ528	1	pm	
15 Aug	FL K G Taylor-Cannon	JN808	1	pm	
16 Aug	FL H M Sweetman	EJ693	1	pm	NW Dungeness
16 Aug	WO O D Eagleson	JN794	3	pm	Rye/Maidstone/Ashford
16 Aug	FL W L Miller	JN803	1	pm	Tonbridge
16 Aug	PO K A Smith	JN808	1	pm	NW Tenterden
18 Aug	FL N J Powell	JN860	1	am	Haywards Heath
19 Aug	FS W J Campbell	JN802	1	eve	N Rye
23 Aug	WO C J Sheddan	EJ577	1	eve	
27 Aug	FL J R Cullen	JN758	1	am	Nr Tenterden
28 Aug	PO W A L Trott	JN869	1	pm	W of Tenterden
29 Aug	WO B J O'Connor	EJ577	1	pm	West Malling
29 Aug	PO K A Smith	EJ858	1	pm	N Ashford
29 Aug	PO B M Hall	JN803	1	pm	
29 Aug	FO R J Cammock	EJ869	1	pm	N of Tonbridge
29 Aug	PO J H Stafford	JN803	1	pm	N of Tonbridge
31 Aug	WO B J O'Connor	JN802	1	am	E of Maidstone

Squadron Pilot Total

WO O D Eagleson	21	PO J H Stafford	8	PO K McCarthy	6	FL V StC Cooke	2
FO R J Cammock	20½	WO G J Hooper	8	PO W A L Trott	6	PO J Steedman	2
FL J H McCaw DFC	19½	WO W A Kalka	8	FO H M Mason	5½	SL J H Iremonger DFC	1½
FL J R Cullen	16	PO K A Smith	8	FL N J Powell	5	FO T M Fenton	1
PO R J Danzey	16	PO B M Hall	7½	FS S J Short	5	FS R J Wright	1
FL H M Sweetman DFC	10½	WO C J Sheddan	7½	FL E W Tanner	4	FS W J Campbell	1
PO F B Lawless	10	FO W A Hart	7	FL L J Appleton	3½	FS J S Ferguson	1
WO B J O'Connor	8½	FL W L Miller	7	FO J G Wilson	2½	FL K G Taylor-Cannon	1
FO S S Williams	8	PO R D Bremner	7				

APPENDIX VI
Some of my 486 pals who didn't make it

Date	Name	Reason
16 May 1943	FO A A "Andy" Brown	engine failed on shipping strike
6 Sep 1943	PO R H "Fitz" Fitzgibbon	lost tail diving on shipping
16 Sep 1943	F/Sgt D Bennett	flak – shipping attack
16 Sep 1943	PO N E "Norm" Preston	flak – shipping attack
16 Sep 1943	F/Sgt M O Jorgenson	flak
10 Nov 1943	PO W B Tyerman	intruder sortie
30 Dec 1943	FO R A Peters	ditched
14 Jan 1944	FO G Philp	flak
13 Mar 1944	WO H W Williams	engine failure
5 Apr 1944	F/Sgt A G Turner	flying accident
28 Jun 1944	F/Sgt R J "Joe" Wright	VI exploded
31 Jul 1944	F/Sgt A A Wilson	collision
17 Aug 1944	F/Sgt J W Waddel	bad weather
6 Oct 1944	FO R J "Ray" Cammock DFC	flak
22 Dec 1944	F/Lt S S Williams	flak
27 Dec 1944	FO B M Hall	shot down by FW190
14 Feb 1945	S/Ldr A E Umbers DFC	flak
25 Mar 1945	FO W A "Wackie" Kalka	flak/drowned
26 Mar 1945	PO A H "Bill" Bailey	hit building evading US fighter
13 Apr 1945	S/Ldr K G Taylor-Cannon DFC	flak – last seen in parachute
14 Apr 1945	WO O J Mitchell	air combat
27 Apr 1945	F/Sgt Ross Mellies	flak – baled out and evaded; killed motor cycle accident the evening before we left for Germany

APPENDIX VII

Where some of my 485/486 pals hailed from

W/Cdr R W Baker DFC	Dunedin, RNZAF Jul 1940
FO R D "Duf" Bremner DFC	Taihope, RNZAF May 1942
FO R J "Ray" Cammock DFC	Christchurch, RNZAF Aug 1941
S/Ldr J R Cullen DFC & bar	Waihi, RNZAF Nov 1941
F/Lt R J "Bluey" Dall DFC	Hamilton, (Australia)
FO R J Danzey DFC	Auckland, RNZAF Nov 1941
FO O D "Eagle" Eagleson DFC	Auckland, RNZAF Mar 1942
F/Lt V C Fittall DFC	Auckland, RNZAF Mar 1941
PO R H "Fitz" Fitzgibbon	Rangiora, RNZAF Mar 1941
F/Lt C N "Norm" Gall DFC	Ngaruawahia, RNZAF Mar 1941
W/Cdr R J C Grant DFC & bar DFM	Woodville, RNZAF Nov 1939
FO B M Hall	Dannevirke, RNZAF Mar 1942
F/Lt W A Hart DFC	Wellington, RNZAF May 1942
FO G J "Gus" Hooper DFC	Wellington, RNZAF Jun 1941
S/Ldr M R D "Marty" Hume DFC	Martinborough, RNZAF Dec 1940
W/Cdr J H Iremonger DFC	Wiltshire, England, RAF 1938
G/Cpt P J Jameson DSO DFC & bar	Wellington, RAF 1936
PO M O Jorgensen	Auckland, RNZAF May 1941
FO W A "Wackie" Kalka	Auckland, RNZAF Sep 1941
F/Lt F B Lawless DFC	Christchurch, RNZAF Mar 1941
F/Lt C J "Colin" McDonald	Christchurch, RNZAF 1941
W/Cdr E D "Rosie" Mackie DSO DFC & bar	Waihi, RNZAF Jan 1941
F/Lt J H "Black Mac" McCaw DFC	Oamaru, RNZAF Jul 1941
F/Lt W L "Dusty" Miller	Invercargill, RNZAF Jul 1940
S/Ldr F "Spud" Murphy DFC	Bolton, Lancs, RNZAF Mar 1941
FO B J "Oc" O'Connor DFC	Napier, RNZAF Aug 1940
F/Lt N J "Pip" Powell DFC	Dargaville, RNZAF Sep 1941
F/Sgt N E "Norm" Preston	Wellington
F/Lt A N "Arty" Sames DFC	Auckland, RNZAF Mar 1941
W/Cdr W E "Smoky" Schrader DFC & bar	Wellington, RNZAF Mar 1941
G/Capt D J Scott DSO OBE DFC	Ashburton, RNZAF Mar 1940
FO S J Short	Cardiff, Wales, RNZAF Jan 1942
S/Ldr A H Smith DFC & bar	Auckland, RNZAF Mar 1941
FO K A Smith	Masterton, RNZAF Oct 1940
W/Cdr R L "Spud" Spurdle DFC & bar	Wanganui, RNZAF Sep 1939
F/Lt J H "Jack" Stafford DFC	New Lynn, RNZAF Mar 1942
FO J "Butch" Steedman	Whangarei, RNZAF Apr 1942
F/Lt M G Sutherland	Otago Heads, RNZAF Jun 1941
S/Ldr H N Sweetman DFC	Auckland, RNZAF Apr 1940
WO W J "Rangi" Swinton	Auckland, RNZAF Aug 1941
F/Lt E W "Rick" Tanner	Tauranga, RNZAF Sep 1941
S/Ldr K G "Hyphen" Taylor-Cannon DFC & bar	Oamaru, RNZAF Apr 1941
FO W A L "Bill" Trott DFC	Wellington, RNZAF Dec 1941
PO W B Tyerman	Taihope, RNZAF Mar 1941
S/Ldr A E "Spike" Umbers DFC & bar	Dunedin, RNZAF Nov 1940
S/Ldr I D Waddy DFC	Blenheim, RNZAF Aug 1940
F/Lt L S McQ "Chalky" White DFC	Gore, RNZAF Jul 1941
F/Lt S S Williams	Wanganui, RNZAF Apr 1941

INDEX

Aldridge, D   17, 19, 20, 22, 25, 26, 28, 29
Appleton, FL L   95, 104
Atkison, Pony   170

Baker, WC R W   39, 40
Barker, R   35
Beamont, WC R P   118-9
Bennett, FS D   59
Bex, Ted   120
Blackie,   33
Brash, J   128
Bremner, FO R D   141
Brooker, WC R E P   145
Brown, FO A A   61

Chisholm, GC P   95-6
Cocks,   56-7
Cole, SL R B   108-9
Collins, FL A   166, 182-3
Cook,   61
Cooper, FO S   174-5
Cotes-Preedy, SL D V C   154
Cowan,   52, 57
Cullen, SL J R   61

Dall, FL R J   160-1
Dolman, J   48-9
Duncan, Sgt J R   158, 169

Eagleson, FO O D   67-8, 94-5, 104, 106, 117, 124, 157, 165, 169
Evine,   52, 57

Fitzgibbon, PO R H   59
Fletcher, FL T   88fn
Frewer, Sgt A   41
Froggatt, WO D   58-9, 61-4, 90

George, S   12
Gordon, D   17, 19, 20-3, 25, 28, 29
Grant, FL G   47
Grant, FO I A C   38
Grant, WO R J C   38

Hall, FO B M   106-7, 137-8
Hannsen, Miss R   140fn
Harrison, M   42
Healey, FL L R   88fn
Helleen, FS N J   77
Holmes, A   16, 27
Holmes, SL M P C   74-75, 146, 178
Hooper, FO G J   133
Hume, SL M R D   42

Ingle-Finch, WC M R   156, 173-4
Iremonger, WC J H   94, 111, 124, 130, 143, 162, 178

Jameson, GC P G   38, 93-5, 145-6, 153, 167
Johnson, GC J E   153, 156, 159-160, 165, 167, 169, 172-4, 178-9
Jordan, Sir W J   164

Kalka, FO W A   138-140
Keenan, W   17-18
Kendall, FO J   142, 154

Law, G   62-3
Lawless, FL F B   14, 77-9, 83, 98, 103, 113, 120, 124

Maddaford, WO G   142, 160, 164-5
McCaw, FL J   60, 114, 117
McCarthy, FO K   60, 114, 117
McDonald, FL C   14, 67, 78, 133-4, 142, 154, 165-8
Mellies, FS A R   179
Miller, FL W L   95, 114-7
Montgomery, FM B   167
Moorhead, FO G   39, 42
Muller, S   166
Murphy, SL F   58-60, 64-5, 75, 78

Nelson, J   12-13, 31
Norris, Sgt F W   40

O'Connor, FO B J   78, 105, 148-9

Parks, N   97
Peters, FO R A   81-2
Powell, PO J R   77, 79, 98-9, 100-1, 105-6
Powell, FL N J   134-5
Preston, PO N E   59, 61, 93

Raffer, FL   50, 52
Ramsey, C   33-4, 36
Ross, FL A I   141, 179

Sames, PO A N   59
Sanders, FL   32
Schrader, WC W E   132, 145, 147
Scott, GC D J   51, 56, 61, 65-6, 68, 77, 81, 87, 93, 98
Shaw, WO W J   149, 179
Sheddan, A B   10, 40-1, 53, 120, 174-5
Sheddan, Joan   120
Short, FO S J   79, 148
Smith, SL A H   61
Smith, H   12
Stafford, FL J H   123-4, 141, 146
Steedman, FO J   105, 107, 124-5
Sutherland, FL M G   42, 46fn
Sweetman, FL H N   60, 143
Swinton, PO R   59

Tanner, FL E W   109, 110
Taylor-Cannon, SL K G   59, 78, 144-7
Thompson, FO D J   149-150
Trenchard, Lord   135-6
Turner, FS A G   102-3
Turner, Sgt W F   145fn
Tyerman, PO W B   59
Tyler, Master   28
Tyler, Miss   26
Tyler, Mrs   26-9
Tyler, Squire   23, 25-6, 28

Umbers, SL A E   51, 65, 94, 138, 140-1, 143-7

Waddy, SL I D   61, 73
Wallens, SL R W   47, 56
Walker, Sgt L   59
Wells, GC E P   178
White, FL L S Mc   41-2, 44-6
Wigram, Lord   10
Wilson, FO J G   22, 58-9, 60-1, 64, 70, 90, 95, 115, 150, 160
Wood, PO J E   157
Worthington, Miss P   143
Wright, FS R J   113, 117-8, 124-5

Jimmy Sheddan was one of the many New Zealanders who joined the RNZAF, then left his native land to go to England to fight the enemies of Great Britain and her Empire during World War Two.

Despite their size of population, New Zealanders rose to the colours in great numbers and through the recollections of Jim Sheddan we can share some of the trials and wartime tribulations they faced. Yet we can read too of the enormous amount of fun these men had despite the dangers of the sacrifices of war. It is this quality which endears his book to us as well as the achievements of the airmen who served with 486 New Zealand Squadron.

Although he got off to a shaky start, Jim Sheddan rose from the rank of Sergeant Pilot to Squadron Leader with 486 Squadron. Whilst to reach such a rank from such a start is not unique, those who managed it were few. After beginning with Spitfires, then going onto the Typhoon, Jim became an exponent of the Hawker Tempest, winning the DFC.

In many ways his is a very special account as, amongst other things, he survived 19 hours in a dinghy off the French coast, a crash landing in a Tempest after a battle with a V1 flying bomb, and the advance across northern Europe in the final weeks of the war. Few Tempest pilots have told their story – but Jim has, and in an honest, self-effacing way that will astound and enthrall everyone.

NORMAN FRANKS

With a Foreword by AVM J E 'Johnnie' Johnson, CB, CBE, DSO and 2 bars, DFC and bar; and an appreciation by Group Captain Johnny Iremonger DFC.

Norman Franks is recognized worldwide for the excellence of his research and writing into the air wars of World War One and Two.